THE PRINCIPLES OF OCEAN TRANSPORTATION

The Principles of
Ocean Transportation

BY

JAMES VERNON METCALFE
Professor of Foreign Trade
Seattle University

SIMMONS-BOARDMAN PUBLISHING CORPORATION
New York

PREFACE

This book is intended to portray the overall picture of the complex operation of vessels in the transportation of merchandise all over the world wherein each of the many elements is set out and balanced in its relationship and contribution to the entire operation. The successful vessel operator takes into consideration in his planning all of these elements, but in the rush and pressure of the business some of his many assistants may become so immersed, in a single phase of the business, as to be unaware of the relationship each individual's activities bear to the total project. The book furnishes these subordinates with a view of the entire operation and seeks to point out the importance of the individual effort to the management objective.

For a college student, the text likewise develops a broad picture of vessel operation with the various components of the business enumerated. If the student is seeking a career in transportation he will find many suggestions for employment in vessel operation and allied activities. If, on the other hand, the student is primarily seeking to relate ocean transportation to the overall operation of our economy, the many components of the business are set out in the book to serve as a practical check list of the elements that bear on the soundness of theoretical applications when measured by current practice.

The several facets of the business are briefly explained. A deeper knowledge of each may be imparted by the instructor who, drawing on his own experience, will expand each item with more detailed explanations. In addition, detailed analyses and research may be developed in maritime law, marine insurance, engineering in vessel construction, management-labor relations, commercial geography, world area studies, financing relative to ships, subsidies and foreign aid, international politics, vessels as war time auxiliaries, competition in domestic transportation, canals and essential trade routes, and Congressional action.

Grateful acknowledgement to many firms and associations is made of the assistance and material used in the preparation of this book. Especial thanks are extended to the following for their interest and help: American Merchant Marine Institute, Inc., Pacific Maritime Association, National Maritime Union of America, AFL-CIO Maritime Committee, Federal Maritime Board, Federal Maritime Administration, Seattle Field Office, U. S. Department of Commerce, Rear Admiral F. A. Zeusler, U.S.C.G. Ret., American Mail Line, Matson Navigation Company, Standard Oil Company of California, "Daily Shipping News," Seattle—Portland, Portland Oregon Public Schools, Fireman's Fund Insurance Company, and to Walter Hamshar, marine editor of the "New York Herald Tribune."

April 1, 1959

J. V. M.

CONTENTS

CHAPTER I

SHIP CHARACTERISTICS

NOMENCLATURE—PASSENGER VESSELS—COMBINATION VESSELS — GENERAL CARGO SHIPS — REFRIGERATORS — GRAIN AND ORE VESSELS—SEATRAINS—ROLL-ON ROLL-OFF SHIPS—LINERS, TRAMPS, INDUSTRIAL CARRIERS—CARRIER CLASSIFICATION

CHAPTER II

SHIP AND CARGO MEASUREMENTS

LOAD LINE—DISPLACEMENT TONNAGE—REGISTER TONNAGE—VESSEL CAPACITIES—CARGO TON—CAPACITY PLAN—IMMERSION SCALE—DEADWEIGHT—PLIMSOLL MARK

CHAPTER III

BEFORE THE VESSEL ARRIVES

INWARD FOREIGN MANIFESTS—DISCHARGE PLANNING—THE "LONG HATCH" — LOCAL CONSIGNEES — DESPATCH FROM MASTER—GOVERNMENT AGENCIES INTERESTED— BERTHING THE VESSEL

CHAPTER IV

ENTERING A VESSEL FROM A FOREIGN PORT

U. S. PUBLIC HEALTH SERVICE—U. S. CUSTOMS—DEPARTMENT OF AGRICULTURE—PREPARATIONS FOR DISCHARGE

CHAPTER V

TERMINAL OPERATION

BASIC TERMINOLOGY—TERMINAL FACILITIES, EQUIPMENT, CHARGES—CUSTOMS PRACTICE—FOREIGN TRADE ZONE—RECEIVING CARGO—HATCH BOOKS—STORAGE AND HANDLING—OVER, SHORT AND DAMAGED REPORTS

CONTENTS

CHAPTER VI

VESSEL IN PORT

REPAIRS—STEWARD'S SUPPLIES—ENGINE ROOM REQUIRE-
MENTS—ACCOUNTING—FOREIGN FLAG VESSELS AND CON-
SULS—SHIPPING COMMISSIONERS—OFFICER REQUIREMENTS
—ABLE SEAMEN—ENGINE DEPARTMENT—STAFF OFFICERS
—INSPECTION OF VESSELS—STEAMSHIP AGENTS

CHAPTER VII

CARGO HANDLING

HANDLING GEAR — CRANES — SLINGS — PALLETS — CON-
TAINERS:—HOW SELECT HANDLING GEAR?—THE ROLE OF
THE LONGSHOREMEN—TIMING AND COSTS

CHAPTER VIII

CARGO PROCUREMENT

CARGO SOLICITATION—CARGO SELECTION—CARGO BOOK—
OPTIONS—FREIGHT ENGAGEMENT—FOREIGN TRADE QUOTA-
TIONS

CHAPTER IX

CARGO STOWAGE

BOAT NOTES—SUPERCARGO—CHECKERS—VESSEL LOADING
RESPONSIBILITY—PREPLANNING OF LOADING—EXCEPTIONS
TO CARGO CONDITION—BROKEN STOWAGE—STOWAGE FAC-
TOR—VESSEL TRIM—VESSEL ROLLING—DUNNAGE—DECK
CARGO STOWAGE

CHAPTER X

VESSEL STABILITY

EFFECT OF STABILITY—METACENTER—RIGHTING FORCE—
COMPUTING THE GM—FREE SURFACE CORRECTION

CONTENTS

CHAPTER XI

CARGO DOCUMENTATION

CHAPTER XII

OCEAN FREIGHT RATES

CHAPTER XIII

VESSEL AT SEA

CHAPTER XIV

VESSEL CHARTERING

CHAPTER XV

FOREIGN FREIGHT FORWARDERS

CONTENTS

CHAPTER XVI

MARINE INSURANCE

CHAPTER XVII

ADMIRALTY AND MARITIME LAW

CHAPTER XVIII

LABOR RELATIONS

CHAPTER XIX

OCEAN SHIPPING VIA CANALS

CONTENTS

Courtesy of Standard Oil Company of California.

Cutaway drawings of tanker T.S. Petersen, 36,280-ton displacement, powered by steam turbines developing 13,750 shaft horsepower. Normal operating speed is approximately 16 knots. Liquid capacity of this tanker is 10,100,000 gallons. Pumps discharge cargo at rate of 20,000 barrels an hour.

CHAPTER I

Ship Characteristics

In the maritime industry, as in other occupations, there has grown a special language descriptive of the ship and her movements. To fail to use the sea-going terminology is to be branded a land-lubber who does not understand sailors and ships.

A *gangplank* or brow is put in place by the pier for the convenience of the vessel to permit boarding the vessel from shoreside. Or the vessel may put over a companion-ladder which is a collapsible stairway which folds up tightly against the ship's side. When at sea, a *Jacob's ladder,* made of rope and suspended over the ship's rail is used.

When aboard a ship, to indicate direction or place on a vessel, any point between the speaker's location and the bow of the vessel is termed *forward.* The opposite direction towards the stern of the vessel or that area, is *aft. Starboard* is the right side of the vessel, or a change in the course of the vessel to the right, or is the direction towards the right from the ship in which an object lies. *Port* is the left side of the vessel, or a change in direction of the ship's course to the left, or is a direction or bearing to the left from the ship.

The forward part of the ship is the *bow.* It is that section from the extreme tip of the vessel, called the stem or sometimes, cut-water, backwards until the ship's sides cease widening and run parallel. The after part of the vessel is the *stern* commencing at the point where the ship's sides begin to converge and onward to the extreme end of the vessel.

1

The center portion of the ship is termed *midships* and usually comprises the section in which the engines, the navigation bridge, and the officers' quarters are located.

Cargo ships usually have three structures built above the main deck. They receive their names from old time sailing ships which had very elaborate houses erected in these portions of the ship called castles, as they were intended to be occupied by the master or ship owner or the crew. The forecastle, pronounced as fo'cas'l, was at the bow of the ship and housed the crew. It was notorious for its dirty and poor accommodations. Now the sailor's quarters are generally midships, above the main deck, and are comfortable, clean and convenient.

The structure in the center of the vessel is called the midships house, sometimes the center castle. The raised section at the stern of the ship is the *poop*. Vessels with these three elevated portions above the main deck are termed three-island type.

The *main deck* of the vessel is the complete, water-tight deck which forms the uppermost part of the hull of the vessel and generally extends unbroken from bow to the stern of the ship.

Below the main deck and parallel to it are platforms called *'tween decks*. Two sets of 'tween decks become *upper* and *lower 'tween decks*. An *orlop* deck is a partial platform located between the 'tween decks in the bow of the vessel.

Erections above the main deck are the ship's *superstructure* and the decks receive their names from their uses, as the *bridge* deck which forms a part of the navigational bridge.

A person's movement between decks also has a special terminology. To go down into a ship is to *go below;* to go up to the main deck is to *go topside;* to go up on a mast is to *go aloft*.

On cargo ships, the various compartments into which the ship is divided are *holds* and are numbered beginning at the bow consecutively towards the stern. Thus No. 1 hatch is the entrance to No. 1 'tween deck and No. 1 lower hold, and No. 2 hatch is the next compartment aft. Areas on any deck within a hold are indicated as, port or starboard, forward or aft, midships towards the center of the ship, and in the *wings* are towards the side of the ship until they touch the side plates of the ships when they are against the *skin* of the vessel. Undefined areas between the holds of the ship are *no-man's land*. All of this terminology becomes of practical use to the agent in designating the place where cargo has been stowed, so that the consignee may secure the prompt discharge of a particular lot.

Basically all ships follow the same rules of construction, but there is infinite variance in the size of the vessels, the fineness of the lines of their hulls and the arrangement of their compartments to carry the cargoes for their prospective employment. In size they vary from a tiny out-board motor to the S.S. *United States*, 990 feet in length with gross tonnage of 53,330 tons. The above-water silhouettes in Figure 1 indicate the more common types of ocean going vessels.

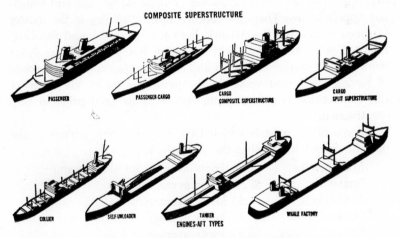

Figure 1. Principal Types of Merchant Ships

In hull design, the craft vary from hydroplanes which strive for minimum displacement to the tremendous ocean going vessels with a draft of 35 feet or more. The underwater bodies of these ships range from the round, full hulls of the freight ships to the speedy fine-lined passenger vessels and extremely slender yachts. The slenderness of the hull designed for speed is referred to as a percentage of *block co-efficient,* which is the ratio between the size of the hull of the vessel and an imaginary block of wood from which the hull was supposed to have been carved. Thus a sleek yacht would be 50%, a fast fine-lined passenger vessel would be about 70%, whereas a fat, round bottomed freighter might have a 90% block co-efficient. Every vessel has its own percentage according to the volume which the hull of the vessel bears to the uncut block.

It is the trade into which the vessel will be placed that controls all of the characteristics of size, shape, speed and compartmentation. The greatest and most costly of all vessels built are those intended for the passenger business, with emphasis on speed and luxurious appointments. Almost the entire underdeck space is used for passenger accommodations leaving only a small area for baggage, mail and express shipments.

Passenger vessels are the highly advertised class of vessels that appeal to the traveling public by their speed, size and luxurious appointments. There has been a historic rivalry in the matter of speed of crossing the Atlantic between New York and the Continent. For years every maritime nation has produced the finest work of their marine architects and engineers to capture the record of having the fastest vessel in the passenger trade. The story of this competition is a fascinating history of national pride in ship construction.

Some of the vessels which have held the blue ribbon in the past for speed in crossing the Atlantic are:

MAURETANIA	26.25 knots average for the crossing
BREMEN	27.83 knots average
NORMANDIE	31.20 knots average
QUEEN MARY	31.72 knots average
UNITED STATES	35.59 knots average

A *knot* is a measure of speed equalling one nautical mile per hour. A nautical mile is one minute of arc measured at the earth's equator and equals 6,080.20 feet On July 1, 1954, in the interest of international relationships, the United States adopted a new standard for the nautical mile, 6,076.10333 feet. The difference of 4.1 feet shorter does not affect navigational calculations.

As the passenger trade is necessarily limited to voyages between large centers of population which supply the volume of travelers required to support these costly ships, there has developed a *combination* passenger and freight type of ship whose passenger accommodations are limited to the ship's superstructure. The area below the main deck is utilized for cargo. These vessels have a cruising speed of 15 to 18 knots and offer a reasonably fast voyage to the passengers and comparatively fast delivery of cargo.

As airlines have seriously cut into the long distance passenger routes in the carrying of passengers, the combination type vessel seems to be the answer to this problem as it retains to the surface craft the transportation of the freight, which is the greater revenue producing operation, and at the same time offers reasonably fast passenger service.

The most usual type of sea-going vessel is the *general cargo*, or dry cargo vessel which is designed to carry the great bulk of cargo in international transportation. Many of these ships are also equipped with tanks which can be used in the hauling of liquid items, as the various kinds of mineral, vegetable and fish oils. Also these ships may have limited refrigerator space, but their primary purpose is the transportation of dry cargo.

One of the most efficient types of carrier is the *tanker*, used mostly in the transportation of petroleum products. It may be so compartmented that it can carry 15 kinds of oil products and deliver them more cheaply than any other form of carrier. They receive their cargoes from specially designed piers which are equipped with numerous pipe lines for the loading and discharging of the petroleum items. The tankers are generally privately owned by the oil companies whose products they are distributing.

The *refrigerator* vessel, "reefer," has her compartments insulated so that the areas may be maintained at the fixed temperatures required by the cargo. The space has two uses. The freezing compartment maintains a temperature of about 15 degrees below zero Fahrenheit, during the transportation of frozen meat and fish. The other areas, "cool rooms," are kept at temperatures just above freezing, 32 to 34 degrees Fahrenheit, for the keeping of vegetables, fruit, dairy products. Very efficient refrigerating machinery keeps the temperature in the compartments constant during the entire voyage, and, as in the case with fruits, the air is withdrawn from the holds and replaced with fresh, chilled air furnishing ventilated refrigeration.

Another type of carrier is the *grain carrying* vessel whose holds are constructed so that grain in bulk may be loaded into them and be transported without leaking into other parts of the vessel. Special loading devices at elevators fill the vessels and other machinery discharges the grain at destination. Nearly any dry cargo vessel can be used for the same purpose by lining the vessel's holds to prevent the grain from seeping out and by constructing shifting bulkheads in the ship to prevent the grain from flowing to one side if the vessel rolls in a seaway. Grain will shift if the inclination exceeds 23 degrees, the angle of repose for wheat. This is corrected sometimes by overstowing the bulk grain with layers of sacked grain.

Ore vessels are specially built for that trade and also have special facilities for loading and discharging efficiently. Some of the ore carriers have the bottom of the lower hold raised so that the heavy ore will not be too low in the vessel thus making an unusually low center of gravity in the cargo. This would cause the ship to suffer strain during a storm. If too low, the ship would become "stiff" and would offer sharp resistance to waves rather than easing the shock by rolling away from the impact of the waves.

Lumberships are designed with as few bulkheads and stanchions as possible below decks to permit the quick and easy loading of lumber and logs. The lumber schooners had unusually long booms to reach as far as possible across a pier to pick up a load of lumber at a distance.

Colliers are vessels that are engaged in the transport of cargoes of coal and they usually ply between ports that are specially equipped with bunkers for the storage of coal to permit its quick loading into the vessels by gravity chutes and those ports which have discharging machinery adapted to handling coal.

Vessels which have been designed for the carrying of the products of a single industry such as oil, grain, lumber are referred to as *industrial carriers* by reason of their specialized type of cargo.

Sea trains allow loaded railroad cars to be rolled into the holds of the vessel. At destination the cars are landed and proceed on rails to inland stations without shipments in the cars having been handled. These ships have been in service for several years between Florida and Cuba.

A new type of vessel has been built for the Navy, called a *Roll-on, Roll-off* ship, which can load wheeled and track vehicles through stern ports and side ports, each vehicle proceeding on its own power to a designated place within the vessel. If the car is going into the lower hold it follows a hydraulic ramp that takes it downward to the selected deck. The purpose of the vessel is to eliminate the use of cranes in loading and discharging and to speed both operations.

These designations of type of ship comprise the more usual varieties of the larger sea-going vessels. There are many other types of commercial vessels engaged in coastwise and interior waters service such as ferries, barges, lighters, tugs, tankers, fishing vessels and yachts. Some of the larger vessels of these types may find employment in ocean-going voyages.

Carrier Classification. A further classification of vessels is made for the purpose of governmental regulation of freight rates and other matters of public interest. This division is made into private, common, and contract carriers as evidenced by the contractual relation between carrier operator and cargo owner.

Private carriers are those owned by a private company for the distribution of that firm's products, as the oil tankers operating for the petroleum companies. The difference in operation lies mostly in the question of ocean freight rates which are considered as costs by the private carrier but must contain a profit in the case of common carriers.

Common carriers are those vessels which hold themselves out to carry the cargo of any shipper, indiscriminately and for hire. This service to the general public is the basis for regulation of rates and shipping conditions by governmental agencies for the protection of the public interests.

Contract carriers are those carriers that make special agreements with one or more shippers to carry the special type of commodity produced by such shippers. The contract between the carrier and the shipper covers the shipping conditions and the rate agreed upon for the transportation.

Ships may be further classified according to the regularity of their services. *Liners* are those vessels scheduled to sail regularly between designated ports. They form a line between ranges which are areas in which sufficient freight is available to keep the vessels constantly employed so that they may offer a regularity of future sailings. They are called berth-line vessels by reason of their advertisement of their loading berths. For the purpose of stabilizing rates and preventing rate wars, the various lines serving the same ports usually form a conference wherein they agree to quote the same rates to shippers.

Tramp vessels are those which are free to accept cargo wherever it may be offered and are in open competition with all other vessels in the matter of rates. Their operations are usually fixed by chartering agents located in various ports of the world who submit offerings of cargo through their associates in those ports.

Chartered vessels are those which are hired for some special employment by an individual shipper under a written contract called a charter-party. The term of employment of the ship may be for a single voyage, or for a definite period of time, or the vessel itself (bare boat) may be turned over to the cargo owner or another carrier for operation. The matter of rates is negotiated in each instance and subject to competition with vessels of many nations and therefore reflects world-wide shipping conditions similar to those among tramp vessels.

It is possible that any individual ship may be classified in several ways and may shift between classes by reason of changes in ownership or operation. Summarizing the classifications, vessels may be listed as:

BY CONSTRUCTION OF PASSENGER AND FREIGHT ACCOMMODATIONS

Passenger vessel   Combination freight and passenger   Cargo vessel

BY CONSTRUCTION FOR SPECIAL USE
   Tankers, ore vessels, fishing vessels, whale factories, etc.

BY CONTRACT FOR REVENUE
   Common carriers
   Contract carriers
   Private carriers

BY REGULARITY OF SERVICE
   Liners with schedules
   Tramp vessels with varying employment
   Charters with special employment

CHAPTER 2

Ship and Cargo Measurements

Consider the ship as a cylinder floating in water. When the ship is empty, she floats high in the water. When weight as cargo is added the ship sinks lower in the water. The measurement of the depth to which the ship sinks permits determination of the ship's carrying capacity, the present amount of cargo loaded, and the ship's margin of safety in carrying capacity. This is possible because a floating body displaces an amount of liquid, and the weight of the body equals the weight of liquid displaced.

A vessel may be loaded with cargo until it is as low in the water as it is safe for the vessel to be and still proceed to sea. This limit of safety is marked on the ship's side as the point beyond which it would be dangerous to add more weight. This is the ship's *load line*. In practice, the position of this line is determined by the ship's builders, officially measured, and then engraved on the ship's plates and painted white. It is located on the ship's side at the midship mark.

The distance from this line upward to the ship's main deck is the calculated *free board*. The free board at any particular time is the distance from the level of the surface of the water on the ship's side upward to the main deck and indicates the state of the vessel's load and the margin of safety. It usually is greater than the distance from the loadline but may be slightly less when the vessel is fully loaded.

Tonnage and vessel capacity. The ship is fully loaded when she is "down to her marks," that is, when her draft coincides with her loadline indicating that she has taken on board all the weight that she can safely carry. The sum of the weight of the ship plus the

9

weight of cargo, fuel and stores, expressed in long tons (2240 lbs.) and sometimes in metric tons (2204.6 lbs.), is the vessel's *displacement tonnage.*

The expression "displacement" has two meanings: (a) the volume of the water displaced by the ship measured in cubic feet, and (b) the weight of the quantity of water displaced expressed in tons of 2240 lbs. When no qualification has been expressed, the term "displacement" relates to the weight factor to describe the vessel and her carrying capacity.

From the ship's plans the following data are used to determine a vessel's displacement tonnage:

Length, breadth and draft of the ship in feet.

The weight of one cubic foot of seawater of specific gravity 1.026 is 64 pounds. One ton of seawater, weight 2240 lbs., is 35 cubic feet, which is the volume of one ton of seawater.

Block coefficient of a vessel is the ratio between the volume of displacement of the vessel and the volume of a block of the same length, breadth and height (draft of ship). As the ship narrows at bow and stern it occupies less cubic volume than the block of the same dimensions. Passenger ships have "fine" lines for speed while freight vessels have fuller lines for freight carrying. The finer the ship's lines, the smaller the block coefficient becomes.

Example: Ship's length 500 feet, times breadth 65 feet times draft 30 feet times block coefficient 0.700 divided by 35 cubic feet to 2240 lbs. equals 19,500 tons (2240 lbs.) ship's displacement tonnage.

The total amount of weight that a vessel can safely carry is termed *dead weight carrying capacity* and is calculated by subtracting the weight of the light (empty) vessel from the displacement tonnage. It is expressed in long or metric tons.

Example:

Displacement tonnage	....	14,245 long tons
Weight of light ship	....	3,364
Dead weight capacity	....	10,881

The displacement tonnage of a vessel is the total weight of the vessel and the limit of weight that she can safely carry. This figure is the statement of the size of the vessel determined from its weight carrying factor. The ship's displacement at any stage of her loading is obtained by reading her draft (depth in water) and with this figure referring to a table (ship's immersion scale) which shows the relationship between the ship's draft at all stages and the vessel's displacement and also shows directly the amount of weight that has been placed in the vessel.

At any draft (depth) of a vessel in water, the weight of the volume of water displaced is known. This is determined from the combined weight of vessel and cargo loaded at that time. The weight of the empty vessel is also known; hence the weight of the load on board can be determined by subtraction of the weight of the empty ship from the displacement shown.

Note these definitions as defined in *Modern Ship Stowage**:

Register Tonnage—Register tonnage is applicable to both gross and net—in other words, it can be expressed as gross register tonnage or net register tonnage. However, it is ordinarily used to refer to net register tonnage. Register tonnages are so named because they are the tonnages shown on the documents of registration issued for each vessel in its home country.

Gross Tonnage—The entire internal cubic capacity of the holds and erections on and/or above the upper deck to the hull of the ship expressed in tons of 100 cubic feet, except for certain spaces which are exempted, such as:

Peak and other tanks for water ballast; open forecastle, bridge and poop; excess of hatchways; certain light and air spaces; domes and skylights; condenser; anchor gear, wheel house; galley; cabins for passengers (when on decks not to the hull); and other items.

Net Tonnage—The tonnage of a ship remaining after certain deductions have been made from the gross tonnage expressed in tons of 100 cubic feet. Among the deductions are: crew spaces; master's cabin; navigation spaces; donkey engine and boiler; shaft trunks; allowance for propelling power; and other items.

Suez and Panama Canal Tonnages—These are arrived at along the same lines as are the gross and net tonnages. Each is,

*U. S. Government Printing Office, Washington, D. C., 1942.

as a rule, larger than the register tonnage because of the inclusion of space which, under national measurement rules, is exempted.

Of greatest interest to the vessel operator from a revenue standpoint is the net register tonnage, because that expresses (in units of 100 cubic feet to a ton) the amount of space available within the ship for cargo carrying. By inspection of the isometric view of the Liberty Ship, Figure 2, it can be noted that the spaces to be deducted are in black and the spaces available for cargo have been left white. The sum of white spaces would be the net register tonnage.

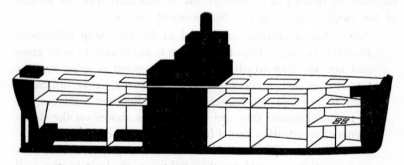

Figure 2. Isometric view of a Liberty Ship. Total Cargo space shown in white equals net register tonnage.

The gross register tonnage of a Liberty Ship is 7176 tons of 100 cubic feet. The net register tonnage of a Liberty ship is 4375 tons of 100 cubic feet.

Both of these tonnages are carefully measured by government agencies and are certified on the ship's register, which is a document describing the vessel and indicating her nationality and home port. The certifying agency for the United States is the American Bureau of Shipping; for Great Britain, Lloyds Register; for France, Bureau Veritas; for Norway, Det Norske Veritas; for Italy, Registro Italiano Naval.

These two tonnages give the ship operator the exact data on the capacity of his vessel. The net register tonnage tells the operator the exact size of the cargo spaces into which he must fit his shipment. The dead weight tonnage tells him just how heavy that cargo can be for the ship to be able to transport it safely.

The *capacity plan* of a ship, indicates the total amount of space available for cargo on the vessel listed as net register tons. The cubic capacity of each hold is also indicated. Both upper and lower sections have their capacities expressed in cubic feet. The height, breadth, and length of each compartment are likewise indicated. Hence, the agent knows the size of each compartment and its shape into which he must fit his cargo. Even the narrowing of the ship at bow and stern is shown.

For oil and liquid cargoes, the capacities of the tanks are given in tons. This figure immediately gives the amount of liquid that can be carried and at the same time how much weight will be added when the tanks are filled.

Liberty ships have tanks which may be used either for liquid or dry cargo. These are located in No. 1 lower hold and forward of No. 4 hold. Tank tops can be removed to insert dry cargo, or the tanks can be filled with oil through pipe lines.

Other data on cargo spaces includes the refrigerator spaces. Certain holds are insulated for reefer purposes, and again the cubic footage is given and also the three dimensions of each compartment. These reefer spaces may also be used for dry cargo, but a part of the space which would otherwise be available for cargo has been used in insulating the compartments. This insulation is about a foot thick on all sides and top and bottom of the reefer compartment.

These dry cargo spaces are given "bale" and "grain" capacities and are measured in cubic feet. As there are many curved sections and angles in these compartments, it is estimated that considerable space will not be usable for cargo. Hence the *bale capacity* is a practical measurement slightly less than the accurately measured volume of the holds. When grain in bulk is loaded in the same compartments, the grain flows into corners and fills curved spaces into which bales or boxes would not fit. Hence, the *grain capacity* is slightly larger than the figure for the bale capacity for the same compartment.

Tanks in the double bottom of the ship are used for carrying fuel oil, cargo oil, fresh water, or water ballast. The capacity of each of the tanks is given in tons which indicates the amount of liquid each tank will hold and indicates the weight added to the ship's cargo which must be accounted for in the safe loading of vessels.

Measurements of the clear spaces on deck suitable for deck cargo are also given. In this case only the length and breadth are given. The weight of cargo that can be loaded on these deck areas is dependent upon the stability of the ship as affected by the weight of cargo laden underdeck.

The *cargo ton* is used by shipping companies for the purpose of assessing freight rates and for data on the cargo. It shows the two elements of each piece of cargo: its weight and its cubic measurement. Information as to the weight of each item is necessary to insure that the vessel will not be overloaded. Its size is important to ascertain that the space under deck is large enough to hold all of the cargo booked. The steamship companies have worked out the ratio between the volume of a shipment and its weight so that when the ship is completely filled under deck she will have all the weight she can safely carry. The selection of cargo to meet this end is the work of the ship's agent and is important from the point of view of producing a maximum amount of revenue.

This ratio is 40 cubic feet to 2240 lbs. (East Coast); 40 cubic feet to 2000 lbs. (West Coast); 1 cubic meter to 1 metric ton, or 35.3 cubic feet to 2204.6 lbs. (Foreign).

For the steamship company, this cargo ton is the unit of measurement of the amount of cargo the vessel can accept from shippers. The total amount of cargo the ship can carry is the total weight of the cargo offered divided by tons of 2240 lbs. (2000 lbs.), and the sum must not exceed the tons dead weight the vessel is registered to carry. At the same time the same cargo in its total measurement of cubic feet must not exceed the available space under deck.

The cargo ton also serves the operator and the shipper as a form of quotation of ocean freight, particularly where the volume and weight of the shipment are not definitely known prior to shipment. The operator will make a quotation which provides that the ship has the option of charging freight either on the basis of the item's weight or on its measurement, whichever will produce the greater revenue for the vessel.

For example, the quotations on two items, a table and a safe, could be stated as $20.00 per 2000 lbs. or 40 cubic feet, ship's option. The table measures 2 x 4 x 5 feet totaling 40 cu. ft., but the weight of the table as shipped is only 100 lbs. If the freight were calculated on the measurement basis of $20 per 40 cu. ft., the charge would be $20.00, but if made on the weight basis of $20 per 2000 lbs., the table's weight of 100 lbs would produce a revenue of only $1.00. The ship exercises the option stated in the quotation and makes the freight bill $20.00. On the quotation made for transporting the safe of $20 per 2000 lbs./40 cu. ft., ship's option, the freight calculated on the weight of the safe of 4000 pounds would return $40.00 in revenue. If the freight were figured on the measurement basis of the safe, then this item measuring 2 x 4 x 5 feet totaling 40 cu. ft. would produce a revenue of only $20.00. The ship would figure the freight bill at $40.00 on the weight basis, thereby exercising its option of assessing the freight by the method which produces the greater revenue. The steamship operator, then, will charge $20 for carrying the table and $40 for transporting the safe. Both operator and shipper must agree upon the weight ton to be used, for there is a difference of over 11% in the weight of a long and a short ton.

Capacity Plan. This plan serves many practical uses in the loading of a vessel, since the sheer plan gives the general layout of each hold and its dimensions and capacities. From such a plan the following details may be ascertained:

Cargo booms are shown with the masts upon which they are mounted and the directions in which the booms tend.

The cubic volume of each compartment is shown in cubic feet and the heights of each compartment and to the hatch combings which extend down into each hold by about two feet and thus lessen the headroom.

The positions and capacities of all fuel and cargo tanks are shown in tons of oil and salt water and fresh water. Other compartments not available for cargo are also shown together with any obstructions which may reduce cargo space.

The overall length of the vessel is shown and the position of the midship line is indicated. For convenience in spotting cargo on the pier within reach of the booms before the vessel arrives, the distances between the centers of the hatches are indicated.

The purpose of the trimming scale is to indicate to the officer loading the vessel the effect of placing 100 tons of cargo at various distances either forward or aft of the center of the vessel. For instance, if 100 tons were loaded at the very bow of the vessel it would increase the draft readings at the bow by 10.0 inches but the stern of the vessel would raise and decrease its draft reading by 5.9 inches. These figures would apply when the mean draft of the ship was 27 feet. If the draft of the ship was about 17 feet mean, then the lower line of figures would be used and the change of bow reading would be plus 11.3 inches and the reading at the stern a minus 7.5 inches. This is the greatest possible change to be accomplished by placing the weight at the extreme end of the ship. The vessel must be evenly trimmed so that the readings of the draft at bow and stern are the same or with a slightly greater draft at the stern. If the ship is "down by the head," that is a greater draft at the bow, the ship will not steer easily and will veer off her course frequently.

In the immersion scale, the large central figures are the mean draft of the vessel at any time during its loading. The mean draft is obtained by reading the draft figures which are painted both on the bow and on the stern of the vessel so that they can be read from the pier. The draft is read in feet and inches by observing the height of the water on the draft figures. The figures indicate the vertical distance from the keel line and are six inches tall and spaced one foot apart. Hence, when the water touches the lower edge of the figure the draft is, for example, 17 feet. When the figure 17 is covered the reading is 17' 6''. As the water touches 18 the draft is 18'. Draft is read to the nearest inch. The mean draft is the mean between the bow and stern readings.

First column is the *deadweight* in salt water. There are allowances made to the salt water figure if the vessel is loading in brackish water or fresh river water. The draft reading extended into this column will give the amount of weight that is aboard the vessel consisting of cargo, fuel oil, water, ballast, that is, all weights exclusive of the weight of the empty ship itself. The load line and the Plimsoll Mark are shown near the top of the column.

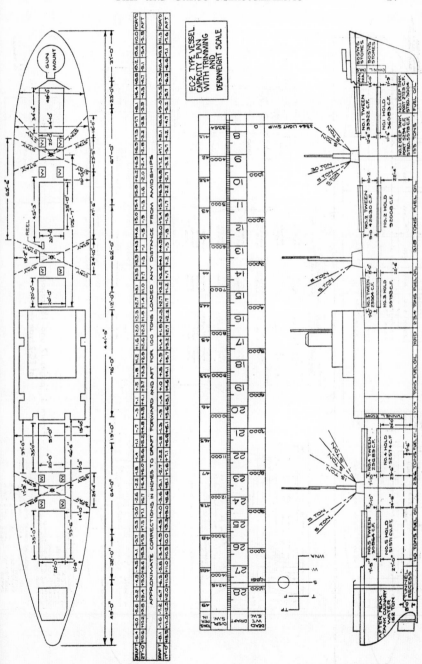

EC-2 TYPE VESSEL
CAPACITY PLAN
WITH TRIMMING
AND
DEADWEIGHT SCALE

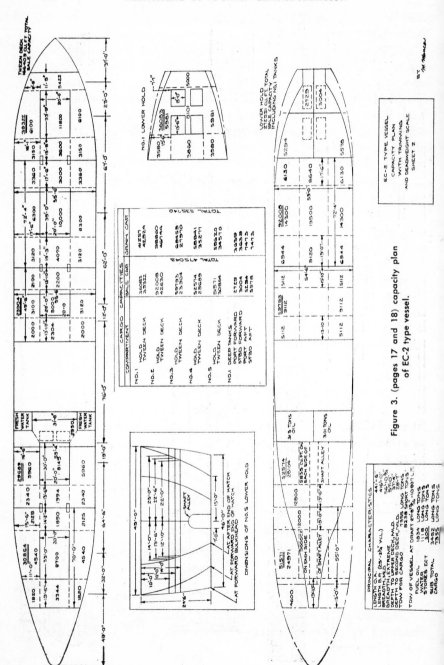

Figure 3. (pages 17 and 18) capacity plan of EC-2 type vessel.

The latter indicates the extreme depth to which the ship may be laden under various conditions of season and voyage.

The third column is the ship's *displacement* tonnage in salt water. It is the total weight of the ship, cargo, fuel oil, stores, crew and gear.

The final column is the *TPI*, tons per inch of immersion. It tells at various drafts how many long tons of weight must be added to cause the vessel to increase its draft by one inch. It takes 49 long tons to cause a fully loaded Liberty ship to sink one inch lower in the water. To the officer loading a ship, this scale serves as a measure of the cargo weight loaded and the available dead-weight for additional cargo loading.

Caution. Before converting the readings of the ship's draft into cargo loaded or the reading of the ship's inclinometer showing a list, check with the chief engineer and find if he has taken on water or oil or has shifted the contents from one tank to another.

The data from the deck plan shows the location of the hatches, the size of the hatch openings, and the location of the winches used to load into the holds. All obstructions are indicated, such as stays which support the masts and the distances between the stays which indicate the possibility of loading very long pieces of cargo without fouling the rigging. Finally, the clear deck space is shown as it is available for stowing deck cargo.

Coincident with the load line on the side of a vessel is the *Plimsoll Mark*. This mark takes its name from a member of the British Parliament who caused it to be officially adopted in Britain as a measure of a vessel's safe loading in any water and in any season.

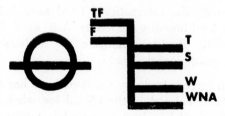

Figure 4. Load Line and Plimsoll Mark

The load line marks the maximum mean draft to which a vessel may be lawfully submerged. It is a circle 12″ in diameter, bisected by a line 18″ long and 1″ in breadth, the upper edge of the line passing through the center of the disc. The load line extended into the Plimsoll mark coincides with the line "S" which indicates the point to which the vessel may be safely loaded in salt water in summer.

To the left of the vertical line of the Plimsoll mark are depths to which the vessel may be loaded in fresh water, "F", and in tropical fresh water, "TF". A vessel loaded in fresh water to the mark "F" will immediately lessen its draft to mark "S" as it enters the ocean and is buoyed up by denser salt water. On the salt water side of the line, the vessel may be loaded according to season to "T" in the tropics, to "S" in summertime, to "W" in wintertime and only to "WNA" when her voyage will be in the North Atlantic in wintertime. The marks apply when the voyage is in the ocean, but a vessel loading in fresh water to proceed to sea is given allowances to compensate for the difference in densities of the waters to be encountered.

The distances between the lines in the Plimsoll mark vary slightly with each vessel. For a Liberty-type ship the distance between "S" and "W" is seven inches. This means that a fully loaded Liberty ship can lawfully load in summer 343 more long tons of cargo than she can in winter.

The United States Coast Guard enforces the regulations regarding the load line. The American Bureau of Shipping and Lloyd's Register of Shipping have been appointed to determine the position of the line in accordance with "An Act to Establish Load Lines for American Vessels" approved March 2, 1929, and in conformity with the International Load Line Act of 1930. At the ends of the load line disc the letters "A B" or "L R" (American Bureau or Lloyd's Register) indicate the authority which has determined the position of the line.

A vessel in foreign trade by sea must have her draft and her load line positions entered in the official log when leaving port. Violations of the load line laws may be for: failure to have load lines on one or both sides of the vessel; failure to have load lines conspicuously marked on both sides of vessel; failure to have a valid load line certificate on board; failure to enter in the log the

positions of the load lines and the drafts forward and aft; sub-
mergence of the load lines; alteration, defacement, obliteration or
concealment of load lines.

A penalty of $100 may be imposed on the master if he fails
to show whether or not the applicable load line is submerged.

The data on ship's draft is of vital importance to marine
underwriters who insure ship and cargo upon the understanding
that the ship's operators have sent the vessel to sea in a seaworthy
condition and not overloaded as evidenced by the submerging of
her loadline.

CHAPTER 3

Before The Vessel Arrives

To a great extent, the efficient handling of a vessel in port and her prompt dispatch depend on careful and thorough preparation made before her arrival. The extent of this planning is limited by the agent's advance information concerning the vessel's cargo and operating needs.

Inward Foreign Manifests. Details of the cargo are usually available from *inward foreign manifests*. forwarded by air mail by the overseas agents who have dispatched the vessel from each foreign port. These are carefully studied by the local ship's operator to determine the disposition of each item of cargo and to provide for the prompt transshipment to oncarrying vessels or for inland and local delivery. If the cargo is intended for transshipment by another ocean vessel, it must be made available to the oncarrying ship either by storing it on the pier of discharge, waiting the call of the other vessel, or by providing for its transfer to the berth of such vessel. If the cargo is to go inland by rail or motor truck, appropriate carriers must be notified of the amount of the transshipment and the character of the cargo so that they may supply the proper number and type of cars. This may require gondola cars for steel shapes, boxcars for general merchandise, and refrigerator cars for perishable items.

In the carrying out of these details, the designations used in this text of ship's "operator" or "agent" or "representative" are used to identify some individual whose duty is to expedite the discharge of the vessel. The authority of such individual to give these orders may come from a number of sources. He may be an employee of the company that owns and operates the vessel, or he may be individually commissioned to take care of these details. Sometimes the vessel is owned by another company or a foreign concern and may be consigned to the individual or his company as agent for the vessel owner in the discharge of the vessel. At other times the charterer of a vessel may be operating the ship for his own account.

Discharge Planning. Whatever the source of his authority, this individual receives instructions and requests from many sources. These directions may appear on bills of lading, or on the ship's inward manifest, or be contained in separate communications from the overseas agent, or by request of the shipper or the consignee, or by foreign freight forwarders, or customs house brokers who are acting as agents for the shipper or the consignee. These special instructions and the normal distribution for forwarding of cargo, require many prompt actions on the part of the representative.

Many items of cargo for delivery at destination carry the specification made by the shipper or the consignee of *"ship's tackle delivery."* This means that instead of the usual across-the-pier movement by the cargo, the consignee will take delivery from the ship's tackle at the instant of its being unloaded. This may be necessary because of the nature of the item itself or may save the consignee a part of the terminal expenses; namely, those of moving the cargo across the pier to the warehouse, and a part of the wharfage charge, and the further expense of loading the item on to a carrier which will remove it from the pier to consignee's specified destination.

To take delivery in this manner the consignee will require the proper form of transportation, according to the type of cargo, to be available at ship's side when his item of cargo is ready for discharge. The item might be, for example, a heavy piece of machinery to be unloaded onto a flat car on rails at the ship's side, or onto a barge on the offshore side of the vessel, or into the water offshore, as logs, which must be received by a tug with boomsticks. All of these facilities must be at the proper spot and at the exact time they are needed in order that there be no delay. This coordination sometimes necessitates intricate planning by the ship's agent in advance of the ship's arrival.

Local cargo, and cargo which does not have further routing instructions, will be discharged directly to the pier and into the custody of the terminal operator, who also studies the manifests and selects the areas on his pier into which the cargo will be assembled according to bill-of-lading, ready for delivery to the individual consignee or to the transshipment carrier. The operator further arranges to have the proper cargo handling gear available for various kinds of cargo and estimates the number of longshore gangs needed to receive the cargo. He must also instruct his checkers concerning the plans for the spotting of the shipments on the pier.

The "long hatch." Vessel agent and terminal operator will confer with the stevedore manager as to number of hatches to be worked, the number of gangs to be ordered, and special equipment needed for discharge. The discussion will center around the "long hatch", meaning the hold containing cargo which will require the longest time in discharging. This fixes the length of time required to unload the vessel. It may be necessary to work this hatch overtime or even around-the-clock in order to expedite the discharge of the vessel. The period of time necessary to unload this one hold should have been foreseen by the loading agents and balanced by equalizing the amount of cargo in other holds of the ship so that all hatches will work out at approximately the same time. This "long hatch", therefore, determines the number of stevedore gangs required and the length of time the ship will be occupied in discharge.

The vessel operator has the further duty of notifying all interested parties of the presence of their cargo aboard the ship and of receiving their instructions concerning the delivery, storage or forwarding of each consignment of cargo.

Local Consignees. *Local importers* are concerned with arrival time of goods in order to plan their delivery to purchasers or for forwarding to other destinations. They are often impatient to get possession of their merchandise by having it discharged first from the vessel. This can be accomplished if a stowage plan of the cargo on the ship has been received showing where larger blocks of cargo have been stowed in the vessel. From this plan the availability of the particular lot for prompt discharge can be learned. If the item of cargo is small it may not be shown on the stowage plan but can be located in "hatch books" which have been compiled by the purser during the inward voyage and made available upon arrival of the ship. The "hatch books" name each item of cargo alphabetically by shipping mark and give the place of stowage on board the ship.

Freight forwarders who represent importers in other cities have the interest of their clients in mind and use the advice of the prospective arrival of their client's cargo to expedite the delivery of the cargo or its transshipment.

Custom house brokers also can begin preparation of their customs entries according to the wishes of their clients as to whether the items will be entered for consumption and payment of duty, or go into a bonded warehouse for storage or be entered for immediate transportation to another customs port of entry in a distant city.

The physical disposition of part of the cargo as it will come from the ship on arrival, therefore, is determined by these many individual importers and agencies according to their needs. Their desires are communicated to the ship's agent and passed on to the terminal operator, the stevedore manager, and the transshipment carrier for appropriate action. Much of the cargo remaining in the vessel will not be subject to these special orders for distribution but will be coming forward under bills of lading indicating the consignees to whom it must be delivered at the destinations specified. Such cargo must be expedited and forwarded by the ship's agent. If the inward foreign manifests and the stowage plans have not been received prior to the ship's arrival, the ascertainment and disposition of these many details must be accomplished in the first hours after the ship's arrival. There is then the consequent burden of many items having to be accounted for during the actual discharge of the vessel with possible confusion and resulting delay to the delivery of the cargo.

Despatch from master. As to the vessel herself, aside from the cargo, there are many details to be attended to while in port. The most pressing of these needs are communicated by the ship's master by radio a day or two before she is due to arrive in port. An imaginary dispatch from the master of a vessel is inserted here indicating about twenty-five emergencies that the master expects the agent to handle during the brief time the vessel is in port. The troubles listed are typical of thousands to be met in the course of ship operation and cargo handling. As stated in the preface of this book, the vessel agent may not know how to handle the particular emergency but he must know where to look for prompt assistance in order that the ship be not delayed. The twenty-five commissions listed in the dispatch suggest their own remedies.

MACKAY RADIO

083016

SEATTLE SHIPPING COMPANY
   900 BROADWAY, SEATTLE
AT 0800 30 MILES WEST CAPE FLATTERY PROCEEDING AT 10 KNOTS DUE TO CRACKED RUDDER FRAME, ARRIVING PORT ANGELES 1700, FOR SEATTLE 10 PASSENGERS, 220 BAGS FIRST CLASS MAIL, 500 BALES SILK NEW YORK EXPRESS, 3000 TONS OVERLAND CARGO, 1223 TONS LOCAL GENERAL CARGO, 120 TONS COCONUT OIL IN NO. 1 DEEP TANKS, 3322 CASES JAPANESE SEED OYSTERS, 35 TONS FROZEN TUNA, SIX LIVE MONKEYS FOR SPOKANE ZOO, 25 TUBS GOLDFISH, 95 TON LOCOMOTIVE ON DECK NO. 2, 200,000 FEET MAHOGANY LOGS FOR DELIVERY IN RAFT, 300 TONS STEEL SHAPES FOR RAIL CAR DELIVERY, FOR TACOMA 650 TONS GENERAL CARGO, FOR OLYMPIA 15 TONS GENERAL, WILL REQUIRE RETUBING OF STARBOARD CONDENSER, NEED 850 TONS FUEL OIL, PAYROLL $4500, SECOND MATE ANDERSON REQUESTS RELIEF FOR ONE VOYAGE, SEAMAN WITH BROKEN LEG REQUIRES HOSPITALIZATION IMMEDIATELY, SEAMAN VIOLENTLY INSANE IN IRONS, SECURE PASSAGE THREE ADULTS TO CHICAGO SOONEST BY AIR, CANNOT LOAD DYNAMITE FOR YOKOHAMA.

SHIPPEN, MASTER

In addition to the attention required by the ship's personnel and the special items of cargo, the dispatch from the master indicates that the vessel herself must shift from her regular berth to four other berths. (To repair rudder frame at drydock, to discharge cargo in Tacoma, to unload coconut oil at a tank farm and to go on to an oil dock for fuel.) These vessel movements must be scheduled carefully to avoid delay in the ship's discharge and outward loading and be coordinated with the availability of the special type berths.

Government agencies interested. The following agencies have definite interests in ship, cargo or passengers and, therefore, must be notified of the expected hour of arrival of the vessel, both at a point of sanitary inspection and a port of discharge. Notification must be given to the U. S. Customs Bureau, the U. S. Public Health Service, the U. S. Immigration Service, U. S. Post Office, and the Department of Agriculture. Their interests will appear as the ship enters port.

A pilot for the vessel must be procured and notified in time for him to board the vessel at a point where the inland rules of navigation require that a specially trained and licensed officer be in charge of the navigation of the vessel while operating within territorial waters of United States.

Reservation must also be made of a sufficient number of tugs necessary to berth the vessel. As the ship approaches the pier and slows down, she loses steerage-way and her rudder becomes useless in its normal function. If there is a current flowing across the face of the pier, or a strong wind blowing, or if the vessel must be turned sharply to enter the slip, then one or more tugs are required to bring the ship into her berth. If conditions are favorable, the pilot will take pride in berthing the vessel without the aid of tugs by the skillful use of the ship's lines, engines, rudder, and winches.

In either case, there must be provided a gang of men, at least four, to receive and run the ship's lines as she docks. If not already permanently in place, these men will spot camels in the water alongside the pier at the location where the ship will finally rest. These camels are logs or beams that float between ship and pier to keep the vessel from scraping the piling or fouling the pier structure as she rises and falls with the tides.

Berthing the vessel. The technique of berthing a vessel with her own lines involves approaching the pier slowly until she is parallel to her berth and close enough so that light heaving lines may be thrown from ship to pier where they are taken by the waiting linesmen. If the ship should touch the pier while moving, the great weight would crush the pier and cause damage to the ship's hull. Therefore, the ship must be brought in contact with the pier as gently as possible. By direction of the pilot, the linesmen take the heavy mooring lines and place the eye or loop over indicated bollards or cleats spaced along the edge of the pier.

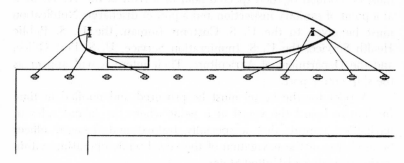

Figure 5.   Berthing a vessell with her own lines

The ship can then haul taut these lines with her winches or use them as spring lines with the aid of the ship's engines, to draw the vessel sidewise against the pier. The *bow line* leads ahead of the ship on the pier and is used to pull the vessel forward. The *stern lines* lead from the stern of the vessel to pull the vessel backward. *Breast lines* lead directly from ship to pier and are used to pull the ship sidewise toward the pier. *Spring lines* lead from the bow backwards to the pier so that when the vessel uses her engines to go ahead slowly, the *bow spring* draws the bow of the vessel towards the pier. The *stern spring* acts to draw the stern inward, as the vessel is backing. See Figure 5.

When a vessel is moving, she is *underway* and when backing, she has *stern way.* Legally speaking, a vessel, though not moving, is still considered to be underway if she is not moored to a pier, nor at anchor, nor aground.

As the vessel approaches her berth, she is moved to an exact position alongside the pier to a point indicated by a moveable sign, reading, "Place Bridge Here." The reason for this exact location is that certain heavy items of cargo, either for discharge or loading, have been so placed that they can be handled with the ship's gear without further moving of the cargo or that heavy cargo on the ship's deck will be positioned within reach of a fixed crane on the dock. The ship is made fast at that spot; the mooring lines are doubled for strength and safety. The pilot telegraphs to the engine room, "Finished with Engines" and leaves the navigating bridge. The vessel has been berthed.

CHAPTER 4

Entering A Vessel From A Foreign Port

Before a vessel which is inbound from a foreign port may commence to discharge her cargo, several governmental agencies must inspect the ship documents and personnel to determine the vessel's proper condition to enter the United States.

U. S. Public Health Service. Before the vessel proceeds to her berth, a *U. S. Public Health Service* representative boards to ascertain if ship or crew or passengers are infected with any dangerous disease which could be communicated to others upon the arrival of the ship in port or by the landing of the sick personnel. The ship must produce sanitary statements from the foreign ports she has visited which report the presence or absence of epidemics in those ports of serious diseases such as plague, small pox, yellow fever. If the ship has called at an infested port and has been exposed to the disease, then it is probable that all of the personnel on the vessel will be examined by the doctor to ascertain if any individual has contracted the disease and exposed others on board to it. If the presence of the disease is detected, the vessel will be ordered into quarantine for many days until the danger of the spread of the disease has been overcome.

The situation can become extremely serious if the vessel enters the U. S. port and causes an outbreak of the disease. Then the port itself may be quarantined and all vessels forbidden to enter or leave the port which effects a maritime paralysis for many days. The crews of the vessels found to be infested are put ashore, while the ships are being fumigated to kill any rats on board for it is the fleas on the rats that are the plague carriers. The finding of a single rat with plague is ground for ordering all ships to be breasted off the piers a distance of at least four feet, all mooring lines to be equipped with rat guards, and ships' gangways either raised or guarded in hours of darkness. The rat guards are large iron discs hinged to fit around the mooring lines so that rats can neither leave the ship nor climb aboard via the lines.

If the Public Health doctor finds that the sanitary conditions are satisfactory, he issues permission to the vessel to proceed inward to a U. S. port and land passengers and crew. The technical expression is that the vessel has "Passed Pratique".

U. S. Customs. When the vessel has been made secure in her berth, gangway guards from the *U. S. Customs* department station themselves so that no one may leave the ship nor go aboard until permission is given by the immigration and customs representatives following their preliminary inspection. The immigration n-spector checks a crew list and passenger list to ascertain whether any individuals should be barred from entering the United States. If such are found, the vessel is required to detain them aboard and to be responsible for producing them later when the vessel is ready to sail to a foreign port. Vessels entering from a non-contiguous U. S. port, as from Alaska, also have their passenger lists examined and the individuals are required to give evidence of their United States citizenship.

U. S. Customs inspectors examine the inward foreign manifest to determine the character of the cargo, its origin, and its suitability to be landed in the United States. A list of the ship's stores is also submitted and if objectionable items are noted, it may be required that they be placed under custom's seal and locked up during the stay of the vessel in port.. Permission is then given for the vessel to commence discharging during daylight hours.

To prevent any delay occasioned by this customs' examination, a bond may be given to U. S. Customs providing for the permission of a vessel to commence discharge before she has been entered in customs or for discharge at night. If the bond has not been given, the ship's master must promptly go to the Customs House and enter his vessel before the marine section or execute a sworn statement before a custom house broker as a notary for the same purpose. The master exhibits the ship's register which determines the identity of the vessel and her nationality, also, a list of clearances from the ports from which the vessel has sailed on the present voyage and an inward foreign manifest showing the cargo on board, the ports at which it was loaded, its destinations and the consignees. This entering of the vessel may be performed by the master in person but the details are usually done by a custom house broker who accompanies the master on this errand. All being found in order, the vessel is given permission to discharge its cargo.

Usually the permission to commence discharging will be given by the U. S. Customs Inspector who boards the vessel as she docks and makes a preliminary inspection of the inward foreign manifest sufficient for that purpose. The waiting stevedores, ship's repair men, and others having business with the ship then go aboard, and in the case of a foreign vessel, identifying themselves and their business with the customs' gangway guard.

The stevedore gangs then open the hatches, which will be worked, by removing the steel clamps holding the tarpaulins covering the hatches, folding the tarpaulins, taking off the wooden hatch covers, which exposes the cargo. At the same time, the gangs have rigged the ship's loading gear, tried out the winches, raised the cargo booms and trimmed them for discharging and lifted out and stored the big steel hatch beams. All of this service takes about 30 minutes and is a charge made against the ship outside of the contract price for actually working the cargo. Sometimes a mate of a vessel will have this work done in advance of arrival by the ship's crew in order to save his ship this expense.

The first cargo out is usually sacks of mail which are delivered directly to the waiting trucks from the United States Post Office. Then the general cargo comes out.

Department of Agriculture. This Department is concerned with items of cargo intended for human consumption, or which may cause spread of disease, such as certain items of cargo packed in straw which might carry infection. If animals or birds or other live creatures are to be landed, then inspection, clearance, and permission to land them must be obtained from the Department of Agriculture. These inspections are made aboard the vessel or in the case of canned goods, by sampling before their removal from the pier.

The Plant Quarantine Branch of the Department checks the importation and presence on board the vessel of any plant life which could spread plant disease among its American counterpart. Thus the importation of Mandarin "Christmas" Oranges from Japan has been forbidden; the oranges have an infection that might spread among the California oranges. The presence of the infection at point of shipment controls and the same species of plant may be imported if coming from a healthy growing area. A plant disease is apt to spread very quickly among American grown plants; as, such plants have not been immunized by nature and experience against the specific disease. The Quarantine Branch may condemn and destroy the import or confine it aboard the ship till its departure.

In the animal industry, imports of live stock or the products thereof are forbidden entry if coming from a source infected with hoof-and-mouth disease.

Preparations for discharge. The unloading continues until the cargo destined for discharge has been landed or the hold completely emptied. The hold is then cleaned and made ready to receive outward cargo. The outward loading may be commenced but usually is postponed until the ship has made her shifts to other ports and piers and all of the cargo discharged.

If the vessel has foreign cargo on board for discharge at another American port, a certificate must be obtained from the Bureau of Customs for permission to proceed to such port with the foreign cargo. The Certificate is addressed to the Collector of Customs of the port to which the ship is sailing and is accompanied with a copy of the entire inward foreign manifest.

CHAPTER 5

Terminal Operation

Basic terminology. *Terminals* are those facilities used to berth ships, to receive and deliver cargo to vessels, to transship some items of cargo and deliver others to the consignees, and in general to complete and account for the inland disposition of the cargo, thus terminating the carrier's contract of transportation. Similarly, it is at the terminals that outbound cargo is received, thus commencing the carrier's obligations.

To berth the ships, there are wharves which are shore structures with warehouses and open areas for the receiving and storing of cargo. When the wharf is built parallel with the shoreline, it is known as a *quay*, and when it extends from the shore into the water at an angle, it is called a *pier*, sometimes a finger pier.

The word *dock* is used interchangeably in meaning with pier and quay, but it also is used to designate the basin in which the ship berths. It is termed a wet dock if the ship remains afloat and is called a drydock if the ship is lifted out of the water or is locked in with a gate and the water pumped from around the vessel. In another type of dock, the ship enters at high tide and is locked in with a gate. It remains afloat until the next high tide when the gate can be opened and the ship may leave.

Wharves vary greatly in construction depending upon the type of cargo they are equipped to handle. A general cargo wharf has a large warehouse for the receipt and storage of cargo out of the effects of bad weather and also open areas where large items of cargo and items not affected by weather may be stored. Bunkers are wharves equipped with special machinery to load or discharge

34

ore and coal. Tank farms have a number of storage tanks for oils of many kinds and pipe lines connecting them to ships for loading or discharging by pumping the oil. Lumber wharves have large areas where lumber can be piled in preparation for the loading of a ship. Grain elevators as wharves have large storage facilities from which grain can be loaded onto ships in bulk through chutes. For ships that carry loaded motor trucks and trailers, an extensive parking area near the wharf must be provided.

Terminal facilities, equipment, changes. The terminal comprises the wharf and all of the facilities added for the handling of cargo, its storage and its transshipment including cranes, railroad trackage, and motor freight delivery areas.

The ownership of a terminal may be by a public corporation such as Port Authorities or Port Commissions which manage the terminal for the use and benefit of the general public. Terminals may also be owned or leased by steamship companies for their own use, and in some cases the terminal is a part of the industry supplying the cargo. A terminal may also be privately owned but available for public use.

The constituted authorities in various ports issue descriptions of their harbors, their facilities, and a tariff of charges for the various services available to visiting vessels. The following items for example are contained in Seattle Terminals Tariff No. 100 (Port of Seattle) as illustrative of the information furnished to vessel operators who intend to berth their vessels in that port.

Several aerial photographs of the port of Seattle showing the extent of the harbor and typical docks and terminals.

Dockage assessed against ocean vessels, its period and charge.

Dockage during repair of vessel.

Availability of drydocks.

Transshipment of cargo at same pier.

Handling of cargo.

Direct loading or discharge of cargo to other carriers or to the water.

Heavy lifts in excess of five tons.

Handling rates on enumerated items of cargo.

Service charges for: Providing terminal facilities, arranging berth for vessel, arranging terminal space for cargo, checking cargo, receiving cargo from shippers, delivering cargo to consignees, preparing dock manifests, preparing over, short and damage reports, ordering cars or barges required by vessels, information on cargo and ship for shippers and and consignees, lighting the terminal.

Heavy lift charges from 5 tons to 100 tons.

Rental of equipment, cargo boards, clamshell buckets, conveyors, marine elevators, piling machines, electric magnets, tractors, cargo handling trucks, four wheeled trailers, bridge crane, hammerhead crane, locomotive crane, sheerleg derrick, switching locomotive, Gantry crane, McLean boom, hand trucks.

Man-hour rates:
At average base scale of $2.50 per hour
    Straight time $4.17
    Over time $5.51
    Penalty overtime 7.54
Weighing of cargo charges
    Weighing by public weighers
Wharfage charges—Overside wharfage
Supply of dunnage
Car loading or unloading
Free time on wharf on overseas shipments—10 days.
    Wharf demurrage and storage.
    Time storage
Pumping of liquids from vessel to tanks
Cold storage facilities and charges
Bulk grain handling and storage facilities
Coal bunkers

In the movement of cargo across a pier, three items of charge are common to all cargo but are assessed at different rates for items handled. *Handling* is the term which designates the carrying of cargo from the spot where it is discharged on or picked up from the pier by the ship's tackle and the place-of-rest on the pier. *Wharfage* is the charge made for the use of the pier by cargo moving across the pier, between vessels or overside from vessels moored at the pier, to a vessel moored in a slip adjacent to the

SEATTLE TERMINALS TARIFF NO. 2-D

| SECTION 2 | WHARFAGE - CARLOADING, CAR UNLOADING | RATES AND CHARGES |

‡ WHARFAGE, HANDLING, CARLOADING, CAR UNLOADING, AND STORAGE RATES, AS WELL AS ALL OTHER PROVISIONS OF THIS ITEM, APPLY ON TRAFFIC MOVING IN ALL TRADE ROUTES.

✦ EXCEPT AS OTHERWISE PROVIDED IN INDIVIDUAL ITEMS, RATES ARE IN CENTS PER 2,000 LBS.

				✦ RATES IN CENTS		
					‡ CAR		ITEM
COMMODITY	‡ STORAGE	‡ WHARFAGE	‡ HANDLING	LDG.	UNLDG.	NO.
FISH AND SEAFOODS, CANNED, VIZ.: N.O.S. IN CASES	NOTES 1 AND 4	NOTE 1	NOTES 1, 2 & 3	NOTES 1, 5,6 & 7	NOTES 1, 5,6 & 7	
30 LBS. OR OVER	① 65	50	✦ 346	✦ 346	✦ 346	⊕
UNDER 30 LBS.	① 100	50	✦ 397	✦ 397	✦ 397	910
SALMON IN CASES 48-1 LB. TALLS OR FLATS ⟩ 12-4 LB. CANS .... PER CASE ⟩	① 1.75	1.5	✦ 7.8	✦ 7.8	✦ 7.8	
24-1 OR 48 HALF LB. CANS .. PER CASE	① 1	1	✦ 5.1	✦ 5.1	✦ 5.1	

NOTE 1: THE MINIMUM CHARGE FOR ANY SINGLE SHIPMENT SHALL BE 50¢. MINIMUM STORAGE CHARGE ON ANY W/R SHALL BE 50¢. CHARGE FOR ISSUING NEW W/R SHALL BE 50¢. NEW W/R'S CONSOLIDATING MINIMUM STORAGE LOTS MAY BE ISSUED UPON REQUEST.

NOTE 2: WHEN CANNED FISH IS RECEIVED FROM ALASKAN VESSELS DURING OVERTIME HOURS, THE DIFFERENCE BETWEEN STRAIGHT TIME AND OVERTIME SHALL BE CHARGED AGAINST THE FREIGHT IN ACCORDANCE WITH PROVISIONS OF ITEM 460.

NOTE 3: HANDLING CHARGE IS THE CHARGE ASSESSED AGAINST THE CARGO (SEE EXCEPTION) FOR MOVING CANNED FISH AND SEAFOODS FROM END OF SHIP'S TACKLE ON THE WHARF TO FIRST PLACE OF REST ON THE WHARF, OR FROM PLACE OF REST ON THE WHARF TO WITHIN REACH OF SHIP'S TACKLE.

    EXCEPTION: HANDLING CHARGES APPLYING ON CANNED FISH AND SEAFOODS, FOREIGN IMPORTS OR EXPORTS, WILL BE ASSESSED AGAINST THE VESSEL.

    HANDLING CHARGES WILL ALSO BE ASSESSED AGAINST THE CARGO FOR MOVING CANNED FISH AND SEAFOODS TO OR FROM STORAGE WHEN RECEIVED FROM OR DELIVERED TO DRAYS OR INLAND WATERWAY VESSELS.

NOTE 4: NO STORAGE CHARGE WILL BE ASSESSED ON CANNED FISH MOVING FORWARD FROM TERMINALS WITHIN 10 DAYS FROM RECEIPT OF SAME. BALANCES ON HAND AT EXPIRATION OF 10 DAYS WILL BE PLACED ON MONTHLY STORAGE BASIS, DATING FROM DAY SUCH FISH WAS RECEIVED ON TERMINAL.

NOTE 5: ON CANNED FISH RECEIVED FROM DRAYS FOR CONSOLIDATION IN CARS APPLY ITEM 730.

NOTE 6: WHEN IT IS REQUIRED THAT RAILROAD CARS BE LOADED WITH COMMODITIES NAMED IN THIS ITEM IN SUCH MANNER AS TO PERMIT PARTIAL UNLOADING AT DESTINATIONS AND/OR THAT CARLOADS FOR ONE OR MORE DESTINATIONS CONSIST OF BRANDS AND/OR LOTS FROM DIFFERENT WAREHOUSE RECEIPTS OR DIFFERENT BRANDS AND/OR DIFFERENT LOTS UNDER ONE WAREHOUSE RECEIPT, THE FOLLOWING SCHEDULE OF RATES WILL BE ASSESSED ON THE ENTIRE CARLOAD, IN ADDITION TO THE REGULAR CARLOADING RATES NAMED IN THIS ITEM:

    NUMBER OF LOTS AND/OR BRANDS - PER 100 LBS.

    5 TO AND INCLUDING 10 - 1-1/4¢   16 TO AND INCLUDING 25 - 3-3/4¢
    11 TO AND INCLUDING 15 - 2-1-2¢   26 OR MORE - 5¢

† NOTE 7: CARLOADING AND CAR UNLOADING RATES APPLY BETWEEN THE HOURS OF 8:00 A.M. AND 6:00 P.M., MONDAY THROUGH FRIDAY. CARLOADING OR CAR UNLOADING PERFORMED ON SATURDAYS, SUNDAYS, HOLIDAYS OR OTHER HOURS NOT HEREIN NAMED WILL BE ASSESSED CHARGES IN ACCORDANCE WITH ITEM NO. 460, PARAGRAPH (A).

    ① ON W/R PER MONTH OR FRACTION THEREOF.

| ISSUED JULY 22, 1958 | EFFECTIVE: | INTRASTATE TRAFFIC - SEPTEMBER 1, 1958 ALL OTHER TRAFFIC - AUGUST 1, 1958 |

ISSUED BY J. J. USHER, AGENT, PORT OF SEATTLE, P.O. BOX 1878, SEATTLE 11, WASHINGTON

| CORRECTION NO. 206 | OTHER REFERENCE MARKS AND ABBREVIATIONS ARE EXPLAINED ON PAGE NO. 13. |

Figure 6. Sample page from terminal tariff

pier. *Loading* or *unloading* is the charge made for moving the cargo from place-of-rest on the pier to or from freight cars.

The reproduction of a page from a terminal tariff is an illustration of these charges. See Figure 6. In various ports of the United States these charges are assessed directly against the cargo owner and in some ports the charges are absorbed in the ocean or rail freight rates so that in ascertaining a through freight rate care must be taken in the computation of the total transportation cost to the shipper.

Customs practice. In the receipt of cargo from a foreign port, United States Customs procedure for entry of the goods into the United States is similar for any wharf over which the cargo passes. The selection by the consignee or his representative of one of three most commonly used types of customs entry will serve as a directive to the terminal operator in the forwarding of the cargo: (1) the immediate transportation (IT) entry will direct the terminal operator to transship the cargo to a bonded carrier which will transport the goods to some interior port of customs entry or to another carrier for export; (2) the bonded warehouse entry which directs the removal of the goods into a bonded warehouse for storage purposes, (the bonds executed by the carriers are conditioned that the carrier transport and deliver the goods to the order of the customs department at destination); and, (3) the consumption entry which means that the consignee has had his shipment appraised by Customs and has paid the duties, if any, on it, and the terminal operator may deliver the cargo as the consignee may direct.

By law the cargo inbound from foreign ports is discharged into the custody of the United States Customs who place guards over the landed merchandise until the consignee makes his entry of the merchandise to be consumed, or stored, or shipped to another port of entry. This decision must be made within five days after entry of vessel. Any manipulation or reconditioning of the cargo must be done in the presence of a custom's guard, who is paid by the consignee for the time occupied. If the consignee has not made his entry, the customs will remove his shipment to general order warehouse at the cargo owner's expense.

Foreign Trade Zone. To postpone this decision or to avoid the expense of the guard are advantages of landing cargo in a *Foreign Trade Zone*. The Zone is a sort of no-man's land into which cargo is moved. Possession of the goods is not immediately in the Customs department, which only guards the fencing around the area to see that nothing is removed from the Zone until the usual regulations have been complied with. It is this ability of the consignee to get physical possession of his cargo without Custom's supervision that is a valuable service that the Zone offers. The consignee may enter the Zone, manipulate, recondition, display and sell his merchandise. He may store it in the Zone indefinitely, mingle it with U. S. goods or re-export it.

Some of the operations performed by consignees within the Zone are the importation of wine in casks and rebottling to save transportation costs; the combining of imported alcohol with domestic essences and re-exporting the fluids without the payment of duty on the alcohol and the obtaining of a drawback of duty when it is re-exported; the cleaning and shelling of imported nuts, entering only the meats through U. S. customs; the importation of woolens in bolts then cutting to patterns in the Zone and entering the cut pieces and waste under lower rates of duty.

Under the present Custom's regulations, duty must be paid at one time on the entire quantity imported whereas through the Zone duty is paid only on the actual amount brought in at any one time. For instance in the importation of automobiles, instead of tying up capital in paying duty on the entire shipment, duty can be paid as each car is taken from the Zone.

The cost of handling the cargo in and out of storage in the Zone, the storage in the area, and all services furnished by the Zone are strictly competitive with other commercial piers in the port so that there is no advantage in using the Zone for cargo that is intended for immediate transportation or for prompt entry for consumption.

The management and operation of the Zones are in public service bodies which are finding it difficult to carry on the Zones by reason of actual losses in operation. Several Zones have been discontinued. There are now (1958) only four open: Seattle, San Francisco, New Orleans, New York.

To the steamship operator there are several advantages in the use of a Foreign Trade Zone for both loading and discharging cargo. There is no delay occasioned by the customs boarding officer in his examination of the vessel's inward foreign manifest before discharging operations may commence. The vessel's operator does not have to procure bonds to the Customs to permit immediate discharge of the vessel or discharge during night hours. There is no requirement that a Custom's inspector be present during nighttime discharge of the vessel and no expense for his overtime pay.

Receiving cargo. On outward loading, the vessel may proceed at will. Notice to Customs of the intent to load outward bonded items is not required. Notice of the loading of exports upon which the shipper is claiming a drawback or refund of duty paid is not required. If the cargo is in the Foreign Trade Zone, it is clear for export.

The other problems of the receiving of cargo, storage and delivery or transshipment of it are identical, if moving through a Zone or over a commercial pier. The commercial piers have a real problem in allocating space for the reception of cargo as it comes from the ships and placing it for prompt delivery to a consignee. For example, a large item of cargo covered by one bill of lading may have been stowed in several holds of the vessel, but it must be reassembled on the pier for easy delivery. This is accomplished by channeling this item of cargo as it comes from the several holds to a common place-of-rest on the pier. The placement or spotting of the cargo for delivery to other carriers or for local delivery has been mentioned in the preplanning that was done before the arrival of the ship. All of this must be carefully coordinated with the areas reserved for outbound cargo and with the timing of the arrival of carriers to load inbound cargo and the timing of the arrival of outbound cargo for loading.

Careful check is made of the cargo as it comes from the vessel by reference to the inward foreign manifests to ascertain if the shipments match perfectly in number and quantity specified on the bills of lading. If a shipment checks short, then a search of the vessel's holds can be made to locate the particular item which may have been overlooked in the hurry of discharging.

Hatch books. To assist in identifying cargo there have been compiled, by the purser of the ship during the inward voyage, *hatch books* which list alphabetically by shipping marks each item of cargo. The books list the shipper's or consignee's mark, the quantity, the bill of lading origin and number, the commodity, its weight and measurement, the consignee and the destination, and the spot in the ship in which the item was stowed for shipment. Besides identifying the shipment, its location on board can be determined and the item selected for immediate discharge if possible. The following excerpts illustrate the makeup of the books and their technical abbreviations.

K-SO-5 Mr. Y. Nakajima

K △ T 1 pkg Sample Celluloid Dolls
⟨Z-I⟩
C ▽ L

80 lbs 7'5" cf
3 UTD M/S lkr

Translated: Bill of lading Kobe, to Seattle for Overland shipment No. 5 Y. Nakajima consignee, leading mark *K* contents dolls, 1 package, weight 80 lbs, measurement 7 feet 5 inches cubic feet, stowed in No. 3 hold Upper Tween Decks Mid-ship locker.

TB-9V Jordans Ltd
H △ C 4 bdl carpets
⧄CF⧄   1355 lbs 84 cf
VANCOUVER
238/241   #4 LH A

Translated: Taku Bar lading 9 for Vancouver, Jordans Ltd, consignee, leading mark *H*, 4 bundles carpets, weight 1355 pounds, measure 84 cu. ft., for discharge Vancouver, bundle numbers 238 to 241. Stowed in No. 4 Lower Hold Aft.

Y-12-S Fujii & Co.

F   384 tins frozen Shark Liver
Seattle 16128 lbs 320 cf
POOJ   Reefer Box #8.

Translated: Yokohama lading 12 for Seattle, Fujii & Co. consignee, leading mark *F*, 384 tins frozen shark liver, 16128 lbs., 320 cu. ft., Product of Occupied Japan. Stowed in Refrigerator Box No. 8

Transshipment, storage and handling. As the vessel has completed her unloading, the next duty of the terminal operator in conjunction with the vessel operator, is the proper delivery of the various shipments. Transshipment cargo will move quickly as the carriers or consignees will have applied to the Customs for immediate transportation entries, "IT's," which permits them to carry the cargo to other ports of entry and there redeliver it to the custody of Customs. The carriers give a bond to perform this service faithfully, hence are "bonded carriers." The terminal checks the cargo out of the carrier, which receipts for it, and the duty is thus discharged.

Local cargo is delivered to the consignee upon surrender of a bill of lading and the issuance of a delivery order by the vessel operator, which becomes the acknowledgement of the receipt of the item of cargo upon the actual taking physical possession by consignee. If the shipment moves on a straight bill of lading, then the cargo may be delivered to the consignee named on the lading by proper identification of the individual. If the cargo is moving on an order bill of lading, then delivery will be made only to the person who has possession of a properly endorsed, original bill of lading, and who has apparently received the lading in the regular course of his business. The delivery to any other person will render the terminal liable, for improper delivery, to the person who does possess the original lading. In the case of a consignee who claims that the original lading is delayed or lost, the terminal may accept that person's bond conditioned upon the production of the lading or damages caused by the delivery of the shipment to him.

Certain irregularities may occur which change the normal delivery procedure. If the consignee has not made his Custom's entry, then his cargo is removed to a general order warehouse under the care of the Customs. If the consignee does not wish to receive his cargo, he may abandon it to the Customs which department will sell the merchandise and apply the proceeds to the payment of duty. The consignee may wish to store the goods on the pier. This may be done by agreement with the terminal after Customs regulations have been met. The consignee may wish to store his goods in a bonded warehouse. This removes the shipment from the pier but retains it under Customs regulation.

The terminal operator immediately gives written notice to all consignees of the arrival of their shipments on the pier ready for delivery to them. This notice serves to terminate the liability of the ocean carrier for the safety and care of the shipments under the bill of lading clauses. The goods then are at the risk of the terminal only as a warehouseman. The notice may also set the end of the period of free time allowed the consignees to claim their shipments after which the merchandise will be charged storage by the terminal.

Examples:

COMMODITY AND DESCRIPTION OF PACKAGE	Per 1 cu. ft. or 40 lbs. whichever is the greater.	
	MONTHLY STORAGE	STORAGE HANDLING
	Cents	
Sake		
In cases	2	2½
In barrels, per bbl.	50	50
Sardines, canned		
In cases	1½	2½
Silk, manufactured		
In pkgs., per cu. ft. (Value not over $100 per package and so declared in writing)	7	6
Silverware and *Jewelry*		
In packages, per cu. ft.	25	29
Skins, fur (Unmanufactured apparel)		
Per cu. ft.	5	5
Snuff		
In pkgs., per cu. ft.	6	3
Soy Sauce		
In tubs	1½	2½

Over, Short and Damaged Reports. Finally, a few small items of cargo will remain which cannot be identified under any bill of lading or which have been discharged in error or over-carried from some other port. These items are listed on an *"Over, Short and Damaged"* report (OS&D), which is circularized to the vessel and all ports of loading and discharge in order to learn the proper consignee and destination.

All of the records of delivery, bills of lading, manifests, are filed by both the vessel operator and the terminal for reference purposes. The records are kept for seven years, the period within which suits at law must be brought concerning transportation or delivery of the cargo.

CHAPTER 6

Vessel In Port

When a vessel arrives in port, the operator is immediately confronted with many problems in addition to the discharge and loading of cargo. These questions must be resolved quickly and in most cases within the brief and busy time that the vessel will be on berth. The most important of these problems are the repair of the ship, if necessary, and the procurement of her supplies and fuel in order that she may be in a seaworthy condition to sail. The operator is also asked to assist in solving many personal problems of the master, his officers, and crew members. These troubles may be very important to the individuals whose only opportunity of correcting them is during the stay of the vessel in port.

The solution of these varied problems may become the duty of a single individual in a vessel agency office, who has been entrusted with the operation of the ship while in port, and he issues directions for the benefit of the owners of the vessel. In other types of business organization, these duties may fall into various departments which have been established to handle each type of operating problem. Or in the case of established steamship lines, the solutions of these problems have been allocated to many departments and individuals who can anticipate the needs of the vessel as a matter of routine.

Repairs. The urgency of the ship's problems is measured by their bearing on the ship's seaworthiness or her prompt despatch on her voyage. Thus, in the case of a needed repair, if it can be postponed it may be more efficiently and cheaply made if done at the vessel's home port where repair facilities are available and preparations may be made in advance. In the case of a foreign vessel, the lower wage scale in the foreign country may be the controlling factor in making the decision. When the problem affects the time of sailing of the vessel, it should be corrected at once with the consent of the owners.

In the supposed case of our vessel coming in with a cracked rudder frame (page 26), such questions as the following may arise: should tugs be sent to her aid? will tugs be needed in berthing? can a shipyard repair her immediately? is a drydock available?

At this port of call, the vessel must take on fuel oil. This raises the question of whether she will be refuelled at her own berth from barges or will proceed to the oil docks and refuel directly. If the latter the availability of a berth at the oil dock is so involved.

Steward's supplies. The procurement of steward's supplies seems to be the prerogative of that officer. He guards it carefully. He is the first man ashore in port, and before the next meal time a succession of deliveries of fresh milk and vegetables arrive at the ship. Shortly before the vessel is ready to sail, the galley supplies arrive in great quantity and usually require considerable stevedore time in loading them from pier to ship. The stewards seem to know their way around in every port and appear to be members of a fraternity with the ship supply firms. There is little chance of checking the efficiency of his purchases except by noting an undue amount of spoilage and the complaints of the crew members over the meals served. This latter check is probably a very practical one as the steward for his own sake must reasonably satisfy the crew members.

Bos'n's requirements. The Bos'n's requirements are generally for some item of deck gear to replace a broken counterpart and his requests are backed with the approval of one of the mates with the approval of the master.

Engine room requirements. Likewise from the engineering department come requisitions for tools, packing and greases and such items that are considered necessary for the smooth operation of the engines and boilers. A large quantity of fresh water is taken aboard by the engineering department which will question the purity of the water for culinary use, crews' washing and for making steam in the boilers. The amount of water taken on board is a considerable item running into the hundreds of tons. Engineers use the opportunity while in port to clean the water tanks, emptying some and filling others. This operation frequently causes the vessel to take on an unexpected list.

All of these are routine needs of each ship in port, but if the vessel is calling for the first time in this port these matters must be handled by the ship's agent for the guidance of the ship personnel. Such items are apart from the serious problem of a major repair or overhaul.

Accounting. Accounting and payment for the requirements of the vessel are relatively simple if it is not the vessel's home port and does not involve the general financing of the ship's operation. The agent renders an account of each call of the vessel at his port. His receipts are the prepaid ocean freight that he has secured for the outward loading of the ship. From this he deducts his commission, the items which the ship has requisitioned and other port fees and expenses necessary to the ship's call. The balance is remitted to the vessel owners. If there is not a sufficient amount of money on hand, the vessel owners must cable funds or make other arrangements. As a last resort, the master would have the authority to pledge his vessel for sufficient funds to continue the voyage.

Foreign flag vessels and consuls. If it is a foreign flag vessel, then many of these problems must be solved in conference between the ship's master and the consul of her country. The captain generally consults with the consul on many matters not involved directly with the voyage in question but concerning nationals who are crew members. Sick seamen who have been landed for hospitalization by other vessels of the same nationality are to be returned to their home land. Confidential instructions from the vessel's owners are forwarded through the consul. The consul will also verify an invoice for each item of cargo intended for delivery into his country, certifying the value for export purposes, quantity of the goods shipped, and the country of origin of manufacture or product. The official documents prepared for the custom's department of the foreign country are entrusted to the master for delivery to customs when he arrives in his home land. Though these documents are not the immediate concern of the ship's agent, it is his duty to see that they are procured in order to provide an orderly account of the cargo on the ship.

The accomplishment of many of these commissions is done in many cases with the consultation and approval of the master or after communication with the vessel owners. These meetings are on ship's business. But there are also courtesy calls on the captain and often entertainment and assistance extended to him in his personal capacity. These also must be scheduled to fit into the intricate pattern of the vessel's operation in port.

If she is an American Flag vessel, the laws of the United States require that her crew be composed of licensed officers and certified and registered crew members. The vessel operator must comply with this provision which renders his ship "seaworthy" in this particular, for unless the ship is "seaworthy" she will not be cleared for sailing nor can she obtain marine insurance.

Shipping Commissioners. Shipping Commissioners are appointed under the Commandant of the United States Coast Guard to enforce the provisions of the shipping laws. Their general duties are to supervise the signing on of a crew and the paying off of the crew upon the completion of the voyage. The shipping articles, which constitute a written contract between the vessel and her crew for the prospective voyage, are signed in their presence. This contract sets out the various ratings and rates of pay at which the men will be employed. Crew men signify their acceptance by signing the articles. Before the individual crew member is permitted to sign, he must exhibit to the Shipping Commissioner his certificate of proficiency in his rating or his registration as a staff member. The shipping articles are prepared in quadruplicate for the vessel, the Commerce Department and the Coast Guard.

On completion of the voyage, the crew is paid off in the presence of the Commissioner. In a sense he has acted as an arbitrator between crew and vessel, so that there is a complete understanding of the terms of the employment and a satisfactory payoff after the voyage.

Officer requirements. Vessels must be placed under command of *licensed officers.* A license as an officer is obtained by taking a written examination before the U. S. Coast Guard to prove that the applicant is proficient in the duties of his command.* For a master of ocean vessels competency is indicated by proficiency in the following: latitude by Polaris, meridian altitude, ex-meridian; longitude by position line or time sight; star identification; deviation of compass by amplitude, by azimuth; position by dead reckoning — great circle sailing; magnetism, deviation, compass compensation; chart navigation; aids to navigation; tides, currents and use of tables; ocean winds, weather and currents; international and inland rules of the road; seamanship; cargo handling and stowage; life saving apparatus; ship sanitation; regulations for vessel inspection; United States navigation laws.

Able seaman. Every seaman employed on any merchant vessel of the United States of 100 gross tons or more, except vessels employed exclusively in trade on the navigable rivers of the United States, must produce a continuous discharge book or certificate of identification or merchant mariner's document representing such certificate before signing articles of agreement before a Shipping Commissioner.

For advancement in rating, the seamen aboard a vessel must be certified by the U. S. Coast Guard that they are *able-bodied seamen*. To secure this certificate, the applicant is examined by the Coast Guard and is required to demonstrate his ability as a seaman. To be rated an able seaman, the applicant must demonstrate: that he has been trained in the launching of lifeboats; that he can handle the boats themselves; and that he is capable of taking command of a boat's crew.

He will be given a written or oral examination in: life boats and life rafts; clearing and lowering boats; handling of boats under oars and sail; nautical terms, ship's compass, running lights; fog and distress signals; knowledge of orders passed to wheelmen; and construction and function of davits.

Every person employed in a rating of able seaman on any United States vessel requiring certified able seaman, must present his certificate to the Shipping Commissioner before signing articles of agreement of employment on the vessel. While the ship is in port, the Coast Guard conducts drills in fire fighting aboard ship and abandoning ship by lowering a life boat and opera-

*Regulations for Licensing and Certificating of Merchant Marine Personnel, U. S. Coast Guard CG 191, July 2, 1951.

ting it under oars and sail. (See *Manual for Able Seaman,* Coast Guard 175 June 1, 1955.)

Engine department. In the *engineering department,* the officers must demonstrate to the Coast Guard their knowledge of engines, boilers and auxiliaries and show a length of service in the engine department which would qualify them for a license as an engineering officer. Under the officer rank, men in the engineering department must be certified in various ratings before they may be employed in these capacities on vessels. The certificate rates them as qualified members of the engine department in the specific ratings of a Refrigeration engineer, Oiler, Watertender, Fireman, Deck engineer, Junior engineer, Electrician, Boilermaker, Machinist, Pumpman. When the applicant qualifies in all of these he is certified as "QMED — any rating." (See *Coast Guard Manual 175 for Members of Engine Department June 1, 1955.*)

Staff officers. These officers are registered for employment on vessels requiring staff officers such as Purser, Surgeon, Pharmacist's Mate. The registration of a purser comes after two years service in that capacity. The Surgeon must have his license under the authority to practice from any State or Territory of the United States or the District of Columbia.

A serious problem confronts vessel operators in securing a crew for each voyage in the fact that maritime law requires that owners of vessels warrant their seaworthiness. The United States Supreme Court has recently held that a drunken seaman aboard a ship can render the vessel a perilous place and therefore unseaworthy.* The warranty is not that the seaman be competent to meet all emergencies but that he is equal in disposition and seamanship to the ordinary men in the calling. Steamship men would not argue against the logic of the Court's ruling, but the problem arises in the selection of the individual seamen in that members of the crew are supplied by their unions in accordance with a union plan of work rotation, rather than through selection by the steamship employer.

Inspection of vessels. Under Title 52 of the REVISED STATUTES OF THE UNITED STATES, the Coast Guard is required once a year to inspect all of the steam vessel hulls within each district and motor

---

*Boudoin vs. Lykes Bros, SS. Co. 348 U.S. 336, 99 L.ed. 354, 75 S.Ct. 382, 1955.

driven hulls over 300 gross tons to ascertain if the vessel is of a suitable structure for the service in which she will be employed, has suitable accommodations for passengers and crew, may be navigated with safety to life, and that all requirements of law have been complied with in relation to fires, boats, pumps, hose, life preservers, floats, anchors, cables, etc. Written application for this annual inspection is made by the vessel operator to the Officer in Charge, Marine Inspection, U. S. Coast Guard (*Coast Guard Vessel Inspection Rules,* June 1, 1950. CG 170).

Articles inspected are davits, life boats and means of lowering, buoyant apparatus, life boat equipment, compass and distress signals, lantern, mast and sails, drinking water, storm oil, construction and stowage of life rafts, number of life buoys, embarkation ladders, bulkheads on passenger vessels, steam and inert-gas fire extinguishing systems, pumps, couplings and fire hose, fire detection system, sprinkler systems, fire-resisting bulk heads, engine room signal, whistles and fog bells. Detailed rules and regulations are provided for the inspection of hulls and propelling power.

To have his vessel pronounced seaworthy by the Coast Guard, the vessel owner must prepare his vessel to meet the specified rules and regulations. There is considerable variance in the requirements of the rules for vessels in ocean or coastwise service and those operating on bays, sounds, and lakes, and still other rules for vessels on the Great Lakes.

Steamship agents. According to the circumstances of the vessel owner, he may appoint an agent to perform any or all of the services required by the vessel while she is in the port wherein the agent is representative of the owner.

The remuneration to agents for the operation and care of vessels for the owners is dependent upon the services expected of the agents. The General Agent is entrusted with the entire operation of the ship within his area. This agent discharges the inbound cargo, takes care of the vessel's requirements while she is in port, procures outbound cargo and loads the ship. For these services he receives 5% of the ocean freight on the out-bound cargo. In some cases this percentage may be as high as 8%.

A sub-agent's commission often is divided into 1¼% for the care of the vessel in port, 1¼% allowed to be paid to foreign freight forwarders for procuring out-bound cargo, and 1¼% to the sub-agent. All percentages are based upon the ocean freight money on the out-bound cargo from the agent's area.

The ship owner may appoint an agent to act as "Ship's husband." Such an agent carries out all of the instructions of the owner for the operation of the vessel while she is in the agent's port. His pay is ordinarily $400 for a period not exceeding 10 days.

As the loading of the vessel progresses, reports are made to the agent and an estimate is formed of the completion of the work. When sailing day arrives the signal flag, P, is hoisted as an indication that the ship is ready to sail. A check is made of all the necessary preparations, the steward has his supplies aboard, the ship's crew has been signed on, the pilot has been notified of sailing time, the ship's outward foreign manifest has been prepared, each item of cargo has been substantiated with a shipper's export declaration for customs regulation, the U. S. Customs has issued the vessel's clearance, consular documents are in possession of the master, manifest of cargo with copies of the ladings have been placed aboard, the engineer is warming up the engines, linesmen are standing by to cast off the mooring lines, the gangway is rigged in.

The pilot comes to the bridge, signals "let go lines," telegraphs to the engine room "engines astern," gives the whistle a long blast. The ship gathers sternway and commences her outward voyage.

CHAPTER 7

Cargo Handling

Although the supervision of operating gear for handling the ship's cargo is the duty of the stevedore department, the general agent must have a broad knowledge of the use of this equipment and applicable labor rules. Otherwise he can contribute little to the efficient handling of cargo. The handling of the cargo also gives rise to the problem of the charges to be made against the ship for use of special gear and for delay caused by the ship in the process of working cargo. Either the contract stevedore or the ship must pay when the "hook hangs," that is, when the work stops and the cargo hook on the ship's gear is idle and the stevedores are standing by, yet drawing pay.

If the stevedoring contract provides for handling cargo on a per ton basis, then such delays and special services become extra charges against the ship. Such charges typically may be for delays in effective cargo work, uncovering and covering the hatches, rigging the cargo gear, failure of the ship's winches or gear, switching of rail cars alongside the ship, failure to supply cargo for loading, waiting for the ship to berth. These charges must be justified to the vessel operators by the loading officer in as much as they will be billed in addition to the charge for loading or unloading of cargo on a per ton basis.

Handling gear. The most usual system of gear for cargo handling is the ship's booms, which are arranged in pairs at each hatch. One boom extends over the pier and lifts the item of cargo from its place at ship's side. The other boom, with its falls matched to the same cargo hook, draws the load across and over the hatch opening at which point both booms lower the load into the hold.

This requires the use of two winches and their skillful operation by either one or two winch-men. On a Liberty ship, these booms have a maximum lifting capacity of 5 tons, 10,000 pounds. Other single booms on the same ship have a maximum heavy lift of 15 tons, and there is also a jumbo boom which can lift 30 tons. Use of these heavy lift booms requires special rigging by the stevedores and involves additional charges for lifting heavy weights.

Cranes. Some newer vessels have deck cranes mounted at each side of a hatch so that their booms can reach over the hold, lift the cargo, swing it overside and lower it to the pier. Some piers have mobile cranes or cranes on rails which can reach from the pier over the side of the vessel with their booms and raise or lower the cargo within the ship's holds.

For lifts beyond the capacity of the vessel's booms, two types of cranes are available. The stiff-leg crane is built on the pier and requires that the vessel be moved into position so that the crane can reach the heavy lift. The floating crane is constructed on a barge. The barge comes along the ship's off-shore side and makes the heavy lift from the vessel to another barge or into the water, as in the case of discharging a small boat. Either type of crane has a lifting capacity in excess of 100 tons.

Slings. To hold the cargo while it is being loaded, steel or wire slings can be used. These *slings* are in the form of a double loop. They are passed around the item to be loaded and looped into the cargo hook. In the case of lumber, rope slings are used. Wire cable has a tendency to cut into the edges of the item being loaded which, in the case of lumber, would damage the edges of the load. Small, irregular shaped items, such as reels of barbed wire, are loaded in net slings which are squares of woven rope netting about eight feet to a side.

Pallets. During World War II, the use of salmon boards or *pallets* became very extensive because of the speed and convenience they afforded in handling cargo. Such devices were used much earlier to expedite the handling of cases of canned salmon. The cases are piled evenly on these pallets, which are about five feet square and elevated approximately 8 inches above the pier floor so that ship's slings can be inserted under the pallet's edges for lifting and unloading. A lift truck can insert its forks into the same space,

1. Crane moves outboard

2. Spreader frame comes down

3. Spreader frame hooks onto container

4. Container being raised

5. Container starts moving inboard

6. Container lowered into hold

Figure 7. Loading Operation

lift and carry the loaded pallet and stack it to a height of three or four tiers of other palletized cargo. Handling from the ship is made more efficient and the ability to pile goods higher in the warehouse effects a saving of floor space. During war time operation, to facilitate speed of handling, some items of cargo were steel-strapped to the pallets in the warehouse of the manufacturer and remained so fixed during rail haul to the ship, loading, discharge and transport to destination in the theatre of operations before the straps were cut. The Navy found that when pallets were unloaded on vessels in the war area, the empty wooden pallets were often thrown overboard and became a floating menace to small vessels. To avoid this hazard, some wartime pallets were made of metal which would sink when thrown into the sea. In peace time, however, consideration must be given to the return of the empty pallet and to the loss in cargo space by reason of the volume of space occupied by each pallet. A considerable loss of revenue would result unless compensated for by a higher freight on the item of cargo.

Containers. A successful device to secure unitization of cargo handling, transportation, and storing, is the *container*, which is a box about eight feet square. Small and irregular items of cargo are loaded into it and when full the container is closed and loaded as a single unit. The advantages of the container are that the cargo itself does not require such sturdy packing to stand handling and stowage, and small items are not individually handled by the stevedores. A saving of time, breakage, and loss by pilferage results. The containers are small enough to be handled directly from ship to rail or motor trucks for inland delivery at destination.

The same economies which are obtained by the use of containers are secured by the use of trailer bodies as large containers. These trailer bodies, either in full size or one-half the size of a trailer body, are readily detached from trailer chassis or motor trucks and are loaded as pieces of unitized cargo. At destination, they are discharged by the ship's gear or by cranes onto motor trucks or trailer chassis which are then hauled to final destination. The use of these trailer bodies as containers effects a means of transportation of the goods from shipper's warehouse to consignee's warehouse with a minimum of handling. However, an economic disadvantage may arise when trailer bodies are returned empty because of lack of return cargo. When motor truck trailers are carried on rail cars the operation has been popularly called "Piggy Back"; when loaded on vessels, the name is varied to become "Fishy Back."

Figure 8. TRAILERS GO TO SEA—Gateway city leaving Port Newark

The newest type of carrier is the "Roll On, Roll Off" ship which is designed so that motor vehicles roll on board under their own power and by means of a series of ramps move to the spot in the vessel's holds where each will be secured for the voyage. At destination the vehicles roll off the ship under their own power. The advantage of this type of vessel is the speed of loading and discharge, saving in stevedoring charges, and the ease of the operation. It might be likened to the familiar motor car ferry, except that the ship and its cargo placement is designed for ocean transportation. An economic disadvantage is of course the loss of cargo space taken up by the trailer's chassis and wheels.

The "*Sea Train*" is an adaption of the same principle. In this case an entire train is moved on rails into the vessel. On arrival, after the sea voyage, the train is again placed on rails and the cargo moved inland for distribution to the consignees of the individual freight cars.

How to select handling gear? The character of the cargo itself determines the type of handling gear to be used. Thus, bananas are unloaded by an endless belt with pockets designed to hold a stem of bananas. The force of gravity is frequently used in the loading of ore, coal, and grains, which are distributed into the vessel's hold from spouts fed by conveyors from storage bins. In the case of scrap iron, large electromagnets are hooked to the ship's gear. Their magnetic attraction holds many pieces of scrap until the load is moved to the desired position where it can be released by shutting off the electric current. The use of the many types of gear designed to render the handling of cargo more efficient requires the skilled technique of the stevedores acquired in loading cargoes of many kinds.

The role of the longshoremen. The individual longshoreman is proud of his ability to handle and stow cargo. He has obtained his proficiency from years of experience. He associates with others in a team where each man understands the actions to be expected from his fellow worker under conditions of constant danger. He understands the precautions each must take for himself and for others about him. A gang for handling general cargo consists of fifteen men composed of a hatch tender, two winchmen, two hook-up men on the pier, and ten men in the hold, five on each side.

Timing and costs. An important decision made by a ship's agent is the number of stevedore gangs necessary for the unloading and the time at which these gangs are to report for work. If the vessel is due to arrive at night, the gangs must be ordered the previous day to insure a prompt 8 o'clock A.M. start. If the ship's arrival is delayed for any reason, then the cost of the stand-by time of the men falls on the ship. Likewise the decision must be made as to whether to work the gangs overtime or on holidays in order to expedite the sailing of the vessel. These times of work involve considerable differences in rate of pay of the men and corresponding differences in the cost charged to the account of the vessel.

The following excerpts from the Seattle Dock Workers Agreement illustrate the problem of timing the ship's work efficiently:

The basic rate of pay is $2.27 per hour for straight time and $3.405 per hour for overtime.

Six hours shall constitute a day's work. Thirty hours shall constitute a week's work, averaged over a period of four weeks. The first six hours worked between the hours of 8:00 A.M. and 5:00 P.M. shall be designated as straight time, but there shall be no relief of men before 5:00 P.M. All work in excess of six hours between 8:00 A.M. and 5:00 P.M. and all work during meal time and between 5:00 P.M. and 8:00 A.M. on week days and from 5:00 P.M. on Friday to 8:00 A.M. on Monday and all work on legal holidays, shall be designated as overtime.

Eleven holidays are specified.

Additional wages are paid for handling penalty cargo at 10c per hour straight time, 15c per hour overtime. If shoveling is required the rates are 20c ST and 30c OT. Penalty cargo includes: alfalfa meal; offensive bones in sacks; caustic soda in drums; coal in sacks; cement; creosoted products; fertilizers in bags; glass, broken, in sacks; green hides; herring in boxes and barrels; iron blisters; lime in sacks; lumber and logs loaded out of the water; meat scraps in sacks; nitrates in sacks; ore in sacks; phosphates in sacks; rough piled pig iron when hand handled; plaster in sacks; refrigerated cargo; baled rubber covered with talc; salt blocks in sacks; scrap metal in bulk and bales; soda ash in bags.

All of these charges are in addition to the contractual rate of pay to a stevedoring company based on a per ton loading or discharge of cargo. A sample of such rates follows, indicating the variance of rates in the handling of different types of cargo. The rates are listed per cargo ton as manifested by the vessel, weight or measurement, 2240 lbs. or 40 cubic feet.

Agriculture machinery	W	$1.35
	M	.77
Automobiles	W	1.60
	M	.64
Cement	W	.90

Coffee, loading	W	1.10
discharging	W	1.29
General cargo	W	1.04
	M	.85
Wines	W	1.75
	M	1.25
Heavy lift exceeding 3 tons		1.20

The officer in charge of the loading and unloading of a vessel is actually present while the ship is working cargo. He is usually called upon to authorize the use of special gear for cargo handling, to coordinate the stevedoring services to the ship and in addition must provide cargo to prevent delays in cargo handling. He must account to the vessel operator for cargo handling expense. These duties are in addition to his major responsibility for properly stowing the cargo, for the safety of the vessel, and for efficient discharge of the cargo at destination.

CHAPTER 8

Cargo Procurement

Cargo solicitation. Cargo generally is secured by personal solicitation. This is the case because the number of sources from which cargo can be secured is limited. The greater part of cargo offerings come from the same large firms, all well-known to steamship operators. Advertising keeps the names of the line and the operator before the shippers constantly and for the convenience of shippers by the publication of schedules.

As to the question of rates, the condition is that if full cargoes are being offered the tramp vessels have the advantage of being able to quote lower rates than the regular lines. If the cargo is less than a shipload the exporter is required to use regular berth line vessels on which the rates are identical, as the operators of the vessels are probably members of a conference in which all steamship lines have agreed, as a conference rule, to quote the identical rates.

In the solicitation of cargo for steamship lines, the condition is identical with the railroads: all the lines issue the same tariff and quote the same rates. Therefore, successful solicitation must be made on the basis of superior service to the exporter by the individual line.

Pleas for cargo are likely to reflect any or all of the following elements:

1. *National pride.* American flag ships very properly urge their shippers to use U. S. vessels from a patriotic duty to support our own merchant marine. This argument also has force as a saving in subsidies probably being paid the U. S. line and in more taxes paid by the U. S. line on incomes and materials.

2. *Dependability of Service.* The exporter must know the exact time of the proposed sailing of a vessel. He is dependent on that ship to load and carry his cargo on the date set. The exporter has made his contract with the foreign connection wherein he agrees to ship before a certain date. Failing to ship on time, the exporter has broken his contract and the sale can be refused by the foreign connection and the overseas association may be broken. The exporter is working against a fixed deadline on which the letter-of-credit established to pay for his merchandise will expire. Therefore, the reliability of the steamship line in meeting its sailing schedule is a matter of utmost concern.

3. *Care of Cargo.* A steamship line may have a reputation for being careless in the handling of an exporter's cargo. Rough handling in the course of loading, careless stowage in the vessel so that the cargo becomes loose and is injured by the vessel's rolling or is crushed by heavy cargo, or damage from moisture within the holds of the vessel all result in claims against the steamship company. Proper cargo handling, on the other hand, gives the cargo solicitor an important advantage.

4. *Accurate Documentation.* The bill-of-lading issued by the steamship company is the evidence of title to the goods shipped and the bill must be in absolute accurate form in order that banks will accept it from the exporter and pay him for the merchandise. If the bills are inaccurate, have too many exceptions placed on them by the vessel, or are "foul", the exporter will experience difficulty in financing his shipment. Accuracy of documents is thus another strong selling point for the cargo solicitor.

5. *Speed of Delivery.* Speed of delivery of cargo to destination is extremely important but is considered secondary to certainty of shipment. The exporter has completed his duty when he puts the goods on the vessel. The time of delivery is the first worry of the foreign importer.

6. *Responsibility of Carrier.* The berth line vessels are usually financially responsible for any damage to cargo for which they are liable. Some lines fight hard to be relieved of claims. Responsibility for final payment may be presumed. The question of responsibility of the carrier, when tramp vessels are being used, is measured by

the value of the vessel itself which may be held by court procedure
to answer a judgment.

Securing the best paying cargo for the ship must be carefully
coordinated with the vessel's ability to carry the cargo and with
the possibility of stowing different kinds of cargo together in the
same holds. The cargo clerk might wish to take additional steel
rails bringing in a high freight rate, but he may find that the
heavier cargo will exceed the vessel's dead weight carrying capacity.
Then, he must choose available light-weight cargo, such as lumber,
to fill the vessel's holds to capacity

Selection of cargo. The selection of a vessel's cargo from the
freight offering therefore requires careful and scientific handling.
Successful loading of the vessel results in her holds being completely
filled underdeck at the maximum weight allowable. When this is
accomplished, the resulting freight revenue will be found generally
to be the greatest possible from the cargo offering.

The complexity of the selection is increased when some items
of cargo may not be stowed with other cargo by reason of contam-
ination or because certain items are "penalty cargo," such as green
hides. The characteristics of these items are fully set out in *Modern
Ship Stowage*, U.S. Government Printing Office, 1942.

The following records are kept to reflect transactions between
the shipper of the cargo and the steamship company from the time
the shipper first considers making the shipment until the cargo is
actually booked for the vessel.

The cargo book. This book is usually a ruled book with convenient columns which records the name of the shipper, the item of
freight to be shipped, its weight and its measurement, the rate of
freight and its destination. This record is kept for each vessel so
that the prospective load and freight offerings are immediately
available to the person in charge of the selection of cargo for the
vessel.

As the cargo offerings are accepted, they are listed in the book
with notations of the cubic volume of the shipment and its weight.
These items are kept totalled so that a constant check may be made
of the amount of cargo offered. This is necessary to avoid having
more cargo than the vessel can carry with the consequent em-
barassment of "shutting out" cargo.

Options. A situation may arise in which the shipper has a prospective order from a foreign connection and must be able to secure cargo space for the shipment in the event that the order is received. The shipper accordingly secures from the ocean carrier an option on the space necessary for shipment of the goods. He can then make a firm offer to his foreign connection abroad. If the business is secured, then the steamship company is bound to provide the space as optioned and the contract for carriage of the cargo is made definite between the carrier and the shipper. If the option is not taken up it will expire by time limitation. Although the steamship company is bound to provide the space according to the option given, the shipper has no obligation to take up the option if his sales effort abroad fails.

Freight engagement. Confirmation of the booking of cargo is made by the steamship company which executes and sends to the shipper a freight contract or freight engagement in which the details of the shipment to be made are set out. This contract cites the contract number, the shipper, the vessel, expected sailing date, the port of shipment, port of destination, commodity and quantity, weight and measurement of commodity, rate of freight, and suppliers of the cargo if other than the shipper.

Such contracts contain the condition that the obligation of the carrier is contingent upon vessel's safe and timely arrival readiness to load and sail. Should one of these circumstances occur the carrier may cancel the freight engagement and is not obligated to furnish a substitute vessel. This follows the general maritime rule that the ship and cargo are in the same hazardous venture and are not liable to each other for acts beyond their power to foresee and prevent. For good business relationships, however the carrier customarily makes every effort to secure another vessel to relieve the situation. In some cases, where several vessels may be available for carrying the cargo, the expression "*A Vessel*" is entered on the freight engagement. This obligates the steamship company to furnish the transportation regardless of the unavailability of the vessel upon which it had been planned to make shipment.

Failure of the shipper to supply the cargo is a clear breach of contract which gives rise to a cause of action by the vessel operator for "dead freight." This sum is the difference between the entire freight bill under the contract and the amount of revenue from substitute cargo the vessel was able to secure. Although a cause of action exists against the cargo owner, the steamship companies seldom resort to litigation, probably for public relation reasons.

Foreign trade quotations. Although the obligation to procure transportation for a shipment may fall upon the vendor (exporter) of the commodity or upon the vendee (importer), according to the terms of the sale that has been made, an understanding by the steamship operator of the commitments made by the shipper will lead to better business relations between the two. The time of making shipment is most important to vendor and vendee and must be determined in the negotiations between these two parties. The obligation to secure transportation and payment for the cost thereof are expressed in the form of quotations customarily expressed by initials. These quotations, FAS, FOB, CIF, *ex wharf*, etc. are described in *American Foreign Trade Definitions*, 1941 and were originally adopted by the National Foreign Trade Council, The Chamber of Commerce of the United States, and several other organizations whose members were engaged in foreign trade. The purpose of the definitions is to standardize the use of the quotations and clarify their meaning in order to prevent misunderstandings between the American trader and his foreign connection. The definitions are usually made a part of the expressed contract between the two parties.*

Each quotation expresses a physical point in the course of the transportation of the item. When the obligation of the seller is discharged and the duty of the buyer commences relative to further transportation of the item. The terms are also important in determining when title to the goods passes from the vendor to the vendee. This in turn decides upon whom the loss shall fall if the goods, for example are destroyed by fire or otherwise lost.

EX (Point of origin)

> Ex factory, ex mill, ex plantation, ex warehouse, ex wharf (named point of origin)
>
> Buyer must take delivery at agreed place and procure and pay for transportation.

*National Foreign Trade Council, New York.

F. O. B. (free on board) VESSEL (named port of shipment)
Seller may procure the vessel and provide the buyer
with ship's receipt or on-board bill of lading. Buyer
may provide vessel. Must pay further costs and handle
subsequent movement of goods to destination.

F. A. S. (free Along Side) VESSEL (named port of shipment)
Seller must place goods along side vessel or on dock.
Buyer must select vessel and give notice of delivery time
goods from along side. Must pay for ocean transportation.

C. I. F. (cost, insurance, freight) (named port of destination)
Seller must provide and pay for transportation to named
point of destination. Must provide buyer a clean bill of
lading to named point of destination. Where received-
for-shipment lading may be tendered, seller is responsible for any loss or damage to the goods until they
have been delivered into the custody of the carrier.
Where on-board ocean bill of lading is required, seller
is responsible until goods have been delivered on board
the vessel. Buyer must receive the goods on arrival, take
delivery from the vessel, pay all costs of landing at
destination.

The basic requirement of each of these quotations is that the
shipment be physically placed at some definite point in its transportation from its origin to its destination. The division of obligations between vendee and vendor is shown by the chart, Figure 9,
as well as the charges assessed to them for inland transportation,
terminal services, and ocean freight. The chart is based upon the
assumption of the shipment of cargo weighing and measuring one
ton.

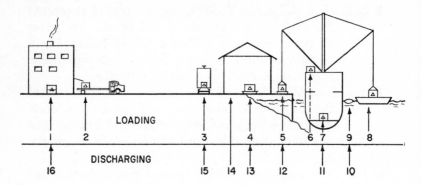

Figure 9. The division of obligations between vendee and vendor
(assuming shipment weighing and measuring one ton).

EXPORT QUOTATION

			QUOTED PRICE
1. Ex factory, Seattle	Manufacturer's cost, profit, packing for export, marking, exporter's profit		$ 1,000.00
2. F.O.B. Truck, factory, Seattle	No. 1 plus loading to truck (car)	$ 2.00	1,002.00
3. F.O.B. cars (truck); wharf, Seattle	No. 2 plus inland freight (cartage)	10.00	1,012.00
4. F.O.B. wharf, Seattle	No. 3 plus car unloading (truck)	2.00	1,014.00
5. F.A.S. vessel, Seattle	No. 4 plus wharfage plus handling to shipside	1.00 2.00	1,017.00
6. F.O.B. vessel, Seattle (on deck)	Same as No. 5 — Stevedoring usually included in ocean freight rate		1,017.00
7. C.I.F. Yokohama	Same as No. 6 — cargo stowed under deck plus marine insurance plus ocean freight to Yokohama	10.00 125.00	1,152.00
8. F.O.B. barge shipside, Seattle	Same as No. 3 plus ½ wharfage $1.00	.50	1,012.50
9. In water shipside, Seattle	Same as No. 8 (for logs)		1,012.50

IMPORT QUOTATION	DISCHARGING INBOUND		
10. C.I.F. Seattle In water shipside	Reverse of No. 7 — All charges paid from Yokohama to Seattle		1,152.00
11. C.I.F. Seattle	Same as No. 10 (Ocean freight and marine insurance included)		1,152.00
12. C.I.F. Seattle	Same as No. 11 — discharge from vessel usually included in ocean freight		1,152.00
13. F.O.B. wharf, Seattle	Same as No. 12 plus handling	2.00	1,154.00
14. F.O.B. wharf, Seattle duty paid	Same as No. 13 — Duty 50% ad valorem 50% $1,1017	508.50	1,662.50
15. F.O.B. cars, Seattle	Same as No. 14 plus wharfage plus loading	1.00 2.00	1,665.50
16. F.O.B. cars (truck), Seattle consignee's warehouse	Same as No. 15 plus inland freight	10.00	1,675.50

CHAPTER 9

Cargo Stowage

Before the hour of the actual loading, a vessel cargo has been accepted, its total weight and measurement ascertained and each shipper alerted to the probable time his cargo has been scheduled for loading. On non-congested piers, cargo may accumulate waiting a vessel's arrival. On busy piers, it is necessary to avoid congestion. Timing of the delivery of cargo alongside becomes a serious problem; therefore, each shipper is given a permit specifying the exact time at which his cargo is to be on hand for loading.

Overland cargo will have been ordered shipped from source with time allowed both for the transit of the shipment to seaboard and the five days usually allowed as free time by the railroads for the unloading of the cars carrying export-import items.

Boat notes. The vessel operator's staff will have prepared *boat-notes,* from details supplied by the shipper, each note describing a single item of cargo or the cargo from one shipper to a single destination. Of prime interest to the officer in charge of loading the ship will be the information of the weight and measurement of each item of cargo, its marks for identification, and the port of discharge. Further information on each boat-note will consist of the supplier of the cargo, the shipper, the inland carrier, and the time when the item has been ordered to be delivered to the vessel.

Supercargo. The individual entrusted with the supervision of loading or the discharge of a vessel is usually a member of the operator's staff whose training and long experience have prepared him to handle the many details of these duties. During the second World War, the armed services hired men who had this experience.

67

They were designated "supercargo" and were in charge of loading of each ship. In the case of a ship under charter, "supercargo" is defined as the person placed on board to represent the owner of the cargo and who by reason of his specialized knowledge of the cargo being transported advises the vessel operator to assure efficient handling and delivery of the cargo.

In civilian practice, an individual entrusted with the loading and discharging of a vessel does not have a title descriptive of these particular duties, but is said to be "in charge of loading or discharging" of a particular vessel. As a definite title for the person commissioned to perform these duties, the text in this chapter will use the military designation of supercargo and differentiate the duties of supercargo when engaged on a chartered ship.

The supercargo is the liaison officer between the ship's officer the vessel operators, the stevedore contractor, and the terminal operator. The usual lines of authority place the prime responsibility for the proper and safe loading of the vessel with the ship's officers. The Chief Mate or First Officer must authorize the loading of cargo aboard the vessel and receipt for each item taken aboard. He must also designate the general disposition of the cargo into various holds and station his junior officers to supervise the loading in each hold. As the cargo comes aboard, it must be inspected to see that it is in "apparent good order and condition," as certified on the bill of lading. If the cargo is not in good condition, the mate and his officers must take and record exceptions to protect the vessel against claims. Or he may refuse to permit the loading of the cargo, if to do so would seem to present a danger to the ship or to cargo already loaded.

Checkers. Naturally, much of the responsibility must be delegated by the mate to his junior officers or to the supercargo and his checkers. Usually, the mate and his juniors are either busy with ship routine while the vessel is in port or on shore leave. Often this personnel is selected and joins the vessel only shortly before sailing. The amount of supervision given to the vessel loading by the mate and his juniors reflects their loyalty to the interests of the vessel owner.

Vessel loading responsibility. The responsibility of the vessel operators is to secure the best and most profitable cargo, to bring it alongside the vessel available for loading, and to manifest it and account for each item.

Directed by the vessel's officers, the stevedore contractor must load the cargo as efficiently and safely as possible, and at the required time.

The terminal operator must have the cargo available at the instant call of the officer in charge of the loading. This requires efficient management to avoid congestion and confusion since a vessel may discharge and load full cargoes totalling 20,000 tons or more within the space of a very few days.

The coordination of all of these agencies to produce efficient, speedy loading, and proper stowage is the on-the-spot duty of the supercargo. His duty must be accomplished under pressure. The wages of those engaged in vessel loading are very high. Each minute that the stevedore gangs are not working is charged against the expense of the vessel, and each delay and every time the "cargo hook hangs" must be explained by the supercargo.

Preplanning of loading. Before the vessel loads, the supercargo takes the boat-notes and from them determines the manner of the loading of the ship, what cargo is to be loaded into the different holds to produce the proper vessel trim and stability. Generally, he selects the heavier cargo to go into the lower holds, distributing it evenly fore and aft. The lighter cargo will probably be placed in the 'tween decks. The arrangement of the deck cargo is planned, and the hatches over which it will be stowed are noted.

All of these details are carefully studied and noted on a tentative stowage plan. This plan serves as a guide until the cargo is actually on board and has been listed on a smooth stowage plan, which is a record of the location of the cargo as it has been stowed in the vessel. With the tentative plan in hand, the supercargo, the stevedore superintendent, and the wharf manager, "walk the pier" selecting the items of cargo which will form the first day's loading.

The complexity of this preplanning is greatly increased when the vessel is scheduled to discharge in several ports. The problem then becomes one of placing the cargo in the ship so that it will be available for discharge at each port in its proper order, the first in the vessel to be the last in order of discharge. It is an error to have cargo for a port overstowed so that other cargo must be handled before the desired lot can be secured for discharge.

During World War II, the preplanning of fleet issue ships became a national problem. These vessels would be fully loaded with many items of ammunition or of food supplies, any item of which was required to be immediately available for delivery to vessels at sea under advanced war area conditions. Each fleet issue vessel was, thus, a floating ammunition supply or supermarket on hand for the convenience of the battle fleet and transports.

Exceptions to cargo condition. As the loading commences, a checker is stationed at each hatch or on the pier. His duty is to count the cargo as it goes aboard and tally it against the boat-note which the supercargo has furnished him. As he is acting for the ship, he is required to be very accurate as to marks and numbers, and the condition of the cargo. The making of the ship's bill of lading will be based upon his record on the boat-note. Cargo being loaded which is not in apparent good order, should be immediately reported to the supercargo or the ship's officers. In case of doubt the loading of that cargo should be stopped. If the decision is to load the cargo with exceptions, the form of those exceptions should be approved as: "M/L rusty" (more or less rusty) or "3 cases recoopered, contents unknown." Such notations on the boat-notes are recopied on the bills of lading and serve to protect the vessel from claims involving the defects shown.

When a particular lot has been loaded, the checker initials the boat-note and indicates the location in the hold where the cargo was stowed and returns it to the supercargo for signature by the ship's officers. The supercargo enters the cargo lot on the stowage plan and returns the boat-note to the office to serve as the basis for a bill of lading.

If loading is interrupted for any cause, the checker should make a note of the exact time of stoppage and its cause as, "10:43 winch broke down—repaired—loading resumed 11:11." This standby time by the stevedores will be charged to the ship and the checker's notation will be a verification of the claim.

At the end of each day, the supercargo enters the cargo loaded on the stowage plan, totals the weight of the cargo loaded and checks it against the draft of the vessel, approves the stevedores' time sheets, and instructs the officer in charge of the night loading.

Broken stowage. The amount of cargo that can be stowed below decks can be greatly increased by the stevedores carefully fitting cargo into every available cubic foot of space. In stowing cargo along the curved sides of the ship and around stanchions, pipes, and projections within the holds, some space will be unusable and will, thus, cause *broken stowage;* i.e., space unavoidably lost in the stowage of general cargo. Even though the exact measurement of each bag or box or barrel is known, certain irregularities exist which keep pieces of cargo from fitting closely, therefore, the amount of cargo space actually used will be the item's measurement plus lost space around it. This practical difference is learned by long experience and is a part of the specialized knowledge of the supercargo. Mathematically, a thousand board feet of lumber, (a board foot is a unit of measurement 1 foot by 1 foot by 1 inch), will measure 83⅓ cubic feet, but by reason of being in small sizes with spaces between and straight lengths in a curved ship, the actual volume of hold space occupied will average approximately 120 cubic feet to the thousand feet board measure. This difference between actual measurement and practical stowed volume could result in overbooking the cargo for the vessel and a consequent "shut out" because of lack of space.

Even in bulk type cargo broken stowage may run as high as 10% in coal, 10% in grain, 50% in lumber, 20% in ore, 5% in brick. In package cargo, the estimates run from 10% to 25%. These percentages are added to the actual volume of the commodity to give the space occupied within the ship.

Stowage factor. Information on how much space an item of cargo occupies when stowed in a vessel's holds was collected by the government for use in the American Expeditionary Forces in 1918, and was named the *stowage factor.* The stowage factor of a commodity is the figure which represents the number of cubic feet of cargo space in which a long ton (2240 lbs.) of the commodity may be stowed. The data is arranged in columns:

Commodity	Package	Gross weight	Measurement	Stowage	Remarks
Salmon canned	case	70 lbs.	1-6 (1-6/12 C.F.)	50 (C.F.)	
Peanuts	bag	113 lbs.	3-8	72	Shelled

This information has been produced by the government. In 1942, the U.S. Department of Commerce published a book, *Modern Ship Stowage*, which is a basic text on terminal operation, cargo handling equipment, vessel loading, and special cargo handling. It includes a complete list of the stowage factors of all usual cargoes. To the above information on stowage factors have been added a description of the inner and outer packaging of a commodity, its gross net and tare weights, and the stowage factor.

Stowage factors are of two kinds: (1) the actual volume of the commodity as packaged for shipment with no allowance made for broken stowage caused by the commodity's peculiar shape and/or the use of dunnage to secure the cargo and protect it in the hold of the ship; (2) a figure in which allowance for broken stowage and the use of dunnage has been made—the actual amount of space occupied by the item as stowed in the hold of the ship.

Because of the many variable conditions which affect the stowage of a commodity, the stowage factors listed in *Modern Ship Stowage* are generally of the first type and do not make allowance for broken stowage and the use of dunnage. Therefore, the knowledge of the actual space occupiable within the ship is of great practical use and this information is obtained only through actual experience in vessel loading. The efficient loading of the vessel is directly dependent upon the use of this specialized knowledge by the loading officer (supercargo).

Vessel trim. Some of the basic considerations must bear the supercargo in mind while planning the loading of the vessel are related to the ship's trim and stability. The ship must be trimmed to an even keel; that is, her draft forward and aft must be the same or slightly deeper at the stern, in order that the vessel can be easily maneuvered. Vessel trim is accomplished by mathematically distributing the cargo by weight evenly throughout the vessel. Each hold must have its weight load proportioned to the size of the hold. The effect of placing weight at each spot, fore or aft, in the vessel can be read from the ship's trimming table. The weight of cargo must be evenly distributed to prevent structural injury to the vessel in case of a storm at sea.

If very heavy weights are placed at bow and stern, the vessel will probably be in trim, but in a storm, the upward buoyancy pressure of a large wave amid-ships will convert the ship into a huge balance with heavy weights at each end. The bow and stern, unsupported for the instant, would throw all of the strain on the midship section and the vessel might crack at the main

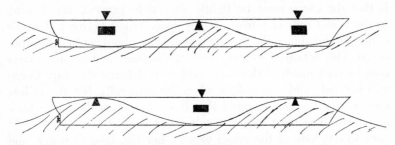

Figure 10. Top—The effect of placing heavy cargo at bow and stern.
Bottom—The effect of placing heavy cargo at midship.
(Note the point of strain in each instance.)

deck. Contrariwise, suppose the weights are concentrated near the midship section. Then the condition could arise in which the vessel is supported at bow and stern by large waves and the heavily loaded midship section, unsupported for the instant, might sag and break.

In order that the ship ride perfectly upright, cargo weight must be evenly distributed towards each side of the vessel to form a perfect balance, port and starboard. With the loading of general cargo this becomes automatic, since each stevedore gang operating in a hold will by custom divide in equal numbers to receive slingloads alternately and stow them in opposite sides of the ship.

Vessel rolling. With heavy cargo, this a-thwartship stowage produces another problem. If the weights are concentrated in the center of the hold, in a storm the ship will roll quickly and sharply return upright. This is because her righting force has been increased by this placement of weight. The snappy roll of the vessel would be most uncomfortable to the crew and could cause damage to the cargo and even to the ship's structure. To prevent this condition, the weights should be placed at the sides of the hold to lessen the ship's righting force and to insure that the vessel returns easily to the upright position. This winging out of weights towards the skin of the vessel will tend to give her a slow, lazy roll.

The proper stowage of cargo within the holds is the primary duty of the stevedores, but must be inspected by the supercargo as a reasonable precaution for the ship's safety. The first rule is that the cargo must be tightly stowed to prevent any shifting as the vessel rolls or pitches. If any space is left between items of cargo, as the ship rolls, the items will slide about and crush other cargo. This action of weights adrift when continued for many days could wreck much of the cargo and even damage the ship. Cargo will not only slide on a deck when the ship rolls, but the rolling motion can become so rapid that it tends to toss the cargo back and forth. The most serious result could be that the cargo would shift to one side of the vessel causing her list, take in water, and sink.

Dunnage. After the first tier of cargo is placed in the hold and secured, it is floored off with *dunnage* which in this case is lumber laid loosely over the cargo to form a floor upon which a second tier of cargo may be stowed. This dunnage not only furnishes a level floor upon which to place other items, but it also serves as a tie to prevent any movement by the lower tier. The locking effect is greatly increased as additional cargo is added in successive tiers. The dunnage also serves to spread the weight of the upper cargo evenly over the under lot, so the effect of crushing by mere weight is minimized. Dunnage is also used to fill in the spaces between irregularly shaped pieces of cargo to prevent movement. Finally, dunnage may serve to keep cargo in place by shoring down each large item with tmber extending from the cargo up to the deck over that particular item, such as a machine. Materials commonly used for dunnage are lumber, matting, and burlap rattans which limit damage from sweat, breakage, chafage, moisture, crushing, and other contacts. When the holds are completely filled, the hatch beams, which are used to close the hatch openings, are put in place with the ship's loading gear. These beams are long, heavy steel beams which extend across the width of the vessel's hatch in intervals of about five feet. They support the hatch boards—small, heavy panels of wood —which in turn, fit between the beams and are put in place by hand by the stevedores. The hatch beams and boards produce a solid floor over the hatch opening over which is stretched several layers of canvas tarpaulins to insure that the hatch opening is watertight. These hatch coverings are secured in place with wide steel bands across the hatch and around the hatch combing which forms the raised edge of the hatch.

When the beams have been placed, there is space between them approximately equal to the area of the hatch opening and about four feet deep. This is available for stowing small parcels of cargo. When this beamfilling is completed, the hatch boards are put in place, the covers are spread and battened down with the steel bands. The hatch is thus prepared for the vessel's going to sea or for the further stowage of cargo on top of the hatch, which thus serves as an area for the stowage of deck cargo.

Deck cargo stowage. The problem of securing deck cargo for sea is more acute than that of under deck stowage. Deck cargo must withstand greater vessel movement, winds of gale force, and constant spray. In heavy storms, the deck load may even be submerged in water.

Deck cargo in the form of large boxes or lumber is secured by running heavy chains from each side of the vessel up and over the cargo and tightened then with turnbuckles. This lashes the cargo securely to the deck until it is almost a part of the ship. However, if any box collapses or any portion of the lumber works loose under water pounding, the whole load may disintegrate and wash overboard.

Other cargo on deck, such as machinery, boats, trucks is usually stowed aft of the midship house where there is less danger from waves coming aboard. Each item of cargo is lashed securely to the deck with steel cable to prevent movement.

If the decks have been completely covered with cargo, then walkways must be constructed so that the seamen may have safe footing in passing over the cargo from the midship area to the bow or to the stern.

Cargo booms must be lowered and secured for sea before the ship is ready to sail.

CHAPTER 10

Vessel Stability

Effect of stability. When the operator intends to load a vessel to cargo capacity, the factors of the ship's action and safety at sea must be taken into consideration. Planning of weight distribution to give a vessel an easy, rolling motion and to lessen the strain of a storm at sea was mentioned in the preceding chapter. Beyond these considerations is the ultimate danger that the weight of cargo may be placed so high within the holds and on deck that the vessel might become unstable or actually capsize. It is therefore, very important to estimate in advance of loading what the safety factor of a vessel will be when the cargo has been finally stowed. The operator must compute what the *vessel's stability* will be at the time of sailing and determine what effect the burning of fuel oil from the double bottoms will have during the course of the ship's voyage. The use of this oil lessens the ballasting effect, and, thus, presents a possible danger to the ship's stability.

The problem is to insure that the vertical center of gravity of the ship combined with the vertical center of gravity of the cargo and fuel oil when stowed in the ship, do not rise above the keel line so high as to capsize the ship. The problem of gravity can be likened to the action of a pendulum. As the weight is raised toward the center of suspension, the effect of the pendulum is lessened; if the weight were raised over the point of suspension, the operation of the pendulum would be ruined.

Righting force. Likewise, the ship has a *righting force* which is the effect of gravity bringing a ship back into a vertical position after it has been inclined from the vertical by load weight, waves or wind. The strength of this force is increased as the weight center is kept low and directed towards the keel of the ship. Its power is lessened as the center of gravity of the cargo rises further above the keel line. The righting force is completely extinguished if the center of gravity of the cargo rises above a calculated point within the ship.

Metacenter. This point is called the *metacenter*. It is the center of gravity of the unsubmerged part of the floating vessel. If the center of gravity of the cargo is further raised above the metacenter, the righting force is reversed and the ship will tip over.

During the loading of the vessel, the reversal of the righting force may become physically apparent. If the ship's loading gear is entrusted to lift from the pier a heavy piece of cargo, two tons or over, the ship will list noticeably towards the pier appearing to strain in almost human effort to lift the weight. To correct such a condition, either cargo must be removed or ballast added in the ship's lower tanks.

To prevent listing while loading, the operator computes before hand the distance between the metacenter and the combined centers of gravity of the ship and cargo and fuel oil. This distance, expressed in feet, is a determination of the vessel's stability. It is, in one sense, an accurate reflection of the vessel's safeness for sea duty.

Computing the GM. The data for computing the problem consists of measurements taken from the ship's plans and details of the proposed cargo loading, fuel and water, stores, crew and ballast.

K, keel is the fore and aft center line of the vessel at the keel.

VCG, vertical center of gravity, the distance that the center of gravity of a full compartment or of a block of cargo in the compartment or on deck, is located above the line K. In the table that follows, the vertical centers of gravity are based upon compartments fully loaded with homogeneous cargo. If the compartment were partially filled with heavy cargo, the center of gravity would be lower. Distances may be measured directly on the ship's plans.

KG is the vertical distance to the line K of a composite center of gravity — the center of gravity of the vessel, of all the centers of the weights placed in the vessel, together with their distances from the keel. This data is readily assembled by using the form below which shows the estimate of the available stability of a Liberty ship. In this example the cargo and oil are presumed to be loaded in even 100-ton lots, with 1000 tons in each lower hold, 400 tons in each 'tween deck, 1000 tons on deck, and so forth. The cargo weight multiplied by its own vertical center of gravity above the keel comprises a *moment*. The total of moments divided by the total of weights (displacement) gives the *KG* or the height in feet of the composite center of gravity from the keel.

M, metacenter, is the point at which the weights of the vessel and its cargo are evenly distributed above and below, and, in turn, the righting force is zero. It is the point about which the ship can be considered to rotate. This point varies at different displacements. Shipbuilders calculate and prove the point by means of inclining tests which are made by placing weights aboard the vessel and measuring the degree of inclination from the vertical. The calculation may be found on the ship's plans in the form of a curve that varies with the ship's displacement.

Displacement is the entire weight of ship, cargo, fuel, fresh water, stores, crew and effects. It is expresed in long tons, 2240 lbs.

KM is the vertical distance from the metacenter to the line *K*.

GM is the distance between the center of gravity of the loaded vessel and the metacenter. *GM* is *KM* minus *KG* and is the indicator of the vessel's stability. From the problem: At 13,600 tons displacement,

KM from table is 24.1 feet
KG, calculated   22.9
GM   1.2

The *GM* of 1.2 feet indicates that the vessel has sufficient stability. This figure means that the righting force is low and that the vessel will have a slow, easy roll in a seaway. A lower *GM* as small as 0.5 feet would show that the vessel is "tender." It would either return slowly to the upright position or even remain inclined at an angle. This condition is dangerous, since it indicates that the vessel might, under certain conditions, capsize. A *GM* of around 5.0 feet would indicate a seaworthy condition. A *GM* much larger than 5.0 feet would mean that the vessel has become "stiff." The righting force is so strong that the vessel would be returned to the upright position with a snap which could cause both structural damage to

the ship and injury to the cargo. The cause of this condition could
be traceable to loading all of the heavy cargo at the bottom of the
ship's holds.

ESTIMATE OF AVAILABLE STABILITY—LIBERTY SHIP

	Weight 100 T.-2240 lbs.	VCG in ft. FULL COMPARTMENT	MOMENT WT. XVCG.
Light Ship (Armed)	35.6	23.3	855.0
Crew & Stores	1.0	38.0	38.0
No. 1 Hold	10.0	21.4	214.0
No. 1 DT P & S	1.0	9.3	9.3
No. 2 DT P & S	1.0	9.0	9.0
No. 2 Hold	10.0	16.0	160.0
No. 3 Hold	10.0	16.0	160.0
No. 3 DT P & S	1.0	17.0	17.0
No. 4 Hold	10.0	17.0	170.0
No. 5 Hold	10.0	19.0	190.0
No. 1 TD	4.0	35.3	141.2
No. 2 TD	4.0	33.8	135.2
No. 3 TD	4.0	33.0	132.0
No. 4 TD	4.0	34.0	136.0
No. 5 TD	4.0	35.0	140.0
Forepeak	1.0	18.5	18.5
Aft Peak	1.0	27.3	27.3
Fuel Oil (D.B.)	10.0	1.9	19.0
Settlers	1.0	12.5	12.5
Fresh Water	3.0	35.0	105.0
Reserve Feed	1.0	1.9	1.9
Deck Load	10.0	45.0	450.0
Displacement	136.6	Moment	3130.9

KG (Mom ÷ Displ)   22.9 ft.

*Includes:

100 Tons F. W. Fixed Ballast at 2.0 VCG

180 Tons Stone Ballast at 5.4 VCG

100 Tons Armament at 50.0 VCG

DT. P and S—Deep tanks, port and starboard

TD—'Tween deck

DB—Double Bottom

FW—Fresh Water

TABLE FOR LIBERTY SHIP

Displacement	KM Feet	Free Surf. Corr. No Cargo Oil	GM Required
5000	29.4	2.7	2.8
5500	28.1	2.5	2.6
6000	27.1	2.3	2.5
6500	26.3	2.1	2.3
7000	25.7	1.9	2.1
7500	25.1	1.8	2.0
8000	24.7	1.8	1.9
8500	24.4	1.8	1.7
9000	24.1	1.5	1.5
9500	23.9	1.4	1.4
10000	23.8	1.4	1.2
10500	23.7	1.3	1.1
11000	23.7	1.3	.9
11500	23.7	1.2	.8
12000	23.8	1.1	.6
12500	23.9	1.1	.5
13000	24.0	1.0	.3
13500	24.1	1.0	.2
14000	24.3	1.0	
14300	24.4	.9	

Free surface correction. In the problem the Liberty Ship has a GM of 1.2 feet upon sailing. As the vessel proceeds on her voyage, fuel oil from her double-bottom tanks will be burned thus lessening the GM. A tank with liquid in it adds to the stability of the ship only when the tank is completely filled or "pressed up." When any of the liquid is subtracted and the liquid can move within the tank, the ballasting effect of the tank is lost. The tank must be immediately subtracted from the vessel's GM. The term for procedure is FSC or *Free Surface Correction*. It is listed in the ship's engineering data along with the corresponding ballasting effect of each fuel tank which can help to correct the deficit. Each large tank averages about 0.5 feet. These corrections are computed in the same manner as determining the VCG of cargo within her holds.

The final column of the table, entitled GM required, is a wartime consideration. It indicates the relative *GM* necessary in the event one compartment of the ship becomes flooded.

Summarizing, at 13,600 tons displacement:

KM (from table)	24.1 feet
KG (Mom - Displ)	22.9
GM (KM-KG)	1.2
FSC (from table) - 1.0	
By ballasting 1.0	0.0
GM available	1.2
GM required (from table)	0.2
Difference	1.0

CHAPTER 11

Cargo Documentation

Some of the record forms used by steamship companies were described in a previous chapter on cargo procurement as these forms pertain to the cargo records kept by the shipper and the company. It will be remembered that during loading, boat notes are issued which record the cargo actually stowed aboard the vessel and the condition of the cargo when it is received on board. The cargo owner may also require a receipt of shipment, which may be issued in several ways.

Dock receipt. If the shipper or the supplier has delivered a shipment of cargo to the pier, he may request a *dock receipt*. This is a simple receipt describing the cargo and acknowledging its receipt at the pier. A dock receipt is important because it provides a check on the condition of cargo at the time of its delivery to the terminal company. Typical wording on the dock receipt is "Received in apparent good order and condition." This is an acknowledgment by the dock company that the exterior packaging of the freight is in good condition and suitable for ocean transport. Once the dock receipt has been signed the responsibility for the safe keeping of the goods is transferred to the dock company. The dock receipt does not, however, determine the question of concealed damage for which the dock or carrier might not be liable.

The dock receipt also fixes the time of the completed delivery of the cargo between the supplier of the product and the exporter, or between the exporter and the carrier. In case of cargo damage from fire or flood at this stage of the operation, a dock receipt would offer some evidence as to the ownership or custody of the cargo and would also help to determine upon whom the loss might fall.

Another benefit of the dock receipt is that it lists not only the commodity being shipped, but also the packaging, quantity, size and weight of the shipment. When the character of a packaged commodity is not readily apparent, the dock receipt may serve to protect the carrier because, in such instances, it will state that the packages are "said to contain" the merchandise described on the receipt.

Usually, the dock receipt is not a negotiable instrument or a part of the set of documents used in foreign trade. The dock may agree with the supplier of the commodity, not to deliver to the shipper an ocean bill of lading, which represents ownership of the cargo, except upon surrender of a dock receipt. The supplier would then attach a dock receipt to the draft on the exporter. This draft which must be paid before the exporter can get the receipt and surrender it, serves as a security for payment to the supplier.

The dock receipt is neither evidence of title to the shipment nor a transportation contract. It does, however, fix the responsibility of the terminal operator as bailee of the cargo until the carrier actually takes possession. If an exporter has quoted his foreign connection free alongside vessel at a given place — "F.A.S. vessel, named port," the dock receipt could be evidence of the completion of the exporter's agreement to place the cargo on the dock and at the disposal of the foreign importer.

Mate's receipt. This receipt is an acknowledgment by the vessel of the receipt of the cargo aboard the ship. It is similar to the dock receipt, except that it means the vessel is subsequently responsible for the cargo. It is also evidence that the shipment has been loaded into the vessel and that the exporter is entitled to an "on board" bill of lading. From this time the cargo is covered by the provisions of the bill of lading issued by the carrier, the Carriage of Good-by-Sea Act. These provisions are considerably different from the simple responsibility of the terminal operator as bailee of the goods. Mates' receipts are issued usually only upon special request of the shipper.

The mate's receipt is merely an interim receipt issued until the bill of lading is formally made up. It is not negotiable but may be used as security for payment to the supplier by the exporter.

When the exporter has quoted the foreign connection — "F.O.B. vessel named port" — the mate's receipt could be evidence of a completed contract between the exporter and the overseas consignee.

It is true that the duties imposed by quotations to foreign importers are the primary concern of the exporter. However, these quotations (FAS, CIF, FOB and the like), because they include the detail and time of shipment, would promote better relations if the implicit obligations were mutually understood by shipper and steamship operator. These duties are fully described in AMERICAN FOREIGN TRADE DEFINITIONS, 1941, referred to in Chapter 8.

Received for shipment lading. Another form of receipt is the *"Received-for-shipment"* bill of lading. This is a receipt issued by the ocean carrier for goods delivered to the dock to be shipped on a vessel which is not at that time on berth or ready to receive cargo. It is no assurance that the vessel will either arrive, or that space on the ship will be available for the cargo. For this reason, the foreign importer usually asks to be furnished with a bill of lading specifying that the goods have been loaded on the vessel bound to his port of delivery.

The received-for-shipment lading is the formal transportation contract. It becomes valid immediately after the goods have been loaded on the vessel. When issued, this bill of lading may serve as evidence of a completed F.A.S. quotation by the exporter or may be accepted by the foreign importer as the exporter's fulfilled contract.

On board bill of lading. The *Shipped* or *On Board* bill of lading is generally used in foreign trade. This receipt from the carrier states that goods have been received in good order and condition; any exceptions are noted on the lading. It is evidence of the actual loading of the cargo aboard the vessel and the date on the receipt fixes the time of shipment from the exporter to his overseas connection. The receipt concludes that part of the contract between the exporter and importer relating to date of shipment. Frequently, the exporter will ship cargo under the provisions of a letter of credit established by the foreign connection which will specify a definite time for shipment. This provision must be met exactly or the local bank acting as the importer's agent may refuse to honor the exporter's draft.

A Received-for-shipment bill of lading can be converted into an On-board receipt by the addition of a clause stating that the goods have been loaded on board the vessel. The wording of the clause is sufficient if it specifies, "Loaded on board the SS Columbia, November 1, 1958", and if the on-board receipt is signed by the vessel's captain, his representative, or by the authorized agent of the carrier whose signature is on the original bill of lading. The phrase "Loaded on board" is mandatory; inclusion of the vessel's name is good practice, since the vessel originally intended may not be the one transporting this cargo. The date is vital; it fixes the time of shipment for sales contract and letter of credit purposes. The signing of the clause is of equal importance to the signing of the Received-for-shipment bill of lading. The converting clause, once signed, represents a legal certification by the carrier.

Foul Ladings. Throughout, this discussion has shown that the dock receipt, the mate's receipt and bills of lading when considered as receipts, include a common phrase, "Received in apparent good order and condition," which serves as evidence of the state of the cargo at the time of its delivery. When the shipment is found not to be in good condition, then it is the duty of the terminal company or the checker for the carrier to record all defects to protect the carrier from cargo claims. Such notations of defects initiate a *foul lading*. This protects the carrier but can slow up the shippers, course of action. A foul lading is evidence that the cargo has not been delivered in good condition and that the exporter is out of contract with his foreign connection. It also means that the bank which is asked to cash the letter of credit must refuse to do so as agent for the foreign importer. Sometimes the shipper will be able to give a bond to the carrier in order that a clean bill of lading can be issued or to the bank to indemnify the bank against a claim for damages by the consignee for having accepted, in good faith cargo shown to be damaged.

Some ordinary exceptions constituting a foul bill of lading follow:

On steel shipments: M/L rusty (more or less rusty).

On case goods: Three cases broken and recoopered — contents unknown. One case recoopered — short three packages.

On sacked goods: Seven sacks torn — resacked — present weight 603 lbs.

On barreled liquids: Four barrels slightly leaking.

General cargo: Four cases more in dispute — if on board to be delivered.

Five cases short — if on board to be delivered.

One case over — all to be delivered.

Some exceptions do not constitute a foul bill of lading as they are accepted as being the custom of the trade, such as:

Ship not responsible for lumber splits, stains or chafing.

Shipper's load and count if it is difficult to tally the cargo.

"Said to contain," if the contents are not known by the carrier.

Ship not responsible for leakage of casks.

Per official weight certificate (of bulk goods officially weighed).

Shipped on deck at owners risk.

Ship not responsible for breakage and loss of contents(of acids in bottles).

Per PLIB certificate (Pacific Lumber Inspection Bureau's certificate on number of pieces and footage of lumber)

The exceptions are not only placed on the bills of lading but are also copied on the ship's manifest of cargo so that the discharging agent will be alerted to the possibility of claim by the consignees.

Contract of transportation. To this point we have considered only the receipt portion of the bill of lading, but it also contains the contract of transportation between the shipper and the carrier for the transport of goods from the port of loading to the port of discharge and for their delivery to a consignee or to the order of the shipper in consideration of freight money usually noted on the lading.

The port of loading is defined on the bill of lading but the place of discharge is qualified by such phrases as:

" . . . .to the port of discharge or so near thereunto as the ship can safely get and leave, always afloat at all stages and conditions of water and weather. . . ."

"In any situation . . . . which in the judgment of the carrier or master is likely to give rise to capture, seizure, detention, damage, delay or disadvantage to or loss of the ship or any part of her cargo or make it unsafe, or unlawful . . . to enter or discharge the goods at the port of discharge. . . . the master may proceed or return, either directly or indirectly, to or stop at such other port or place whatsoever as he or the carrier may consider safe. . . . and discharge the cargo or any part thereof. . . ."

Exceptions on lading. Each bill of lading begins with a list of between twenty to more than one hundred paragraphs, printed in very small type, of conditions under which the ship disclaims responsibility towards the carrying of the cargo. Each paragraph represents the advised opinion of the carrier's legal department based from years of study as well as the carrier's own experience in practical transportation. A superficial glance at a bill of lading might provoke a shipper to remark, "Why doesn't the ship merely print — NOT LIABLE — across the lading?"

The general rules under which the legal effectiveness of these exceptions are measured are:

1. Exceptions must not contravene the responsibilities and limitations nor the rights and immunities of the carrier as set out in the American Carriage of Goods by Sea Act, 1936.*

2. If the bill of lading is of a foreign vessel, then the exceptions must lie within the provisions of the Carriage of Goods by Sea Act of the nation to which the ship belongs.

3. The exceptions must be reasonable and within the custom of the trade of the commodity carried.

4. The ship may not take an exception against its own negligence.

5. But the ship may contract with the shipper concerning the mutual responsibilities of ship and cargo.

The American Carriage of Goods by Sea, 1936, is included as an appendix to this text. Comparing sections of the Act with paragraphs of a bill of lading reveals that the Act states a general duty or liability, while the bill of lading clauses contain the same thought

*See Appendix 2.

but are qualified in terms of specific commodities and special conditions that fall under the general rule. For example: Carrier not liable for—

From the Act Sec. 4 (m): Wastage in bulk or weight or any other loss or damage arising from inherent defect, quality, or vice of the goods.

From the lading: Ship not responsible for splits, stains or chafing of lumber.

Short form lading. Some steamship operators have adopted a *short form* bill of lading which annotates only the parties involved in loading of the commodity, freight charged, and the ports of loading and destination. All of the exceptions, found in the long form bill of lading, are omitted. Each party assumes that the commodity will be carried according to the custom of the trade and the Carriage of Goods by Sea Act or a charter party included by reference.

Straight lading. Ladings are issued in a straight or negotiable form according to the financial arrangements of the shipper and the foreign importer. If the lading is not to be used as security for the payment of money, then a *straight form lading* is issued. Under this type of lading, the carrier is bound to load the goods, transport them to a port of discharge and there turn the goods over to the consignee named in the lading. The carrier's responsibility ends when the goods have been delivered to the consignee. Usually the consignee actually has the original lading and, in fact, surrenders it to the carrier at port of discharge. It then is marked "accomplished" and becomes only a matter of record.

Order lading. An *order form* of lading is subject to the rules of law governing negotiable instruments. The holder of the order lading is during the transaction owner of the merchandise listed on the lading and is entitled to possession of the goods. An order lading may pass from the shipper through a succession of domestic and foreign banks to the consignee or some other delegated person, each of whom is the legal owner of the goods during the period he holds the lading. The passing of title among the various banks and individuals is negotiated by endorsement of the document and

AMERICAN MAIL LINE LTD.

HEAD OFFICE · SEATTLE, WASH.

TRANSPACIFIC ORDER BILL OF LADING

Shipped on Board from the Shipper hereinafter named, the goods or packages said to contain goods hereinafter mentioned, in apparent good order and condition, unless otherwise indicated in this bill of lading, to be transported subject to all the terms of this bill of lading with liberty to proceed via any port or ports within the scope of the voyage described herein, to the port of discharge or so near thereunto as the ship can always safely get and leave, always afloat at all stages and conditions of water and weather, and there to be delivered or transshipped on payment of the charges thereon.

It is agreed that the custody and carriage of the goods are subject to the following terms which shall govern the relations, whatsoever they may be, between the shipper, consignee, and the Carrier, master and ship in every contingency, wheresoever, and whensoever occurring, and also in the event of deviation, or unseaworthiness of the ship at the time of loading or inception of the voyage or subsequently, and none of the terms of this bill of lading shall be deemed to have been waived by the carrier unless by express waiver signed by a duly authorized agent of the Carrier:

Ship: { M.S. ....Voy.............................Port of Loading...........................
{ S.S. ....

Shipper:..

Consignee: Order of...

Notify (If consigned to Shipper's Order)..
(without liability to carrier, see clause 11 hereof)

Port of Discharge from Ship:...Destination of Goods: { If goods to be transshipped {
{ at port of discharge { (subject to clause 11 hereof)

SCOPE OF THE VOYAGE: The carrier's general trade is between ports on or adjacent to the North Pacific Coast of North America in any order and ports in Hawaiian Islands and Far East in any order.

PARTICULARS FURNISHED BY SHIPPER OF GOODS

LEADING MARKS	DESCRIPTION OF GOODS	GROSS WEIGHT POUNDS	MEASUREMENT CUBIC FEET

1. This bill of lading shall have effect subject to the provisions of the Carriage of Goods by Sea Act of the United States, approved April 16, 1936, which shall be deemed to be incorporated herein, and nothing herein contained shall be deemed a surrender by the Carrier of any of its rights or immunities or an increase of any of its responsibilities or liabilities under said Act. The provisions stated in said Act shall (except as may be otherwise specifically provided herein) govern before the goods are loaded on and after they are discharged from the ship and throughout the entire time the goods are in the custody of the Carrier. The Carrier shall not be liable in any capacity whatsoever for any delay, non-delivery or misdelivery, or loss of or damage to the goods occurring while the goods are not in the actual custody of the Carrier.

2. In this bill of lading the word "ship" shall include any substituted vessel, and any craft, lighter or other means of conveyance owned, chartered or operated by the Carrier; the word "Carrier" shall include the ship, her owner, operator, demise charterer, time charterer, master and any substituted carrier, whether the owner, operator, charterer or master shall be acting as carrier or bailee; the word "shipper" shall include the person named as such in this bill of lading and the person for whose account the goods are shipped; the word "consignee" shall include the holder of the bill of lading, properly endorsed, the receiver and the owner of the goods; the word "charges" shall include freight and all expenses and money obligations incurred and payable by the goods, shipper, consignee, or any of them.

3. The scope of voyage herein contracted for shall include usual or customary or advertised ports of call whether named in this contract or not, also ports in or out of the advertised, geographical, usual or ordinary route or order, even though in proceeding thereto the ship may sail beyond the port of discharge or in a direction contrary thereto, or depart from the direct or customary route. The ship may call at any port for the purposes of the current voyage or of a prior or subsequent voyage. The ship may omit calling at any port or ports whether scheduled or not, and may call at the same port more than once; may either with or without the goods on board, and before or after proceeding toward the port of discharge, adjust compasses, dry dock, go on ways or to repair yards, shift berths, make trial trips or tests, take fuel or stores, remain in port, sail with or without pilots, tow and be towed, and save or attempt to save life or property, and all of the foregoing are included in the contract voyage.

IN ACCEPTING THIS BILL OF LADING the shipper, and consignee of the goods agrees to be bound by all of its stipulations, exceptions, and conditions, whether written, printed, or stamped on the front or back hereof, any local customs or privileges to the contrary notwithstanding.

IN WITNESS WHEREOF, the Master of the said ship has affirmed to.......................................bills of lading, all of this tenor and date, ONE of which being accomplished, the others stand void.

ATTENTION OF SHIPPERS is called to Sec. 235 of the United States Criminal Code (Act of Congress, March 4, 1900): Every package shipped containing explosive or dangerous articles shall have plainly marked thereon its contents, and whoever delivers to any common carrier any explosive or dangerous article under false or deceptive marking, description, invoice, shipping order, etc., is liable to a fine of not more than $2,000, or imprisonment for not more than eighteen months or both; also to the act of June 16, 1936, imposing a maximum penalty of $5,000 for obtaining or attempting to obtain by any unjust or unfair means transportation at less than the rates or charges which otherwise would be applicable.

OCEAN RATE AND CHARGES
RATES, WEIGHTS AND/OR MEASUREMENTS SUBJECT TO CORRECTION

FROM	TO	FREIGHT

B/L NUMBER

CONTRACT NUMBER

Dated at..
this..............day of..19.........
FOR THE MASTER:

AMERICAN MAIL LINE LTD.

By..

Terms of Bill of Lading continued on back hereof

Figure 11. A typical Order Bill of Lading.

usually upon the payment of money therefore. The order lading is thus a security for the payment of money upon the transfer of the title to the merchandise.

Negotiability. At destination the carrier then is bound to deliver the cargo only to the person who surrenders the original bill of lading to the carrier. To make delivery to any other person renders the carrier liable for the value of the cargo to the person who in fact holds the original negotiable bill of lading in due course of business. The phrase due course of business means that the holder of the lading must have given consideration (money) for the lading and not be a mere finder of the paper itself.

The importance of the order bill of lading as a valuable commercial document is stressed because all holders of the lading by law may depend upon the representations on the lading and its accuracy in description of the shipment. The order lading is generally issued in sets of three original, signed ladings, which according to the wording of the instrument, "one of which being accomplished, the others stand void". That means that the first original lading presented at destination to the carrier, is the only valid claim for possession of the shipment. The other two original ladings are valueless. Of the three original ladings issued, two are included in duplicate sets of financial documents and are negotiated through banks. One set is sent by mail immediately; a second set is mailed later to provide a check against accident or loss. The third original is required by the exporter to be surrendered to the consul of the country to which the goods are being shipped. It is used by the customs department of that country. As many originals can be issued as the exporter requires. As many as ten have been noted issued for a transaction. The shipper is always responsible for the distribution of the document.

Non-negotiable copies of the lading may be issued in as many copies as desired. These copies serve the carrier, its agents, the exporter and his connection as file copies.

Parties to lading. The parties to a straight bill of lading are the consignor, the consignee, and the carrier. The consignor is the shipper of the merchandise usually an exporter or some person or firm he may choose. The consignee is the person or firm that will receive the merchandise at its destination. When a bill of lading reads

CARGO DOCUMENTATION

91

(CONTINUED FROM OVERPAGE)

FORWARDING AGENT—REFERENCES		PERMIT NO.	EXPORT DEC. NO.
DELIVERING CARRIER TO STEAMER:	CAR NUMBER—REFERENCE		

ABOVE SPACES FOR SHIPPERS MEMORANDA

BILL OF LADING (Continued From Reverse Side)

SHIP	FLAG	PIER	PORT OF LOADING
PORT OF DISCHARGE FROM SHIP			

SHIPPER--------

CONSIGNEE: ORDER OF-----------

ADDRESS ARRIVAL NOTICE TO--------------

WITHOUT LIABILITY TO CARRIER. SEE CLAUSE 12 HEREOF

PARTICULARS FURNISHED BY SHIPPER OF GOODS

MARKS AND NUMBERS	NO. OF PKGS	DESCRIPTION OF PACKAGES AND GOODS	GROSS WT. IN KILOS	GROSS WEIGHT POUNDS

23. At Rosario, the Gas Mole charges shall be for account of the goods.
24. At Montevideo, should it be found impossible for the steamer to discharge owing to there being no berth, shed, deposit, wagons available, or for lack of space on wharf at berth assigned by Port Authorities, or for any other cause of "force majeure" or anything else which should prevent the steamer from discharging on arrival, which will be verified by a declaration of the "Administracion Nacional del Puerto" (Port Administration) the cargo will be discharged to lighters sent by the Agents for account and risk of the Consignees.

25. All agreements or freight engagements for the shipment of the goods are superseded by this bill of lading, and all its terms, whether written, typed, stamped, or printed, are accepted and agreed by the shipper to be binding as fully as if signed by the shipper, any local customs or privileges to the contrary notwithstanding. Nothing in this bill of lading shall operate to limit or deprive the Carrier of any statutory protection or exemption from, or limitation of, liability. If required by the Carrier, one signed bill of lading duly endorsed must be surrendered to the agent of the ship at the port of discharge in exchange for delivery order.

Where the authorities at destination consider cargo to be corrosive, inflammable, explosive or injurious, Owners of such cargo agree to take delivery immediately when vessel, whether in berth or not, is ready to discharge same, otherwise vessel, without any further notice and notwithstanding any custom of the port to the contrary, may discharge such cargo into lighter or other conveyance at the risk of the Owners of such cargo, all expenses beyond vessel's tackle, including lighterage and/or transportation incurred in conveying such cargo to the warehouse or place designated by the Port Authority for the storage or reception of same to be for account of the Consignees, and/or Owners and/or Shippers of such cargo.

Freights named herein are subject to such rates, charges or surcharges as may be in effect on date of sailing from loading port.

IN ACCEPTING THIS BILL OF LADING the shipper, consignee and owner of the goods agree to be bound by all of its stipulations, exceptions, and conditions, whether written, printed, or stamped on the front or back hereof, any local customs or privileges to the contrary notwithstanding.

FREIGHT PAYABLE AT   FREIGHT

cf. @ per 40 cf.	$
cf. @ per 40 cf.	$
cf. @ per 40 cf.	$
cf. @ per 40 cf.	$
lbs. @ per 2240 lbs.	$
lbs. @ per 2240 lbs.	$
@ Surcharge	$
@ Brazilian Merc. Marine Tax	$
@ Consul fee	$

IN WITNESS WHEREOF, there have been executed **3** Bills of Lading. Total $_____
exclusive of non-negotiable copies all of the same tenor and date, ONE of which being accomplished, the others to stand void.

For The Master, By **AMERICAN REPUBLICS LINE** Dated at **NEW YORK**
MOORE-McCORMACK LINES, Inc.

B/L No_____

BY..........

UNIFORM NORTH ATLANTIC CLAUSES 1937, REVISED PRINTED IN U.S.A.

A.R.L. 4 9-50

TO AND FROM U.S.A.—BRAZIL AND RIVER PLATE PORTS

Figure 12. Another Bill of Lading form.

"to order," the ultimate consignee may not be known, when it is made to "shipper's order," the shipper by negotiating passes title until the lading finally reaches the individual who wishes to take possession of the goods. Sometimes there is a restrictive form of order lading such as, "ship to the order of the Shanghai Hong Kong Banking Corporation." This indicates that the bank has some interest in the transaction; therefore, the carrier can not legally deliver the goods unless the surrendered lading carries the bank's endorsement, indicating that its claim has been satisfied.

Notify party. When an order lading has been issued, there is added a *notify party*. This provides the address of the party, usually the foreign importer, most deeply interested in the transaction. This party has no standing in the negotiation of the lading but is mentioned to protect the carrier at destination. Upon arrival of the goods at destination, the carrier can officially advise the "notify party" that the goods have arrived. This notification terminates the contract of carriage and the carrier then becomes a mere bailee of the goods until the negotiable lading is surrendered. A reasonable time after notification by the carrier, the terminal will begin to charge the cargo for storage.

Thru export lading. The *thru export lading* has been devised for the convenience of exporters whose offices are not located in the seaport through which their cargo will move. This lading is a transportation contract issued by the rail line providing a thru rate by rail from inland city to seaport, the transfer of the goods at that point to a vessel, and ocean transport to a foreign destination, as from Chicago to Seattle to Manila. The transfer of cargo at seaboard is accomplished by an agreement between the rail and ocean carriers. This agreement affords the inland shipper immediate possesion of a thru lading for use with his foreign trade documents and it saves him from having to employ a forwarding agent who would attend to the cargo transfer and procure an ocean lading at seaboard. Thru import bills of lading are available also for cargo inbound from foreign ports.

Since the thru export lading is a combination of rail and ocean ladings there is twofold responsibility for the safe carrying of cargo. The first is the rail line which is considered to be a practical insurer of safe carriage of goods, except for an Act of God. The second is the ocean carrier which bears while carrying the cargo the risks and perils of the seas independently.

The availability of the thru export lading to the shipper depends upon the existence of contractual relations between the ocean carrier and the rail line to provide this type of service which includes the details of trans-shipment of goods at port of export from rail to ocean. The shipment may possibly be delayed at the port while awaiting a vessel of a designated line to arrive. For this reason some exporters prefer to use a foreign freight forwarder at seaboard in order to expedite shipment. Cargo can be placed on the first available vessel and an on-board ocean lading procured. This procedure is more acceptable to the foreign importer. The forwarder secures the ocean lading and other export documents for the exporter, pays the trans-shipment and terminal charges, and sends them to the shipper as details of a completed shipment.

These same charges which are present under the thru export lading procedure may or may not be absorbed in the rate charged on the thru export lading. The source of payment of these charges is decided upon by the carrier and the shipper.

The form and type of lading to be issued on a particular shipment is determined by the requirements of the shipper who indicates by letter to the carrier what form is needed and all of the details sought for the lading. Such a letter will specify the parties, the the loading and discharge ports, describe the commodity and its shipping marks, and include the number of needed negotiable and non-negotiable copies. The bill of lading is based on this data. Some carriers furnish the exporter with the blank ladings. The exporter, then makes the lading conforming according to his needs; returning them to the carrier for signature.

Shippers export declaration. Another instrument, not included in foreign trade documents but required by the Commerce Department and the Treasury, is the *shipper's export declaration*. A facsimile is herein included, Figure 13. This is a sworn statement by the shipper attesting to the character, quantity and value of the commodity at seaboard. It served originally for determining statistically exported commodities, value and destination. Recently,

Form 7525-V
(Rev. May 1954)
(See Instructions on
Reverse Side)

U. S. DEPARTMENT OF COMMERCE
BUREAU OF THE CENSUS—BUREAU OF FOREIGN COMMERCE
SHIPPER'S EXPORT DECLARATION
OF SHIPMENTS TO FOREIGN COUNTRIES OR NONCONTIGUOUS TERRITORIES OF THE UNITED STATES
EXPORT SHIPMENTS ARE SUBJECT TO U. S. CUSTOMS INSPECTION
READ CAREFULLY THE INSTRUCTIONS ON BACK TO AVOID DELAY AT SHIPPING POINT
Clearance will not be granted until shipper's declaration has been filed with the Collector of Customs. This declaration shall not be used to effect any exportation after the expiration date of the export license referred to herein, except as specifically authorized by export regulations.
DECLARATIONS SHOULD BE TYPEWRITTEN OR PREPARED IN INK

Form approved. Budget Bureau No. 41-R397.4.

CONFIDENTIAL For use solely for official purposes authorized by the Secretary of Commerce. Use for unauthorized purposes is not permitted. (Title 15, Sec. 30.5 (b) C. F. R.; 50 U. S. C. App., 2026c.)

Do Not Use This Area

Do Not Use This Area	District	Port	Country (For customs use only)

FILE NO. (This Space for Use of Customs)

1. EXPORTING CARRIER (if vessel, give name, flag and pier number)   2. FROM (U. S. Port of Export)

3. EXPORTER (Principal or seller—licensed)   ADDRESS (Number, street, place, State)

4. AGENT OF EXPORTER (Forwarding agent)   ADDRESS (Number, street, place, State)

5. ULTIMATE CONSIGNEE   ADDRESS (Place, country)

6. INTERMEDIATE CONSIGNEE   ADDRESS (Place, country)

7. FOREIGN PORT OF UNLOADING (For vessel and air shipments only)   8. PLACE AND COUNTRY OF ULTIMATE DESTINATION (Not place of transshipment)

(9) MARKS AND NOS.	(10) NUMBER AND KIND OF PACKAGES, DESCRIPTION OF COMMODITIES, EXPORT LICENSE NUMBER, EXPIRATION DATE (OR GENERAL LICENSE SYMBOL) (Describe commodities in sufficient detail to permit verification of the Schedule B commodity numbers assigned. Do not use general terms. Insert required license information on line below description of each item)	(11) SHIPPING (Gross) WEIGHT IN POUNDS (required for vessel and air shipments only)	(12)	(13) SCHEDULE B COMMODITY NO.	(14) NET QUANTITY IN SCHEDULE B UNITS (State unit)	(15) VALUE AT U. S. PORT OF EXPORT (Selling price or cost if not sold, including inland freight, insurance and other charges to U. S. port of export) (Nearest whole dollar; omit cents figures)

16. WAYBILL OR MANIFEST NO. (of Exporting Carrier)   17. DATE OF EXPORTATION (Not required for shipments by vessel)

18. THE UNDERSIGNED HEREBY AUTHORIZES____
TO ACT AS FORWARDING AGENT FOR EXPORT CONTROL AND CUSTOMS PURPOSES.   (Name and address—Number, street, place, State)
(DULY AUTHORIZED
EXPORTER____   BY ____   OFFICER OR EMPLOYEE)____

▶ 19. I DECLARE THAT ALL STATEMENTS MADE AND ALL INFORMATION CONTAINED IN THIS EXPORT DECLARATION ARE TRUE AND CORRECT. I AM AWARE OF THE PENALTIES PROVIDED FOR FALSE REPRESENTATION. (See Paragraphs I (c), (e), on reverse side.)

20. Subscribed and sworn to before me on ____, 19 ____   SIGNATURE ____
(Duly authorized officer or employee of exporter or named forwarding agent)

FOR ____
(Name of corporation or firm and capacity of signer, e. g., secretary, export manager, etc.)

ADDRESS ____
(TITLE OR DESIGNATION) Notary Public, etc., or those authorized to administer oaths under Sec. 486, Tariff Act of 1930.

▶ Declaration should be made by duly authorized officer or employee of exporter or of forwarding agent named by exporter.
* If shipping weight is not available for each Schedule B item listed in column (13) included in one or more packages, insert the approximate gross weight for each Schedule B item. The total of these estimated weights should equal the actual weight of the entire package or packages.
* Designate foreign merchandise (reexports) with an "F" and exports of domestic merchandise produced in the United States or changed in condition in the United States with a "D." (See instructions on reverse side.)
CARRIERS, FORWARDERS AND EXPORTERS ARE REMINDED THAT IF A DESTINATION CONTROL STATEMENT IS REQUIRED ON A SHIPPER'S EXPORT DECLARATION COVERING A GIVEN SHIPMENT, SUCH STATEMENT MUST ALSO APPEAR ON ALL COPIES OF THE BILL OF LADING AND COMMERCIAL INVOICE. (See Comprehensive Export Schedule.)   16—66603-6

Do Not Use This Area

Figure 13. Facsimile of a Shipper's Export Declaration.

under the Office of International Trade, the export declaration has become the means by which the shipper may be prosecuted if cargo or destination are not as declared.

The exporter submits the declaration to U.S. Customs where the status of the commodity to be shipped is checked. It must be determined if this cargo is permitted to be shipped under a general license, if the validated permission from the Office of International Trade must be obtained, or if OIT regulations forbid shipment of the commodity. When customs has cleared the cargo, the shipper's export declaration is delivered to the ocean carrier, allowing the shipment to be loaded on the vessel.

The carrier is forbidden by law to load a shipment before receipt of a customs-cleared, shipper's export declaration. By law the carrier, in order to clear a vessel for travel to a foreign port, must supply customs with an outward foreign manifest itemizing the cargo slated for foreign delivery. Each item of this manifest must be substantiated by the shipper's sworn declaration.

Provisions of the Law, from Par. 1 (Commerce Form 7225-V)

(a) Vessels shall not be cleared for foreign ports until export declarations verified by oath, of the cargo, or its parts have been delivered to the collector at the point of exportation by the owners, shippers or consignors thereof . . . . .

Since the master of the vessel is subject to a fine if this law is violated, in common practice he will authorize loading of the specific cargo only after the shipper's export declaration has actually been delivered to the carrier.

Cargo manifest. The *cargo manifest* contains the pertinent data recorded from all issued bills of lading. Ladings covering cargo to be delivered at different ports are grouped on a separate sheet for each port. Each port agent is thus provided with a list of all cargo intended for unloading at his port.

The complete manifest also records the vessel's freight, the amount and sources of revenue for all cargo operations. This manifest can—minus the amounts of the freight rates and collections—be used as the vessel's outward foreign manifest which is required by the U.S. Customs for clearance of a vessel for travel to a foreign port.

A reproduction of the heading of a manifest is attached Figure 14. The following are comments on the material entered in the various columns:

No. of B/L: Usually each port of discharge is numbered, starting with the figure 1.

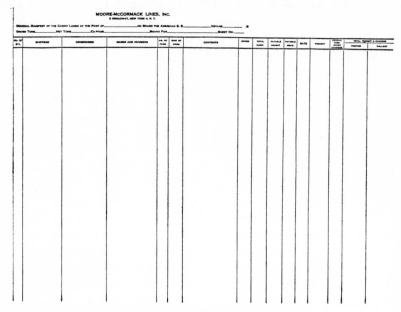

Figure 14. A reproduction of a General Cargo Manifest.

Shippers: As shown on the lading.

Consignee: As shown on the lading, or ORDER, together with the Notify Party, address and destination.

Marks: Carefully reproduced as the customs may be interested in them.

Quantity: As per B/L.

Contents: As described in the lading. Note any exceptions to the condition of the cargo.

Kilos gross: A requirement in South American and some other trades. It pertains to foreign customs and port charges.

Cubic feet: for size and freight purposes.

Lbs. Gross: For total weight and freight calculation.

Freight rate: The agreed rate of freight, assessed in some cases by weight or measurement from the two previous columns.

Freight: The total in dollars.

Handling: Terminal charges for handling cargo to ship.

Wharfage: For use of terminal.

Advance charges: Inland freight, storage cargo packaging.

Freight collect: The total in dollars that the agent in port of discharge is to collect on delivery of the cargo.

To apply beyond: In case the shipper has prepaid a transshipment charge to cover transport of the cargo beyond the vessel's discharge port.

At the bottom of the sheet, the columns of account are totalled. Sheets are signed by the carrier who may add the notation: E. & O. E. (errors and omissions excepted).

Hatch books listing cargo alphabetically by mark and showing the place of stowage in the vessel are prepared by the purser during the voyage, since shoreside staff does not have time after the loading to complete these records.

CHAPTER 12

Ocean Freight Rates

Bases for rates. A quoted ocean freight rate is a simple figure from which the shipper can easily compute his freight bill. The underlying bases of the quoted figure are, however, infinitely complex. For most general cargo rates are quoted on the standard basis of either the cargo ton of 2240 lbs. or 40 cubic feet depending on which figure when computed, produces the greater amount of revenue. In a previous chapter, the origin of the cargo ton was explained along with the variances between 2000 lbs. and 40 cubic feet, and between 1 metric ton and 1 cubic meter. The total of a shipper's freight cost is calculated on the basis of both freight weight and measurement. Whichever totals the largest sum will be submitted as the transportation bill. The shipper should always ascertain which basis the steamship company will use in quoting a freight cost.

Many items of cargo, because of intrinsic peculiarities or long-established custom, are rate-quoted in individual units depending upon geographical location. For instance, lumber is generally quoted in dollars per thousand feet board measure (a board foot is 1 foot by 1 foot by 1 inch). Lumber moving inbound from South America, however, is quoted at a rate based on per cubic meter.

If a quotation is made on logs, any one of three scales may be used as a basis of measurement. In the past, the "square of the mean" was widely used to figure log freight cost. In this procedure, the mean diameter of a log was squared and then that figure was multiplied by the length of the log. The total represented a timber

27.32% larger than the actual log. The Brereton scale, now in use, mathematically computes the actual cross section of the log and multiplies it by the length, providing the true, accurate mathematical calculation of a log's volume. Logs may also be billed for shipment. This scale based on Scribner scale calculations is used to measure and determine actual merchantable lumber contained in a log. The volume calculated by this scale is less than that of the other two, since defective wood is not included in the volume figure. Certificates of measurement may be presented in any one of the three scales.

On an ocean bill of lading, the freight rate may be expressed in many ways and may include many incidental charges. The rate is often expressed in tons of weight or measurement which means the ship is free to accept the freight calculation which will return the greatest revenue. The rate is also sometimes given based on packaging of the cargo as —per barrel, per case, per bag, per 1000 feet board measure. The units of weight may be in long tons (2240 lbs.), short tons (2000 lbs.), metric tons (1000 kilograms or 2204.6 lbs.), units of 100 lbs., hundredweights (CWT—in the United States equals 100 lbs., in England equals 112 lbs.), piculs (133½ lbs.) or in other foreign units of weight, depending on where the cargo was prepared for shipment.

On the measurement basis, cargo size may be expressed in cubic feet, cargo tons of 40 cu. ft., 50 cu. ft., the cubic meter and other measurements used in foreign countries.

The value of the cargo is sometimes used as a basis of freight cost; the rate is then expressed as a percentage ad valorem. The per cent increases according to the value of the cargo. For instance, the high rate levied on gold or specie shipments, is more a matter of insurance than transportation cost.

Because of costly administrative preparatory detail, a relatively high charge is placed on a minimum bill of lading. Sometimes cargo on which no lading is issued will, however, receive a comparatively small charge. In many cases, a steamship company will charge for preparing a bill of lading, regardless of the size of the shipment.

Penalty charges. There are many penalty charges which can be added to the regular ocean rate if handling the cargo presents unusual difficulties. Generally such charges are included in a quoted rate, but sometimes they are listed separately. Penalty expenses are placed on lumber which is over 40 feet in length, heavy lifts—two tons or over. There is a graduated scale of penalty charge upwards as the weight exceeds two tons. Creosoted lumber is also penalized because it burns the skin of those handling it. Green hides, offensive in smell, also fall in the penalty category. Some other penalty items were enumerated in the chapter on cargo handling.

Port charges are also added to the ladings. These are assessed on vessels entering many foreign ports with cargo for discharge. Port charges may be levied for handling cargo in the foreign port, for customs regulations, harbor dues, import taxes or other reasons. Since their collection must be made in advance by the carrier, port charges are always entered on the bill of lading.

Surcharge. Prompt port loading and discharge is a consideration in determining rate tariffs. Occasionally a port will become congested for a long period of time, seriously delaying shipping. To compensate carriers for losses they may incur under such conditions, to maintain normal rates, a temporary charge is added to the rate. This is called a *surcharge.* It is added as a percentage or fixed amount added to the base rate. The surcharge is removed when port conditions once again become normal.

Occasionally, expenses will be incurred before cargo is loaded. These advanced charges, included on the bill of lading, are collected at destination. Likewise, if shipment must be transshipped before its final destination is reached the transshipping charges are itemized on the lading as arbitraries beyond the first port of discharge if no through rate has been quoted together with the transportation charges from port of discharge to final destination.

Collect and prepaid. In most cases, freight will be collected at the port of loading and the lading will show the entire itemized list of charges as prepaid or with the simple notation—FREIGHT PREPAID—without any details shown. In some instances by agreement with the steamship company, the freight may be shown as COLLECT and will be a charge on the consignee whether the ship is "lost or not lost." In either case, its the obligation of the consignee to pay the freight cost. When the freight is to be collected, the carrier has a lien on the shipment for the transportation charges. This lien provides the right to hold cargo until the carrier is paid or, if he fails to receive payment, eventually to sell the shipment as compensation.

Freight charges on shipments from foreign ports are frequently expressed in the national currencies of those ports of loading. This factor adds an element of uncertainty to the application of a proper rate of foreign exchange.

A practice that was once widespread, but which has nearly passed out of existence is that of primage. This is both gratuity paid to the master of the vessel to insure careful cargo handling and a commission for the procurement of cargo. In the past, procurement was one of a master's most important duties.

In theory, an ocean freight rate can be calculated by totaling the costs of transportation and profit. The figure for transportation costs would include the expense of a vessel's operation based on the length of the voyage, the various foreign agency expenses, and fixed cost of investment and administration, and the expense of loading and discharging cargo. The source of vessel revenue is the number of tons a vessel is permitted to carry or the amount of cargo that can be loaded under and on deck. A theoretical ocean freight rate would have to be scaled down in order to make the rate competitive on a world-wide basis.

Competition in rates. Shipping is characterized by world-wide competition. Any vessel of any nation may bid to carry cargo to foreign ports. This freedom is underscored by the practice of chartering. The work of chartering agents is to contact correspondents all over the world to find what vessels are available to lift cargo and what rates are acceptable to carriers. In practice, the lowest bids are those acted on.

There is no practical governmental control to regulate charter rates, since competitors represent many nations which are not subject in any way to the laws of this nation in establishing their rates. Each country may exercise some control over its own flag vessels but in so doing may prevent its ships from meeting the terms of foreign vessels. National regulations sometimes mean a boost in the costs of vessel operations an actual hinderance to international competition.

Nearly all nations subsidize their own vessels. In the setting of a competitive rate, subsidization is taken into consideration. The result is a quoted rate, actually under the cost of ship operation, that is justified only to the extent that a nation may be trying to build or preserve its merchant marine.

Similarly a subsidy is given if the tariff laws of a country provide a lower rate of duty on imports arriving in vessels of that nation or offer preferential marine insurance rates on the cargo when so carried.

As the cost of vessel operation is a factor in determining rates, it should be noted that the American scale of crew wages and subsistence is far higher than that of most foreign countries. A U.S. built Liberty ship operating under the American flag costs on an average of $5,000 per month more to operate than the same vessel operating under a foreign flag with foreign crews. To compete, many originally high scale vessels have been transferred to foreign flags offering lower wage scales. American ships are registered in such low wage countries as Panama, Honduras and Liberia. A Honduran seaman earns a little over $100 per month; a comparable American is paid $487, plus fringe benefits and possible overtime pay.

To maintain an American vessel in only fair condition involves a great deal of expense which many foreign companies avoid by allowing their ships to rust, and to go without repair until they become unseaworthy. Some companies purchase ships which would be considered useless in well maintained fleets and will operate them until the vessels literally stop or sink.

All classes of ships, operating under the flags of nations the world over, are in competition. Varying costs of operation, maintenance, and primary investment, are all factors effecting the determination of freight rates, and, thus, competition.

During a period when rates are relatively stable, an operator, for reasons of his own, may offer a rate lower than the prevailing average. Others may then under-cut this lowered rate and within a very brief time, a rate-war may develop. In a rate war, each operator underbids, attempting to secure cargo to fill ships coming on berth. Generally in such situations rates fall in descending steps until a leveling off point is reached, representing a rate not profitable to any ship. Paradoxically, bargain rates do not produce a rush of business. On the contrary, the exporter it has been found hesitates to book cargo while rates are falling for fear that he may miss out on the most advantageous rate. Consignees on the other hand hesitate to buy for fear competitors may be getting a lower rate. A rate war results in almost a complete business stalemate. New business will not occur until rates seem to be leveling off.

Conference rates. Rate wars are a source of concern not only to the steamship man but to all foreign traders. Both welcome a comparative rate stability. To try to insure rate stability, representatives of various steamship lines serving the same areas enter into *conference* and agree upon rates to handle cargo. Tariffs are issued for cargo charges. These tariffs insure that shippers quote an agreed upon rate, regardless of the vessel upon which they ship. The exporter and the consignee can thus obtain the same rate for having the same commodity shipped. Thus, traders within the same market work with an identical cost figure. So this element of transportation cost is stable with traders and vessel operators.

Steamship conferences. Members of a conference may have to contend with a competitor who will not join the conference, but chooses to operate independently. The outsider quotes rates which are usually lower than those set by members of the conference, the non-conference line is either viewed as a rugged individualist or as an opportunist operating under an umbrella maintained by the conference members. Though the conference members give a bond to abide by tariffs, sometimes reports of rebates made to shippers come back from foreign lands. The conference prevents a regular berth vessel which is without sufficient outbound cargo and in distress from quoting under-tariff rates in order to get available cargo.

A shipper may negotiate with the conference or the individual ship to get a lower rate to help him to compete in other countries for the discharge of his commodity in the port of discharge. In this case, he submits costs and sales data which the conference lines may or may not accept. Any action, however, is usually in the form of a lower rate. In setting a rate, the steamship operator has to consider all of these factors as well as hundreds of variations of them. The quoted rate thus represents a figure not only of what traffic will bear but also of what the shipper will agree to pay in the light of present business conditions.

PACIFIC WESTBOUND CONFERENCE

LOCAL TARIFF NO. 1-V

EFFECTIVE OCTOBER 1, 1954
ISSUED SEPTEMBER 27, 1954

CORRECTION NO. 1734
CANCELS CORRECTION NO. 1647

Except as otherwise provided herein, rates apply per ton of 2,000 lbs. or 40 cu. ft., whichever produces the greater revenue. COMMODITY	GROUP RATE BASIS	1 YOKO-HAMA KOBE OSAKA	2 MANILA HONG-KONG	*3 CEBU ILO-ILO	4 TAKAO KEE-LUNG	5 SAIGON HAI-PHONG	ITEM NO.
FERTILIZERS, viz: AMMONIUM PHOSPHATE, AMMONIUM SULPHATE, AMMOPHOS, MANURE SALTS, SODA NITRATE, SULPHATE OF POTASH, SUPERPHOSPHATE, UREA COMPOUND,							780 n
Non Contract rate...................	2240#	24.85	24.85	28.35	31.85	28.85	
Contract rate.....................	2240#	21.85	21.85	25.35	28.85	25.85	
Shippers are permitted to furnish with each shipment one and one half percent (1 1/2%) empty bags to be carried without charge for rebagging at destination							
FERTILIZER, PACKED, viz: AMMONIUM NITRATE							780a
Non Contract rate...................	WT.	25.75	26.75	29.25	31.75	29.75	n
Contract Rate....................	WT.	22.75	22.75	26.25	29.75	26.75	
Shippers are permitted to furnish with each shipment one and one half percent (1 1/2%) empty bags to be carried without charge for rebagging at destination							
FERTILIZER, N.O.S., (Not including Fish Meal, Shrimp Husks, Shrimp Husk Bran & Meal, & Dried Rendered Tankage).							781 n
Non Contract rate..................	2240#	24.85	24.85	28.35	31.85	28.85	
Contract rate.....................	2240#	21.85	21.85	25.35	28.85	25.85	
FILLER, COMPOUND, SOLE LEATHER,							783
Non Contract rate..................		38.50	38.50	42.00	45.50	42.50	
Contract rate.....................		35.50	35.50	39.00	42.50	39.50	
FILMS, MOVING PICTURE, EXPOSED,							785
Non Contract rate..................		60.50	60.50	64.00	67.50	64.50	
Contract rate.....................		57.50	57.50	61.00	64.50	61.50	
Minimum Bill of Lading Charge - $ 19.00 See Rule No. 16							
FILM, SCRAP,							790
In Tin Lined cases, hermetically sealed Drums, or tongue and groove Wooden Cases, asbestos lined and double strapped,							
Non Contract rate................		72.50	72.50	76.00	79.50	76.50	
Contract rate.....................		69.50	69.50	73.00	76.50	73.50	
FIREARMS, GUNS AND PARTS (Small Arms), N.O.S., in Boxes,							795
Non Contract rate................		72.00	72.00	75.50	79.00	76.00	
Contract rate.....................		69.00	69.00	72.50	76.00	73.00	

* Rates shown are for direct call. Transhipment rate $ 2.00 per ton higher, or corresponding additional per unit rate as shown in individual item.

Change

Printed in U.S.A.

Figure 15. Reproduction of a Tariff Sheet.

For the mutual benefit of its members, the conference establishes rates and regulations which are made known to shippers in the form of a tariff. All of the conference carriers agree to maintain the tariff and post a bond of faithful performance of the tariff rules and regulations. The tariff insures that shippers are quoted uniform rates in the same manner that they are quoted by American railways. The tariff is thus a means of controlling competition between carriers. It means that competition is based on excellence of service, rather than under-cutting of rates.

For some items of cargo, competition is so keen that no rate can be agreed upon by the conference members. These are "open" items. Conference carriers may quote any rate. When competition from a non-conference carrier exists, the conference may protect itself by opening many rates, thus putting its members in a position of competing with lowered rates.

Dual rate systems. Many conferences use a dual rate system as an inducement to shippers to use their carriers exclusively. The tariff under this dual rate system quotes a contract rate and non-contract rate on each item of cargo. The difference between the two may be as high as $3.00 to $5.00 per ton, or more than 10 per cent. A reproduction of such a tariff sheet is made in Figure 15.

The following is a summary of an agreement that a shipper must sign in order to obtain the benefit of lower contract rates:

1. The agreement covers all export shipments of the shipper to designated countries. All such shipments shall be tendered to carriers. Shipper agrees without exception to confine all shipments to vessels of the conference carriers.

2. If the shipper makes any shipment in violation of the agreement, it shall be cause for the conference to terminate the shipper's right to contract rates until the shipper pays the conference as liquidated damages the cost the shipper would have paid if freight had been moved via conference carrier.

3. This is a rate agreement and is not and shall not be construed to be a space agreement. Space agreements may be entered into with any carrier party to the agreement.

4. Carriers agree to furnish at conference rates, space for shipper's cargo. If space is not available and after

notice to the conference, the shipper is free to use non-conference carriers for that particular parcel of cargo.

5. Agreements for actual carriage of shipments are to be made with the individual carrier.

6. The shipper shall have the option of selecting any of the vessels operated by the several carriers.

7. Shipper shall have the right to request shipping space on any line which hereafter becomes a member of the conference.

8. The shipper shall be given notice of changes in rates. Notices of increases in rates will be given 60 days in advance of the effective date of change. In the event of war, the agreement may be cancelled upon 15 days notice.

9. Additional commodities may be placed on a contract rate basis from time to time, or may be withdrawn, with notice as in paragraph 8.

10. Shipper will be given the full benefit of any reduced rates.

11. In case of dispute, the shipper and the carrier shall submit the matter to arbitration.

12. The agreement shall remain in force indefinitely, but may be cancelled by either party giving 60 days written notice to terminate.

13. Shipper will indicate minimum and maximum annual tonnage to be moved under the agreement.

This agreement is signed by the shipper and for the carriers by the conference secretary.

These tariffs and contracts must be filed with the Federal Maritime Board and be approved by that Board, under section 15 of the Shipping Act of 1916. The United States Supreme Court has declined to review cases brought to test the enforceability of these contracts until the Maritime Board had approved or disapproved of the contract under consideration.

In December 1955, the Federal Maritime Board favorably approved of the dual rate system in a proceeding docketed as FMB No. 730 but the ruling was appealed to the United States Supreme Court where the question was decided. The F.M.B. held that the tendency toward monopoly of service are outweighed by the benefits to be derived from the system. The advantages are greater stability and uniformity of rates with resultant benefits to the shipper and the consignee which permit improvement in conference carrier service.

Supreme Court decision. On May 19, 1958, the United States Supreme Court rendered a decision* on the dual rate system, declaring that it had been instituted in the present case for the purpose of curtailing competition from outside the Conference, and that it was a device made illegal by Sec. 14 of the Shipping Act of 1916. This Paragraph prohibits common water carriers to retaliate against a shipper by specified devices or to "resort to other discriminating or unfair methods."

Section 14 of the Shipping Act of 1916** provides that no common carrier by water shall:

1. Pay or allow a deferred rebate to any shipper.
2. Use a fighting ship.
3. Retaliate against any shipper, or "resort to other discriminating or unfair methods" because the shipper patronized any other carrier.
4. Make any unfair contract with a shipper based on volume of freight offered.

The Court held that the penalties contained in the Conference contract for violation of it by the shipper brought this case under the "resort to" clause of the Shipping Act of 1916, and that the purpose of these penalties was to prevent the use by the shipper of lines outside the conference.

The court further held that the Federal Maritime Board, which had declared in favor of the dual rate system as a deterrent to costly rate wars, has administrative jurisdiction to consider matters of this character and that their experienced judgment may be relied upon by the Courts and litigants for guidance. The rulings and opinions of the Board, however, do not control the ruling of the Court in a matter of law.

As evidence of the use of the dual rate system to curtail out-

*Federal Maritime Board vs. Isbrandtsen Company, et. al.
    356 US 486, 2 Led 2d 926, 78 S. Ct. 382, 1955.
**Shipping Act of 1916
    46 USC Sec. 812.

side conference competition, the Court found that when the outside line (Isbrandtsen Co.) announced that they intended to increase sailings from two to three or four per month to competitive ports, the Conference very shortly thereafter proposed instituting the dual rate system. In summarizing the Court held: "In view of the fact in the present case the dual rate system was instituted for the purpose of curtailing Isbrandtsen's competition, thus becoming a device made illegal by Congress in Sec. 14 third, we need not give controlling weight to the various treatments of dual rates by the Board under different circumstances."

The decision appears to hold that the dual rate system is illegal as used in this case, because its use here violated the Shipping Act of 1916. The decision infers, however, that the dual rate system might be proper "under different circumstances". The contractual rights between shipper and conference were not declared illegal per se.

After this decision, a bill was immediately introduced into Congress. The bill provides that nothing in the Shipping Act of 1916 forbids dual rate contracts between the present time and June 30, 1960 other than the situation as ruled on by the one concerned in the Supreme Court. A full-scale Congressional investigation of the contract rate system is to be conducted between the present time and the June, 1960, deadline.

CHAPTER 13

Vessel at Sea

Harbor regulations. While a vessel is in port and leaving the harbor, it is subject to a system of harbor regulations which vary in each port of call. Generally, a ship is forbidden to pump bilge water as this water contains water-polluting oil. Special regulations provide for the disposition of garbage and other waste materials which the ship is also forbidden to cast overboard.

The movement of the ship within the harbor and the spot at which she may anchor are also subject to municipal regulation. Both within the harbor and through the navigable waters leading to the open sea, the services of a pilot are compulsory. The ship operator is responsible for procuring a pilot and for notifying the pilot of the time that he is expected to move or take a ship to sea, as well as for paying the pilot for his services. Occasionally in the case of a vessel which calls frequently in the same inland waters, the master of a vessel can become qualified to pilot his ship thus, saving the expense of hiring an additional employee.

Pilot rules. Moving from a wharf, a ship is subject to pilot rules, designed to prevent collisions, which have been authorized by several United States statutes. There are two sets of rules, one on the prevention of collisions at sea and the other on piloting rules applicable to inland waters of the United States, published by the Coast Guard. These rules are set out in parallel columns so that it is easy to compare them and to see the variations in prescribed action, depending on whether the ship is at sea or within inland waters*.

*Rules to Prevent Collisions of Vessels and Pilot Rules for Certain Inland Waters of The Atlantic and Pacific Coasts and of the Coast of the Gulf of Mexico. CG169 August 1, 1950.

The moment a ship crosses the geographically drawn line which divides the inland waters of a country from the open sea, the vessel is outside the jurisdiction of that country's pilot rules and territorial-water regulations. The services of the pilot at this time are completed and he is "dropped" or sent ashore in a small pilot vessel.

International rules. The ship is now subject to the International Rules to Prevent Collisions which are observed by all maritime nations and which have been made binding in the United States vessels by several federal statutes enumerated in the Coast Guard pamphlet mentioned above.

When two ships are passing, the rules to prevent collisions set out precisely the responsibilities of each to avoid collision. One ship is termed the "burdened" ship and she is required to change course or speed to avoid the other ship, designated as the "privileged" ship. These obligations and duties are more fully discussed in the chapter on Admiralty and Maritime Law.

Strict adherence to both sets of the rules is mandatory. The slightest deviation from prescribed action by a vessel could cause a collision.

The pilot rules prescribe minutely the lights that all types of vessels must display from sunset to sunrise detailing their colors, arcs, and distances of visibility. These lights, which were in use and required for many years before the modern safety service of radio and radar, are still a vivid means of night communication. The Rules-Of-The-Road are so tersely and well written that they may not be readily condensed here. A careful study of them is recommended in order to understand the liabilities of a ship involved in a collision.

Other sections of the rules cover some of the devices which may be required, including signals (flares and sounding whistle) bells, signal guns, rockets, and horns. Other factors outlined are type of vessel, procedure in fog, the relation of a sailing ship to the wind, small boats, vessels at anchor or crossing in courses, procedure when one vessel is overtaking another, indicating a change of course, asking permission to pass, as well as action when towing, fishing or aground. The smallest pleasure boat under power is not exempt from these rules in the matter of navigation lights, whistles, horns and bells. Only motor boats are not required to have on board copies of the pilot rules which, nevertheless, operators must obey.

A vessel at sea is under command of the master who is responsible for seeing that the ship is navigated in accordance with the Internationl Rules-Of-The-Road, however, when the ship crosses into inland territory, the master is required by law to rely on the services of a licensed pilot to bring the ship into port. The pilot must know all the rules for inland water, various harbor regulations, and also possess an intimate knowledge, gained only by long, firsthand experience, of the geographical contours of the land, water depths, currents and tides, rocks and shoals, The pilot is navigating officer of the vessel at this time. The captain, however, is still master of his ship, and in case of imminent danger of collision, he may take over command from the pilot.

Watches. As soon as the pilot is dropped, the ship is free of inland waters regulations and the captain once again takes full command. He will have ordered the crew divided into three sections, called watches, which handle the navigation of the ship at different times. Each watch is commanded by a different mate.

Each section stands watch for four hours and is off eight, standing daily. The first watch starts at midnight and runs to four in the morning; the second, from four to eight; the third, from eight to noon. This procedure continues in four-hour cycles throughout the afternoon and evening. In order to change the rotation of the three watches, a "dog" watch may be set with one section on duty from four to six in the afternoon, and another section taking over from six to eight.

The captain does not stand a watch but is available in emergencies at any hour. He takes command upon appearing upon deck the bridge of the ship. Generally, he more frequently is on deck during the watch of the third mate who of the three mates is the least experienced. The Rules and Regulations for Licensing and Certificating of Merchant Marine Personnel (Coast Guard 191, from the Seamen's Act of 1915, 46 U.S.C. 672) states: No licensed officer or seaman in the deck or engine department shall be required to be on duty for more than eight hours in any one day except under extraordinary circumstances.

Clocks on shipboard strike in a manner as to indicate the progress of each watch. One bell is struck at the end of the first half hour of the watch; two bells at the end of an hour; three bells at one and one half hours, and so on through, the four hour watch is completed when the clocks will strike eight bells. The clocks strike eight bells at four, eight and twelve, morning and afternoon.

For the purposes of navigation and communication, ship clocks also show the time which is read in a consecutive twenty-four sequence, commencing at midnight.

For astronomical navigation purposes, it is necessary that the vessel's time-keeping chronometers are kept carefully running accurately. Variations from perfect time are noted in the records and the differences recorded in seconds.

It is routine for a ship's officers to ascertain the ship's position daily at noon by taking a meridian altitude sight of the sun, from which the latitude and longitude of the vessel is computed. Other sights may be taken at other times of day or by observation of stars at night. If bad weather obscures the heavens, then the position of the vessel is calculated by dead reckoning. This consists of computing the ship's position from data which includes the speed at which the vessel is steaming, her compass course, allowances for ocean current direction and speed, and the estimated effect of wind and waves upon the vessel's course and speed.

Charts. The ship's course and position are plotted on a navigational chart and the report of her position, by latitude and longitude, are reported by radio either to the ship's operators or to marine agencies that collect data on the movement of all ships and make it available to interested operators. This information enables an operator to know the position of a ship each morning and evening, so that he may accurately estimate its time of arrival.

This procedure involves a limited use of the navigational charts by the operator who wishes to keep track of his vessel movements. Reports are forwarded in degrees and minutes of latitude and longitude, in which one degree equals sixty miles.

Ships position. Latitude is the measurement of the earth's surface in degrees and minutes using the earth's center as a reference point and numbering both north or south to 90° from a zero point at the equator to the North and South Pole. These measurements form parallels of latitude, each equally distant from the equator, on a chart which is a representation of the earth's surface. Each minute of latitude equals one nautical mile (6080 or 6076 feet). The distance between two points on a chart can be converted into miles by using the degrees and minutes of latitude as shown on the sides (not top nor bottom). Each minute is computed as one mile; each degree as 60 miles.

The East—West position of a ship is expressed in degrees and minutes of longitude. Zero point longitude is at a meridian drawn through the astronomical observatory at Greenwich near London, England. Meridians are representations of the degrees of arc, using the earth's center as a reference point, emerging upon the earth's rounded surface. Meridians are furthest apart at the equator. They narrow gradually, eventually converging at the geographic poles. To the east of Greenwich is East Longitude, to the westward is West longitude.

To represent the curved surface of the earth, it is necessary on a flat surface chart to distort the areas. The meridians of longitude will appear parallel which, in fact, they are not. The amount of the distortion is considerable when a chart represents a large portion of the earth's surface but it is negligible when the chart focuses on a small area. The parallel longitude form of the chart is called the Mercator projection.

Greenwich is also the point at which the day begins, for navigational purposes. A ship's position can be computed by taking an observation of the sun as it passes over the ship at noon, and then noting the Greenwich time on the ship's chronometers. The sun passes over fifteen degrees of longitude each hour. Thus, the difference between the ship's time and Greenwich time can be converted into degrees and minutes of longitude.

To the vessel operator ashore these calculations will be reported by radio "At 2000 GMT (8 P.M. Greenwich mean time) Lat.48—30 N, Long. 125—10 W." which represents a point near the northwest tip of the United States and which informs the operaator of the vessel's approaching the port of Seattle.

Nautical terminology describing ships and other objects at sea is quite technical. A ship's course is given in degrees of arc as though it were in the center of a circle of 360 degrees with zero being fixed at true North. A vessel moving East would be on course 90 degrees; South 180 degrees; West 270 degrees; therefore, a vessel's course is read to the nearest degree in this geographic circle. The exact position of a sighted object may be quickly located by translating its true bearing into degrees which are read directly across the ship's pelorus, or gyro compass repeater. The pelorus consists of compass cards, with the ship's head fixed as zero.

The pelorus system is of great practical value in detecting the danger of collision of two ships on converging courses. Frequent bearings can be taken to learn if there is a change of reading between successive bearings. If the bearings in degrees change, it is probable that the other ship is going to pass either ahead or astern. If no change in the degrees of bearing is noted, then danger of collision exists. Collision is prevented by following the International Rules-Of-The-Road's prescribed action.

Gyro compass. Many vessels carry two types of compasses to tell the direction of the ship's course: the *gyro* compass and the magnetic compass. The gyro compass is a very precise machine, activated by a gyroscope, which keeps the compass needle constantly pointed at true North, in spite of changes in course and the earth's daily rotation. From the master compass below decks, the reading of the instrument is transmitted to various repeater compasses located at positions convenient for navigational purposes The accuracy of the gyro compass depends upon the constant rapid rotation of the gyroscope which keeps the compass needle from being affected by the turning movements of the vessel. Should the gyro compass fail, recourse is made to the magnetic compass. As a precautionary measure then, the two compasses will be checked hourly while the vessel is underway. In port, compasses should be adjusted by experts.

Magnetic compass. The *magnetic* compass is activated by the earth's magnetism which directs the needle towards the earth's magnetic pole. The magnetic pole does not coincide with the geographic North Pole, but lies at a considerable distance south of the geographic North Pole. The difference between the two is called magnetic variation; its direction and degree at any location on the earth's surface, is shown by a compass "rose," printed on navigational charts of each area in which a vessel operates. A second correction is made in the magnetic compass reading on the basis of the error which is often induced by the iron contained in the hulls of vessels. This error is called deviation. The algebraic sum of the two errors of deviation and variation, applied to the compass reading, gives a true bearing and course. After adjustment and compensation of the magnetic compass, the vessel "swings ship." That is, it proceeds slowly in circles, checking the deviation with bearings taken on the positions of known fixed landmarks.

In the past, the compass was read by dividing the compass card into 32 points, named from the geographic directions indicated by the needle: North; North by East; North North East; North East by North, North East, North East by East, and so on to South, and then to West and back to North. This form of reading is termed "boxing the compass." In boxing the compass, each of the compass points is further sub-divided into quarters such as North North East one-quarter East.

The relationship of the two methods of direction reading can be readily compared by study of the reproduced, compass card in Figure 16. Readings and change of course in the ship's navi-

Figure 16. Reproduction of a Compass Deviation Card.

gational log. These are important navigationally and as evidence in case of a collision.

The compass card on Figure 16 also shows the terminology used to describe the direction in which an object lies from the ship: dead ahead, on the starboard bow, broad on the starboard beam, on the starboard quarter, and astern. Directional designations for the port side of the ship are also shown.

CHAPTER 14

Vessel Chartering

To make chartering profitable for the vessel, the cargo owner must be able to insure that a sufficient quantity of cargo is available for shipment to thus procure the service of a vessel. A factor in attractiveness of any offer from a cargo owner to a vessel is the opportunity of the vessel to get another cargo in the port of discharge of the first shipload which will assure, through a succession of calls for discharge and loading the vessel's constant employment. For example, a ship may agree to take a load of lumber from the Pacific Northwest to Australia in order to obtain a cargo of wheat which will take her to England where a shipment of machinery is waiting to be transported to the Pacific Coast.

Procuring a succession of cargoes for a vessel is the business of chartering agents who have correspondents in the major ports of the world. The request for a vessel to lift cargo is literally broadcast all over the world in order to determine which ship is "in position" to carry cargo in view of its other commitments. The skill of chartering agents involves profitably coordinating cargo offerings in many ports with the planned itinerary of specific vessels. The factor of freight and charter rates acceptable to tramp vessels is a knotty one which makes the job of a chartering agent difficult.

There are three forms of charters for vessels which vary according to the needs of the cargo owner. The *trip charter* is used when the cargo owner as the charterer has available only a sufficient amount of cargo for a single but profitable voyage between a loading and discharge point. This type of offer is interesting to a vessel owner if his ship is "in position" at the time specified to call

for the cargo and, if the vessel owner has a reasonable assurance
of further employment for his ship when the trip charter is fulfilled
in the designated port of discharge.

Time charter. The *time charter* is used when a charterer has
a succeeding number of cargoes or when he wishes a particular
ship in regular trade. Procuring cargoes, both outbound and return, is the responsibility of the charterer, together with the financial responsibilities of loading, transporting and delivering
cargoes. Under a time charter, a ship owner is assured of his vessel's employment for the duration of the charter.

It is his responsibility to keep his ship seaworthy and to see
that the schedule, specified in the charter, is maintained.

Bare boat charter. The *bare boat charter* is a type used by a
charterer who takes over the complete responsibility for procuring cargo and operating a vessel. It is called a "demise" form of
charter because the charterer is granted the duties and privileges
of the vessel owner as though he had purchased the vessel. Under
the terms of the bare boat charter, the ship owner is obliged to
turn over a seaworthy vessel at the beginning of the charter period.
As soon as the charter is in effect, the charterer is dealt with by
third parties just as if he were in fact owner of the vessel involved.

Trip charter. The simplest form of charter is the *trip charter*.
With it, the agreed upon owner is only committed to supplying
cargo in an amount agreed upon and pay freight on a per unit, per
ton, or per thousand board feet basis or he may have contracted to
pay a lump sum for having his cargo transported. The obligations of
the vessel owner include furnishing a ship at a time and port specified, loading the cargo, transporting and discharging it at the port of
destination. The vessel owner assumes responsibility for the cost of
operating the vessel, hiring the crew, supplies, fuel, maintenance
as well as all of the risks incident to ocean transportation. The costs
of loading and discharging are usually part of the expenses borne
by the operator, but sometimes these are excluded, by agreement,
should the cargo owner wish to perform this service himself. In
that case, a charter will contain a clause to the effect that the vessel
shall be relieved of these expenses and that the cargo shall be "free
in and out— F I O". This term is fully expressed as "loaded, stowed,
trimmed and discharged free of expense to the vessel."

The length of time that a vessel is in port, either loading or discharging cargo, is explicitly agreed upon between charterer and vessel owner. In-port periods are called "lay days." They are granted to the charterer to enable him to get his cargo loaded or discharged. Factors affecting the number of lay days are time usually consumed in loading a particular type of cargo, crew holidays, and weather conditions which might hinder loading or discharge.

The type of cargo is an important consideration in determining the number of lay days. For instance, a cargo of oil can be loaded and discharged in the matter of a few hours, grain in a day or two, while general cargoes require a week or more.

If the lay days granted are expressed in a specific number of "days" or as "running" or "consecutive days," then the period will cover inclusive Sundays and holidays. These terms limit the time in port to a particular number of consecutive calendar days. If the lay-days period specifies "working days," this means only on days which it is usual to work, according to the custom of the port, are included. In this case, Sundays and holidays, would not be figured in the number of lay days. The vessel owner must bear in mind holidays, both national and religious holidays, observed throughout the world.

"Weather working days" are days upon which the weather permits cargo to be worked. If lay days are weather working days, then days on which adverse weather conditions render loading or discharging conditions impossible cannot be figured in the tally. What constitutes adverse weather conditions may become a disputed matter between charterer and vessel owner.

If a vessel should fail to complete loading or discharge within a specified lay-day period, the vessel owner is entitled to compensation for the extra delay imposed on the vessel. Such a charge is called "demurrage" and is usually fixed at an agreed sum per day. Allowance is generally made to the charterer for delays beyond his control such as strikes, machinery accidents, floods, fogs, storms and so on.

Days saved within the allowed loading or discharging time are called "despatch days." This saving in time represents money which is credited to the account of the charterer. If extra expense is incurred by the owner in securing despatch of a vessel, the amount of the despatch credit is usually 50% of the agreed amount of a demurrage charge.

The *time charter* is the form of vessel hire in which the charterer engages the services of the vessel for a specified length of time to carry a succession of cargoes in a specific trade. Efficient use of the vessel's time is the responsibility of the charterer since, under a time charter, the vessel owners are paid for the length of time ships are in the service of the charterer. For the purposes of the charter the main duties of the ship owner are to provide a seaworthy ship which is navigated at the direction of the charterer.

The main concern of the charterer is to have sufficient cargo, both inbound and outbound, available to keep the vessel moving efficiently. As the charter runs for a definite period of time, delays in loading or discharge are expenses assumed by the charterer. He must take into account Sundays and holidays, adverse weather conditions which may prevent cargo working, and other possible delays.

Delays caused by a vessel breakdown or unseaworthiness, or by navigation at a slower than agreed upon speed are chargeable to the ship owner who must make allowance to the charterer for the time during which the vessel operates, according to the charter, unsatisfactorily. Such delays could be caused by time consumed in vessel repairs, deviation from course in order to make necessary repairs, and other causes which render a ship unable to perform agreed upon duties. A charter will specify a normal cruising speed for a vessel of so many knots. Any less speed that is maintained will consume time and will thus be allowed as a credit to the charterer.

Under the time charter, the vessel owner is obliged to keep his ship in a seaworthy condition, ready to work cargo or sail on the day set by the charterer. The vessel owner pays all operation costs, the crew hire, the fuel, water, stores and all navigational charges. Stevedoring charges are subject to agreement between the charterer and the ship owner. They may be paid by the ship owner or charged to the charterer under a clause releasing the ship—the F I O clause.

The *bare boat* is a form of charter in which a vessel owner, in effect, turns over his ship to a charterer, who becomes the vessel's operator. It is called a demise form as a charterer will take complete operational control of a vessel as if he were, in fact, its owner. A ship owner, under a bare boat charter, warrants the seaworthiness of his vessel for an intended operation so far as the vessel's hull and machinery are concerned, but is relieved of the seaworthiness obligation in regard to master, crew, stores and fuel. A charterer will take possession after a survey of the vessel has been made to ascertain her condition. He then proceeds to man the bare boat, put supplies and fuel aboard, load, navigate and discharge the vessel. A charterer must assume all responsibility for details of cargo supply, ship operation, maintenance and discharge. Any loss from accidents or delay in operation is borne by the charterer.

During a bare boat charter period, a charterer is required to keep his vessel in good running order, to overhaul and repair the ship when necessary and to drydock, clean and paint the ship at an agreed time. Redelivery to the owners of a vessel must be made after surveying that it is substantially in the same condition in which it was turned over to the charterer, excepting for normal wear and tear.

In each of these three types of charters, there is provision for delivery of the vessel to the charterer in a seaworthy condition, the lawful trades in which she will operate, the safe ports into which she may call and the redelivery of the vessel to her owners. Delivery to a charterer is specified down to the day and hour when the vessel will be placed at the disposal of the charterer in the port of delivery upon written notice by the captain of the vessel's readiness to load. Owners, accordingly, warrant a vessel to be "tight, staunch and strong and fitted for the voyage." Trades in which a ship may operate are required to be lawful. Safe ports of call are defined as those wherein a ship, fully loaded, may lay safely afloat at all stages of the tide in ports which are ice-free. The final condition is that a ship be returned to the owner in a designated port in good order and condition, ordinary wear and tear excepted.

The rate a charterer pays for the hire of a vessel is a matter decided between charterer and vessel owner. One important item in the affixing of rates is the amount of cargo a vessel is capable of carrying. This is determined by a vessel's dead weight carrying capacity in long tons at her summer load line. In the winter season, a vessel is required to carry less than her summer capacity. The charterer must bear this fact in mind.

Under a trip charter, the rate decided upon may be either a lump sum for the voyage or a rate per ton of loaded cargo, with allowances for dispatch or demurrage. In a time charter, the rate is based upon units of time—days or months—during which a vessel operates in the service of the charterer. The bare boat charter rate is also based upon periods of time during which the vessel is in possession of a charterer.

Any one of these charters becomes valid only after an owner and charterer have agreed upon each detail included. A chartering agent or chartering broker is responsible for effecting these agreements. In many cases charters are accomplished by cable communication with an owner and charterer located in foreign countries.

When one of these agreements has been reached, confirmed by both parties, a charter is then termed as "fixed." A "fixing letter" is sent confirming terms agreed upon, whereupon the chartering agent prepares a formal, signature document. This document is termed the "charter party". The word "party" signifies that the document states the partition of duties to be assumed by both owner and charterer. Preparing a charter party requires highly specialized knowledge and experience.

Charter parties vary considerably depending upon cargo a ship will be transporting and the areas in which a ship will be loading and discharging.

Commodities carried. The following list of commodities illustrates the diversity of the trades which use chartered vessels and the geographic origins of the commodities. As mentioned, the speed of loading specified by charter is reflected in the number of lay days granted to a cargo owner.

Coal from England, and the United States

So many running hours excluding holidays

Grain from Argentina, Australia, and America

At 225 tons to 400 tons per running day (Argentina)

500 tons in bags, 1,000 tons in bulk per weather working day

Lumber from the Baltic, and Pacific Coast
1¼ running days per 100 tons net register
Standards per weather working day
300,000 feet board measure per day

Artificial Fertilizers from European Continent

Asphalt from American ports
tons per hatch per day

Cattle from Canada

Cement from Europe

Copra from the Philippines

Cotton from the United States

China Clay from England

Esparto Grass from North Africa
200 tons per working day

Fruit from Spain

Frozen meat from New Zealand, Australia, and Argentina

Oil and Petroleum from the United States
Cases per day—Pumped per running hour

Hay from Canada

Manganese Ore from India, Brazil and Russia

Oil cake from Gulf of Mexico

Iron Ore from North Africa, Spain, Sweden, Chile, Canada
300—500 tons per day

Phosphate from North Africa, United States, and Pacific Islands
36 hours not exceeding 3600 tons

Pitch from Canada

Pulpwood, newsprint from Canada
500 tons per day

Quebracho from South America

Rice from Burma

Scrap Iron from many sources

Sugar from Philippines, Cuba, and Java
500 tons per weather working day
7000 bags, 330# each, per 24 hours weather permitting

Sulphur from Portugal, and the Gulf of Mexico

Zinc concentrates from the Gulf of Mexico

The rights and obligations involved in chartering a vessel so far discussed have been those existing between vessel owner and charterer. Operation of a ship, however, always involves the rights of third persons who enter the picture either because of contract or accident, such as vessel collision. An aggrieved third party can, in some cases, institute suit against a ship itself, regardless of ownership, or, in other instances, he can personally institute action proceed against an operator—either owner or charterer. Procedure in such cases is more fully discussed in the chapter on Admiralty and Marine Law.

As a ship is a thing, a *rem* in law and can be held liable for supplies for a voyage, fuel, and repairs, it is necessary for an owner to be protected from liens which would be incurred by a charterer acting as ship owner. One form of protection is provided by posting a notice on the vessel for suppliers that the ship is under charter and that neither the charterer nor the master has the right to create any liens against the vessel. Liens for crew wages and salvage are, however, not barred by such a notice.

Charter party. The rights of third parties arising from accidents, damage to cargo being carried, collisions, declarations of general average, and salvage involve extremely intricate questions of law. In actions *in personam* against the operator of a vessel, it is the court's responsibility to decide who is to be held responsible, the owner or the charterer—temporary owner. If the owner has retained any control of his vessel during the period of the charter, he may be liable, but if he has made a complete demise of the ship to the charterer for a period, then risk has in all probability fallen on the charterer. The temporary transfer of ownership is determined from the wording of the charter party, and from the division of operating duties between the two parties.

In settling an account between a charterer and vessel owner, the law gives the charterer a lien—a right to hold the ship responsible for all money paid in advance to the vessel owner and not earned. On the other hand, the law provides the owner with a lien against all cargo on the ship for any amounts due under the charter and demurrage.

A master of the vessel, under all forms of charter, is charged with signing bills-of-lading in accordance with the mate's or Tally Clerk's receipts for cargo loaded on the vessel. To safeguard a vessel, the charter party usually provides that the following clauses be included in any bills-of-lading issued. The first clause provides that a vessel shall have the benefit of the rights and immunities granted carriers and vessels under United States law (see chapter on Maritime Law.) The second clause to be added is the general average clause which provides that claims in such cases shall be adjusted under the American port usage rather than on procedure followed in a foreign port where the claim may be presented. See chapter on Marine Insurance.

Clauses. *U.S.A. Clause Paramount.* This bill of lading shall have effect subject to the provisions of the Carriage of Goods by Sea Act of the United States, approved April 16, 1936, which shall be deemed to be incorporated herein, and nothing herein contained shall be deemed a surrender by the carrier of any of its rights or immunities or an increase of any of its responsibilities under said Act. If any term of this bill of lading be repugnant to said Act to any extent, such term shall be void to that extent, but no further.

General Average Clause. General Average shall be adjusted, stated and settled, according to the York-Antwerp Rules, 1950, at such port or place in the United States as may be selected by the carrier, and as to such matters not provided by these Rules, according to the laws and usages at the port of New York. (San Francisco).

Because of uncontrolled competition in world-wide chartering, rates quoted are subject to rapid and sometimes extreme changes. The recent blocking of the Suez Canal precipitated a very large advance in charter rates; the Canal's reopening caused the rates to sink back to a much lower level. At low level, rates may not be compensatory to the vessel owners. To correct this, it has been reported that Greek vessel owners, who control 40% of the charters, are seeking to agree among themselves on minimum rates on charters between various ranges and on usual types of cargo.

In a widely fluctuating rate market, it is an extremely diffi-cult problem to fix a rate for a long term charter that will be ac-ceptable to both a ship owner and charterer. A plan has, how-ever, been suggested— to use the market rates as an index to be applied to rates on shipments made during the term of a charter and that such rates be subject to a maximum-and-minimum agree-ment.

Both plans reflect an effort to bring some measure of stability to ocean rates for vessel owners seeking to charter their ship. Such a stability would pass benefits on to cargo owners and be reflected in prices paid by consignees for commodities. The search for stability of rates has caused berth line ship operators to enter into rate conferences. See chapter on Ocean rates.

CHAPTER 15

Foreign Freight Forwarders

In 1958, the House of Representatives passed a bill which was intended to give the Federal Maritime Board authority to regulate fees charged by the foreign freight forwarders for services rendered to shipping clients and to standardize the practices of forwarders and shippers, which have been revealed by hearings of the Sub-committee on Freight Forwarding, to be haphazard. The Senate, although it did not find an opportunity to consider this legislation before adjournment, is certain to re-introduce the bill in Congress during the next session.

Definition. As officially defined by the House of Representatives, a foreign freight forwarder is: "any person engaged in the business of dispatching shipments on behalf of other persons, by oceangoing vessels in commerce from the United States, its Territories or possessions to foreign countries or between the United States and its Territories or possessions, or between such Territories and possessions; and who handles the formalities incident to such shipments. This definition includes independent freight forwarders, common carriers, manufacturers, exporters, export traders, manufacturers' agents, resident buyers, brokers, commission merchants, and other persons, when they engage for and on behalf of any person other than themselves, in the aforementioned activity."

Services. It will be noted, from the definition, that a forwarder is one who is engaged in the business of despatching shipment on an ocean-going vessel on behalf of a real shipper. All services performed by a forwarder are, in fact duties and obligations of the shipper. Where fully organized export offices are involved, these administrative details are performed by the exporter himself.

The value of forwarder's services to a shipper can be measured by convenience to the exporter. In many instances, there is a distinct saving of expense, because an exporter can hire, advanteously, employees to do the work.

When a shipper does not have an office or representative in a distant port through which his cargo may be required to move, it is a saving in time and money to make use of the services of the forwarder located in that port who can expedite movement of cargo and thus, secure the ocean bill of lading and other documents pertaining to exportations and who can present a completed set of export documents to the specified bank for collection or payment under the terms of the export order.

The availability of forwarders in the ports of the United States enables a shipper to use any port which is most suitable for the shipment of his cargo. By reason of the forwarder's location in the chosen port, a shipper may rely upon a forwarder's choice of carrier and ship best suited for the efficient cargo shipment.

Since the primary duty of the forwarder is despatching cargo, he is also expected to secure an appropriate carrier, to book freight, to expedite movement of cargo from its source to vessel, to check the condition of cargo and its loading, to supply carriers with information concerning the bill of lading to be issued, to secure a signed bill of lading from the carrier, and to make an accounting to the shipper for a completed transaction. For these basic services rendered, a forwarder usually receives as compensation about $10 per bill of lading from a shipper and a commission of one and one quarter per cent of ocean freight from the carrier.

From the viewpoint of the carrier, the forwarder secures cargo and is conveniently in touch with shipping movements, thus saving communication with distant shippers. The carrier is saved expense of freight solicitation which is impractible for a shipper located in a distant city.

In addition to the basic despatching of shipment, a forwarder is in the position to furnish many incidental services for which he may receive additional compensation from the shipper. A foreign freight forwarder must be capable of securing and executing all of the very intricate documents required for foreign trade and of presenting these documents to banks to procure payment for export in the form of foreign exchange drafts or letters of credit. A forwarder receives bank payment and, in turn, remits it to the shippers thus completing the export transaction. Such a comprehensive service by a forwarder may be either a convenience to a shipper or an absolute necessity should a shipper not be skilled in preparing these documents.

Shipper's Export Declaration. As a service for an exporter, a forwarder may himself execute the Shipper's Export Declaration—the sworn statement required to list each item being exported. This declaration contains the names of shipper and consignee, name of carrier, and ports of loading and destination. It also describes fully the export item, giving its value at seaboard. Furnishing export data, the Declaration is checked by customs to determine the legality of exportation and is a record required by the steamship company to justify each item of cargo on the vessel's outward foreign manifest.

A forwarder also procures a dock permit, if required, which serves as a cargo movement control. It assures convenient pier loading. If required by a cargo supplier or a shipper, a forwarder may secure a dock receipt or mate's receipt—proof of cargo delivery to carrier.

One service performed by a forwarder sometimes is an actual pier inspection of cargo to ascertain if it is in fact in "apparent good order and condition" for shipment upon which a vessel's acceptance of cargo and issuance of a bill of lading are based. This service attests to the termination of an exporter's duty to a foreign buyer, and to the carrier to provide cargo in good condition. A carrier assumes responsibility as transportation agent upon pier inspection.

If cargo is not in good condition, a forwarder can proceed to put it in good order by repacking, marking, stenciling, wire-strapping or other repairs.

A forwarder advises the steamship company of details to be included in a bill of lading or will, in fact, prepare a lading for the carrier's signature. He generally advances freight charges, procures a bill of lading from the carrier and remits it to the shipper.

A forwarder among his other duties secures marine insurance in the form and with coverages stipulated by a shipper in his letter of credit from his foreign buyer.

He may also make and execute a foreign consular invoice, presenting it to the consul of the country to which goods are destined and securing the consul's approval of the invoice.

If a cargo weight certificate or a certificate of quantity and quality is needed, these are obtained and paid for as a service to the shipper.

In the final stage of this procedure, all of the usual foreign trade documents are assembled in duplicate and presented to a bank for collection either from the foreign buyer directly or by means of a letter of credit, whereupon the forwarder reports to the shipper completion of the transaction.

There are many other services, depending upon the peculiarities of the commodity being shipped or incidentals of the individual shipment, a forwarder may be called upon to perform. The variety of duties as well as the unforeseen procedures which must be attended to makes it difficult to fix in advance remuneration of a forwarder by agreement for cargo movement. Such a situation provides unscrupulous forwarders with an opportunity to present extortionate billings. This practice has become so widespread that Congress conducted hearings on the subject. A bill, growing out of these hearings, to correct extortionate billings was passed by the House of Representatives during the last session of 1958.

A foreign freight forwarder has the same competitive opportunity as a domestic forwarder to consolidate shipments of several exporters into carload lots which are moved from interior points to seaboard for transshipping. The difference in the rail rates between an under-capacity carload and a full carload is divided between a forwarder and a shipper. The sharing results in a distinct saving for a shipper who would otherwise be required to pay the higher l.c.l. rates charged for small-size shipments. In addition to domestic consolidation, a forwarder may also be able to consolidate small shipments to be carried by vessel. The saving of expense, in this instance, is made by sending small shipments under a single bill of lading rather than under separate ladings, for which an ocean carrier is entitled to affix a minimum charge on each.

A forwarder prepares his own bills of lading, covering each item of cargo, for use by a shipper in his financing of cargo export. A forwarder's lading is in the nature of a receipt. It represents an agreement to forward goods on a particular vessel of a named carrier. As a forwarder does not actually transport cargo, his lading is not the basic contract of transportation. On the basis of prior exporter—consignee foreign exchange bank—agreement, a forwarder's bill of lading is accepted as a negotiable instrument and proof of cargo shipment.

Branch offices. Some foreign freight forwarders maintain offices abroad which take charge of distributing consolidated shipments to consignees. Foreign branch offices and associated companies perform necessary services required by American importers to expedite foreign shipments to the United States. Branch offices also help to expedite an import's transshipment to consignees located in the interior.

Ocean carriers have found it convenient to deal with foreign freight forwarders who are generally more familiar, because of daily contact, with the technical details of cargo transshipment and transportation than is a shipper. In case of emergency, carriers have also found it more efficient to deal with local representatives, rather than having to communicate with shippers located elsewhere.

Commissions. The greatest service a forwarder may render to a carrier is the procurement of cargo for a vessel. For this type of service a forwarder is paid commission, usually one and one-quarter per cent of the freight bill on a shipment. According to testimony given before the Federal Maritime Board, which is concurrently investigating the matter of forwarder commissions with Congress one and one-quarter per cent is the accepted minimum brokerage fee paid by conference members and ocean carriers. Certain conferences, however, pay from two and one-half to five per cent, while some independent lines are known to pay as high as ten per cent. Brokerage paid the forwarder was estimated during this investigation to constitute one-third of the forwarder's gross revenue. The basic business of a forwarder is to procure the most suitable carrier and vessel for the transportation of his client's cargo. The investigation revealed that the wide range of brokerage rates being offered foster unethical practices.

In House of Representatives, the necessity of correcting mal-practices among foreign freight forwarders was pointed out and the suggestion introduced that foreign freight forwarders be licen-sed and be subject to regulatory powers of the Federal Maritime Board. The conclusion of the House was set out in Section 2 of H. R. 8382:-

SEC. 2. The Shipping Act, 1916, is further amended by rede-signing section 44 as section 45, and inserting immediately after section 43 the following new section:

"SEC. 44. (a) No person shall engage in business as a 'for-eign freight forwarder' as defined in this Act unless such person holds a license issued by the Federal Maritime Board to engage in such business.

"(b) A forwarder's license shall be issued to any qualified ap-plicant therefor if it is found by the Board that the applicant is fit, willing, and able properly to perform the services of a foreign freight forwarder, and to conform to the provisions of this Act and the requirements, rules, and regulations of the Board issued thereunder, and that the proposed forwarding business is, or will be, consistent with the public interest and the national maritime policies declared in the Merchant Marine Act, 1936; otherwise such application shall be denied. Any forwarder who on the ef-fective date of this Act, is engaged in business as a foreign freight forwarder under a registration number issued by the Board may continue such business for a period of one hundred and twenty days thereafter without a license, and if application for such license is made within such period, the forwarder may, under such regula-tions as the Board shall prescribe, continue such business until otherwise ordered by the Board.

"(c) The Board shall prescribe reasonable rules and regula-tions to be observed by any person holding a forwarder's license and no such license shall be issued or remain in force unless such person shall have furnished a bond or other security approved by the Board, in such form and amount as in the opinion of the Board will insure financial responsibility and the supplying of the services in accordance with contracts, agreements, or arrangements therefor.

"(d) Licenses shall be effective from the date specified therein, and shall remain in effect until suspended or terminated as herein provided. Any such license may, upon application of the holder thereof, in the discretion of the Board be amended or revoked, in whole or in part or may upon complaint, or on the Board's own initiative, after notice and hearing, be suspended, changed, or revoked, in whole or in part, for willful failure to comply with any provision of this Act, or with any lawful order, rule, or regulation of the Board promulgated thereunder, or with any term, condition, or limitation of such license.

"(e) A common carrier by water may compensate a foreign freight forwarder licensed hereunder for the extent of the value rendered to such carrier in connection with any shipment and such forwarder may receive such compensation from such carrier when such forwarder has performed one or more of the following services:

"(1) The solicitation or securing of the cargo for the ship or the booking of, or otherwise arranging for space for, such cargo;

"(2) The coordination of the movement of the cargo to shipside;

"(3) The preparation and processing of the ocean bill of lading;

"(4) The preparation and processing of dock receipts or delivery orders;

"(5) The processing of consular documents; and

"(6) Relieving the carrier of bookkeeping and billing expense by advancing or arranging payment of freight and accessorial charges, if any, on all prepaid shipments handled by such forwarder or on a particular vessel."

CHAPTER 16

Marine Insurance

Relationship of vessel to cargo. The theory underlying the relationship between a vessel and its cargo developed at the very beginning of ocean transportation. Then ships were small and frequent victims of storms. Besides poorly designed and often unseaworthy, ships were generally overloaded—a practice that contributed to sea disasters. Early maps were embellished with depictions of seamonsters, personifications of angry winds and other perils of the sea—both imaginary and real. The concept grew that a ship and its cargo were in the same adventure together and that both shared the same perils of the sea. Consequently, there was considered to be no responsibility by either carrier or shipper for losses occasioned by these common risks. The basic duty of an operator is to make available a seaworthy ship; a shipper to provide cargo which is safe to ship. Marine insurance is now used as an assurance that losses to operator and shipper, caused by the perils of the sea and the acts of God, will be made good.

Hull policy. The division of responsibilities among ship operator, vessel, and cargo owner has been enacted into United States law in conformity with the laws of other maritime nations. Although the law relieves the vessel and operator from many contingencies and dangers in so far as their liability towards the cargo owner, the law provides, however, well-thought out list of dangers which could bring vessel loss and damage and which, therefore, should be so far as possible covered by marine insurance. The similarity between the excerpt from the United States code and the brief of a marine hull policy immediately following should be noted. Section 4 of the U.S. Code (46 U.S.C. 1304) on the rights and immunities of Carriers and vessels is set out in full in the chapter on Admiralty and Maritime Law.

Hereunder is a brief of a policy of marine insurance (reproduced in Appendix) intended to safeguard a vessel. The explanations and comments refer to the numbered items of coverage in the policy.

1   "Touching the Adventures and Perils which we, the said Assurers, are content to bear and take upon us, they are of the Seas, Men-of-War, Fire, Enemies, Pirates, Rovers, Thieves, Jettisons, Letters of Mart and Counter Mart, Surprisals, Takings at Sea, Arrests, restraints and detainments of all Kings, Princes and Peoples, of what nation, condition or quality soever, Barratry of the Master and Mariners and of all other like Perils, Losses and Misfortunes that have or shall come to the Hurt, Detriment or Damage of said Vessel, &c., or any part thereof."*

The coverages of a hull policy are further briefed:

2   . . if the Ship hereby Insured shall come into collision with any other Ship or Vessel, and the Assured or Charterers shall in consequence of their undertaking become liable to pay and shall pay by way of damages to any other person or persons any sum or sums in respect to such collision . . . .

3   Clause shall not extend to liability for injury to harbours, wharves, stages, piers or to the cargo or to loss of life or personal injury.

4   If vessels in collision are owned by same owner or charterer, the question of damages will be arbitrated.

5   Claim of Charterer shall be no greater than that of Shipowner.

6   Covered in port and at sea, in dock, at all times, in all places.

7   If the vessel is at sea at the expiration of the policy, it will be held covered to her port of destination.

8   Held covered in case of any breach of warranty, providing notice be given.

9   Should the vessel be sold or transferred, the Policy shall

*American Hulls (Pacific)—F.C.&S. revised December 1951

thereupon be cancelled unless agreed to in writing by Underwriters.

10   Policy specially covers damage to hull or machinery, caused by:

Accidents in handling cargo
Explosions on board or elsewhere
Bursting of boilers, latent defects in machinery.
Negligence of Masters, Mariners, Engineers or Pilots

11   General Average, Salvage and Special Charges payable in accordance with the Laws and Usages of the Port of San Francisco.

12   Policy liable only for its proportion under the Sue and Labor Clause.

13   Average payable on each valuation without deduction of thirds, new for old.

14   Donkey boilers, winches, cranes, windlasses, sterring gear, and electric light apparatus are a part of the hull and not a part of the machinery.

15   Warranted free from particular average under 3% unless the vessel was stranded, sunk, burned or was in collision.

16   Free from part of cost of cleaning and painting the bottom of the Vessel.

17   Grounding in a Canal shall not be deemed to be a stranding.

18   Conditions as to average 3% to be applicable to each voyage.

19   Underwriters not liable for unrepaired damage in the event of a subsequent total loss.

20   In ascertaining a constructive total loss the insured value shall be taken as the repaired value.

21   In the event of a total loss no claim will be made by the Underwriters for freight.

22   In the event of accident the Underwriters shall be notified in writing prior to survey and they shall have the right of veto on the cost of repairs.

23   Warranted that the amount insured for commissions shall not exceed 10% of the insured valuation of the vessel.

24   At the expiration of the policy, a percentage net for every thirty consecutive days the vessel is laid up in port out of commission shall be returned.

WARRANTED FREE FROM ANY CLAIM FOR LOSS CAUSED BY HOSTILITIES, CIVIL WAR, REVOLUTION, REBELLION, INSURRECTION OR CIVIL STRIFE ARISING THEREFROM OR PIRACY.

1. The wording in the first section is archaic but is retained in modern policies to describe the perils traditionally insured against. Every word and phrase has been put to the test of legality before courts of maritime nations; their decisions have fixed with certainty the meaning and the limitation of each phrase. The use today of this old-time language is an acknowledgment of the early beginnings of marine insurance and further serves as a time-tested expression of the risks an insuring company assumes.

"Adventures and Perils . . . of the Seas"——In insurance practice perils of the seas are considered to be four: sinking, stranding, collision, and fire.

"Men-of-War . . . Enemies, Pirates, Rovers Thieves, . . . Letters of Mart and Counter Mart, Surprisals, Takings at Sea, Arrests, Restraint and Detainments of all Kings, Princes and Peoples, of what nation, condition or quality soever"— These perils are insured against under the coverage known as War Risk which has modernized to cover loss to the vessel from any cause attributable to wartime operations or after effects such as damage from stray mines. In order that an insuring company can estimate the possibility of loss under war risk, a policy is written only after careful consideration of the risks a proposed voyage entails, the vessel's proximity to wartime operations, the nations involved and the position internationally of the nation under which the vessel is registered. Even the threat of war, may cause a sudden rise in the premium or the risk may become so great that a company might choose not to write this war risk coverage. In World War II, the U.S. Government provided insurance against war risk for privately owned vessels carrying government cargoes. In practice marine insurance policies carry a clause stating that the company shall be free from claims for capture and seizure (F.C. & S. clause) hence, these risks are assumed by a company when it has consented to write the war risk coverage. In the policy quoted above, the vessel owner is carefully warned in large, capital letters that the insuring company is not assuming these risks:

> WARRANTED FREE FROM ANY CLAIM FOR LOSS CAUSED BY HOSTILITIES, CIVIL WAR, REVOLUTION, REBELLION, INSURRECTION OR CIVIL STRIFE ARISING THEREFROM OR PIRACY.

To be covered against the above, a vessel owner must procure war risk coverage which specifically supercedes the above warranty.

A similar exclusion from the basic marine policies is the Strikes, Riots and Civil Commotion clause (S. R. & C. C.) which states that an insuring company is not liable for loss or damage resulting from labor troubles. This coverage must be also placed specially by a ship owner.

Referring still to paragraph 1 of the quoted policy, a pirate is defined as a robber of ships on the high seas—a rover as a pirate ship.—thieves as those who steal from a ship in port.

"Jettison" is to lighten a ship by throwing overboard all or part of the cargo during bad weather.

"Letters of Mart" (Marque) are government letters authorizing an individual to arm his ship in order to capture the merchant ships of an enemy.

"Barratry of Master and Mariners" is negligence or fraud on the part of the master or crew which results in loss to a vessel owner.

2 Collision clause. This clause covers a claim for damages by another vessel which has been in collision with the policy holder's ship.

3. Injuries to harbors, shore-side structures and loss of life or personal injury are not covered in basic marine policy. This coverage is obtained under Protection and Indemnity Insurance (P. & I.)—a form of casualty insurance covered later in this chapter.

4. This clause provides for arbitration when vessels in collision are owned by the same owner or charterer who has hired one of the vessels involved in collision.

5. Claim of charterer shall not be greater than that of owner—In one form of vessel hiring—the demise form—the charterer assumes the responsibilities of an actual vessel owner.

6. This clause defines the comprehensiveness of marine insurance coverage.

7. A policy does not lapse if the vessel is at sea, but remains valid until its destination is reached.

8. If notice of a breach of warranty is given, a policy remains in force until corrected.

9. Upon transfer of a vessel, an insurance company has the right to consider insurance with the new owner.

10. Bursting of boilers—When this type of accident first occurred, the Court held (in the case of the "Inchmaree") that it was not a marine risk. Policies now provide coverage for this risk and have been broadened in coverage as shown in Par. 10. This is known as the Inchmaree clause.

11. General average (see later in this chapter). Salvage from damaged ship, Special Charges paid according to the usages of the Port of San Francisco (New York). Settlement for maritime losses may involve ships of different nationalities and legal procedures of several countries. This policy provides that settlement will be made according to the procedural rules of the trade in San Francisco.

12. The Sue and Labor clause—A company will contribute, in case of loss, to the assured if it is necessary to sue, labor, or travel to safeguard a vessel's interests.

13. This clause outlines loss payable on the value of each item and prohibits the deduction of one-third of the loss just because a replaced item is new and better than the one which was damaged.

14. Machines subject to coverage by the policy are specified as those which are part of the hull. Propelling machinery which breaks down is not covered.

15. A company is not required to pay damages which total less than three per cent of a vessel's appraised value, unless the vessel under question has been subject to the perils of the sea.

16. Cleaning and painting the bottom of a vessel is a usual item of maintenance, and policy only covers the remaining serviceable period of the paint job on the ship.

17. In a canal a ship is usually towed by tugs and is therefore unable to control its course.

18. The limitation of three per cent precludes trouble from adjusting small claims.

19. If a vessel has not been repaired at the time it becomes a a total loss, the insurance company is excused from paying for these repairs.

20. To determine whether a damaged vessel shall be considered as a total loss, the cost of repairs will exceed the insured value.

21. Marine insurance reflects an interest in preserving of a vessel's hull rather than in the vessel's financial operation.

22. The veto power of an insuring company relative to the cost of repairs is an assurance to a company that the cost of repairs will be a reasonable one.

23. Insurance on commissions and other disbursements are considered excess insurance and is to be limited to 10 per cent of the insured value.

24. This section provides for return of the premium for the time a vessel out of commission is laid up in port.

For full protection, a vessel owner has several forms of insurance available to him:

Marine Insurance basically protects the hull of the vessel against the perils of the sea and other operational dangers. The amount of insurance placed on a vessel is agreed upon by a vessel owner and insuring company in the form of an "agreed value" of the vessel, plus "excess insurance" on commissions and freight interests which are limited to about 25 per cent of a vessel's hull insurance valuation.

Increased value insurance is a protection for a ship owner from claims under general average adjustments and collision contributions. Such claims are based upon percentage of the value of the ship. The insured value might be underappraised because of fluctuating economic conditions or an out-of-line adjuster. A higher valuation, would, of course, increase the amount to be paid on the claim and this is the contingency to be covered.

Freight insurance protects a vessel owner from freight revenue loss in case a vessel or its cargo is lost. If bills of lading are claused with a provision that freight money shill be considered earned at the time of cargo handling, no freight insurance is necessary since the lading is a freight guarantee for the ship owner.

P. & I. insurance. Protection and Indemnity insurance (P & I) is a type of casualty insurance that protects the vessel owner against liability for loss of life, personal injury, for damage to cargo or other property. The principal coverages in a P. & I. insurance policy are:

1. Personal injury, loss of life, illness of seamen. The vessel owner is obligated to insure the health and safety of crew members. P. & I. insurance offers protection against claims from these sources, as well as for injuries suffered by stevedores, longshoremen and other workmen employed occasionally aboard ship.

2. Damage to cargo and personal effects of passengers. The conditions which cause liability to the vessel owner from these causes are very complex and insurance is necessary.

3. Damage to shore establishments. These losses are usually caused by faulty navigation of the vessel are not covered in the marine policy.

4. Fines and penalties of the customs, and immigration departments. This covers—irregularities in vessel entrance and clearing, illegal drugs found on board, fines and penalties for stowaways against which the vessel owner needs protection.

5. Damage to another vessel other than collision. Fire or explosion on one vessel might cause damage to another ship and give rise to a claim which can be insured under P. & I.

6. Repatriating a crewmember. A seaman stranded in foreign country for any of a great number of causes is required to be returned home by a vessel owner. This insurance covers such travel expenses.

7. Removal of a wreck. If a vessel sinks in the navigable waters of a foreign country, a ship owner in many cases is required to pay for having the wreck removed..

8. General average settlements. Some contributions under general average become uncollectable. But if salvage expenditures are made, a vessel owner is required to pay the full amount.

A STOCK COMPANY **The Indemnity Marine Assurance Company Limited** ESTABLISHED 1824

WM. H. McGEE & CO., Inc., United States Managers, 111 John St., New York 38, N. Y.

Specimen

SPECIAL CARGO POLICY

$............

In correspondence refer to these letters and numbers

This Company, in consideration of an agreed premium and subject to the terms and conditions included herein or stamped or endorsed hereon, **does insure**

..................................(PLACE AND DATE)..19......

in the sum of..**Dollars**

on...

MARKS AND NUMBERS

valued at sum insured, to be shipped subject to an "Under Deck" Bill of Lading unless otherwise specified hereon,

by... or other vessel, and connecting conveyances B/L date............................

at and from.......................................via...

to...

Loss, if any, payable to the order of the Assured.

This insurance is against the perils of the seas, fire, assailing thieves, jettisons, barratry of the master and mariners, and all other like perils, losses or misfortunes that have or shall come to the hurt, detriment or damage of the property insured hereunder or any part thereof except as hereinafter provided.

SPECIAL TERMS AND CONDITIONS

SHIPMENTS ON DECK, AIR CARGO and MAIL or PARCEL POST SHIPMENTS, when insured under this Policy, are subject to average terms and conditions specified in clauses 13, 19 and 20 hereof.

SHIPMENTS SUBJECT TO AN "UNDER DECK" BILL OF LADING are insured:—

This Insurance is also subject to the following American Institute Clauses current on the date of Issuance of this policy:—

| MARINE EXTENSION CLAUSES | S. R. & C. C. ENDORSEMENT | WAR RISK INSURANCE |

When goods are so destined this insurance is subject to:—
SOUTH AMERICAN 60 DAY CLAUSE

AMERICAN INSTITUTE CARGO CLAUSES (February, 1949)

1. **WAREHOUSE TO WAREHOUSE CLAUSE:** This insurance attaches from the time the goods leave the Warehouse and/or Store at the place named in the policy for the commencement of the transit and continues during the ordinary course of transit, including customary transhipment, if any, until the goods are discharged overside from the oversea vessel at the final port. Also until the destination named in the policy or until the expiry of 15 days (or 30 days if the destination to which the goods are insured is outside the limits of the port), whichever shall first occur. The time limits referred to above to be reckoned from midnight of the day on which the discharge overside of the goods hereby insured from the oversea vessel is completed. Held covered at a premium to be arranged in the event of transhipment, if any, other than as above and/or in the event of delay in excess of the above time limits arising from circumstances beyond the control of the Assured.

It is necessary for the Assured to give prompt notice to these Assurers when they become aware of an event for which they are "held covered" under this policy and the right to such cover is dependent on compliance with this obligation.

2. **CRAFT, &c. CLAUSE:** Including transit by craft and/or lighter to and from the vessel. Each craft and/or lighter to be deemed a separate insurance. The Assured are not to be prejudiced by any agreement exempting lightermen from liability.

3. **DEVIATION CLAUSE:** This Insurance shall not be vitiated by any unintentional error in description of vessel, voyage or interest, or by deviation, over-carriage, change of voyage, transhipment, or other interruption of the ordinary course of transit from causes beyond the control of the Assured. It is understood, however, that any such error, deviation or other occurrence mentioned above shall be reported to this Company as soon as known to the Assured, and additional premium paid if required.

4. **F. P. A. CLAUSE:** Warranted free from Particular Average unless the vessel or craft be stranded, sunk, burnt, on fire or in collision, but notwithstanding this warranty these Assurers are to pay any loss of or damage to the interest insured which may reasonably be attributed to fire, collision or contact of the vessel and/or craft and/or conveyance with any external substance (ice included) other than water, or to discharge of cargo at port of distress. The foregoing warranty, however, shall not apply where broader terms of average are provided for elsewhere in this policy.

5. **WAREHOUSING & FORWARDING CHARGES, PACKAGES TOTALLY LOST LOADING, ETC.** Notwithstanding any average warranty contained herein, these Assurers agree to pay any landing, warehousing, forwarding and special charges for which this policy is liable under its terms, the Assured having the right to have the cost so incurred determined. Also to pay the insured value of any package which may be totally lost in loading, transhipment or discharge.

6. **LABELS CLAUSE:** In case of damage affecting labels, capsules or wrappers, these Assurers, if liable therefor under the terms of this policy, shall not be liable for more than an amount sufficient to pay the cost of new labels, capsules or wrappers, and the cost of reconditioning the goods, but in no event shall these Assurers be liable for more than the insured value of the damaged merchandise.

7. **MACHINERY CLAUSE:** When the property insured under this policy includes a machine consisting, when complete for sale or use, of several parts, then in case of loss or damage covered by this insurance to any part of such machine, these Assurers shall be liable only for the proportion of the insured value of the part lost or damaged, or at the Assured's option, for the cost and expense, including labor and forwarding charges, of replacing or repairing the lost or damaged part; but in no event shall these Assurers be liable for more than the insured value of the complete machine.

8. **EXPLOSION CLAUSE:** Including the risk of explosion, howsoever or wheresoever occurring during the currency of this insurance unless excluded by F. C. & S. Warranty or the S. R. & C. C. Warranty set forth herein.

9. **SHORE CLAUSE:** Where this insurance by its terms covers while on docks, wharves or elsewhere on shore, and/or during land transportation, it shall include the risks of collision, derailment, overturning or other accident to the conveyance, fire, lightning, sprinkler leakage, cyclones, hurricanes, earthquakes, floods (meaning the rising of navigable waters), and/or collapse or subsidence of docks or wharves, even though the Insurance be otherwise F. P. A.

11. **BILL OF LADING, &c. CLAUSE:** The Assured are not to be prejudiced by the presence of the negligence clause and/or latent defect clause in the Bill of Lading and/or Charter-party. The carriers' negligence clause and/or latent defect clause in the Bill of Lading and/or Charter-party. The servants is not to defeat the recovery by an Assured if a loss recoverable hereunder would have been a loss recoverable under this policy, and also to use all diligence to sail with or without pilot, and to tow and assist vessels or craft in all situations, and so far.

12. **INCHMAREE CLAUSE:** This insurance is also specially to cover any loss of or damage to the interest insured hereunder, through the bursting of boilers, breakage of shafts or through any latent defect in the machinery, hull or appurtenances, or from faults or errors in the navigation and/or management of the vessel by the master, mariners, mates, engineers or pilots.

13. **DELAY CLAUSE:** Warranted free of claim for loss of market or for loss, damage or deterioration arising from delay, whether caused by a peril insured against or otherwise, unless expressly assumed in writing hereon.

14. **BOTH TO BLAME COLLISION CLAUSE:** Where goods are shipped under a Bill of Lading containing the so-called "Both to Blame Collision" Clause, these Assurers agree as to all losses covered by this insurance, to indemnify the Assured for this policy's proportion of any amount (not exceeding the amount insured) which the Assured may be legally bound to pay to the shipowners under such clause. In the event that such liability is asserted the Assured agree to notify these Assurers who shall have the right at their own cost and expense to defend the Assured against such claim.

15. **CONSTRUCTIVE TOTAL LOSS CLAUSE:** No Constructive Total Loss shall be paid hereunder unless the property insured is reasonably abandoned on account of its actual total loss appearing to be unavoidable or because it cannot be preserved from actual total loss without an expenditure which would exceed its value when the expenditure had been incurred.

16. **CARRIER CLAUSE:** Warranted that this insurance shall not inure, directly or indirectly, to the benefit of any carrier or bailee.

17. The following Warranties shall be paramount and shall not be modified or superseded by any other provision included herein or stamped or endorsed hereon unless such other provision refers specifically to the risks excluded by these Warranties and expressly assumes the said risks:—

(A) **F. C. & S. WARRANTY:** Notwithstanding anything herein contained to the contrary, this insurance is warranted free from capture, seizure, arrest, restraint, detainment, confiscation, preemption, requisition or nationalization, and the consequences thereof or any attempt thereat; also from all consequences of hostilities or warlike operations (whether there be a declaration of war or not), but this warranty shall not exclude collision, explosion or contact with any fixed or floating object (other than a mine or torpedo), stranding, heavy weather or fire unless caused directly (and independently of the nature of the voyage or service which the vessel concerned or, in the case of a collision, any other vessel involved therein, is performing) by a hostile act by or against a belligerent power; and for the purpose of this warranty "power" includes any authority maintaining naval, military or air forces in association with a power. Further warranted free from the consequences of civil war, revolution, rebellion, insurrection, or civil strife arising therefrom, or piracy.

(B) **S. R. & C. C. WARRANTY:** Warranted free of loss or damage caused by or resulting from strikes, lockouts, labor disturbances, riots, civil commotions or the acts of any person or persons taking part in any such occurrence or disorder.

This Policy is made and accepted subject to the above terms and conditions and to those on the reverse hereof, which are hereby specially referred to and made a part of this Policy.

IN WITNESS WHEREOF, THE INDEMNITY MARINE ASSURANCE COMPANY LIMITED has caused these presents to be executed on its behalf by Wm. H. McGee & CO., Inc., United States Managers.

WM. H. McGEE & CO., Inc.

President

This Policy not transferable unless countersigned by an authorized representative of this Company or the Assured.

Countersigned: ....

NOTE: NOTICE TO THESE ASSURERS IN ACCORDANCE WITH PROVISIONS OF THIS POLICY MAY BE GIVEN TO THE NEAREST SETTLING AGENTS SHOWN ON BACK HEREOF OR TO Wm. H. McGEE & CO., Inc., 111 JOHN STREET, NEW YORK 38, NEW YORK, U.S.A.

INSTRUCTIONS TO CLAIMANTS ON THE REVERSE SIDE

Figure 16. Reproduction of a new type of ocean cargo special policy.

P. & I. is a recent form of insurance developed by vessel owners to fill out casualty coverages offered by old-time marine insurance.

Lloyds of London. The origin of underwriting began in Lloyd's coffee house, in London, where representatives of marine insurance companies while lunching discussed insurance risks. It was common practice for one company to insure a vessel but, not wishing to assume the entire risk, offer portions of the risk to other companies. Those companies which agreed to accept a share of the risk indicated acceptance by writing their names under that of the original company. This is how the term and practice of "underwriting" evolved.

The insurance companies which first practiced underwriting formed an association which was to become the world center of marine insurance procurement. Taking its name from its place of origin, the association called itself Lloyds of London. In addition to the marine risks that the association will write, Lloyds has now become a market where risks of any character will be considered for insuring, such as, against bad weather on a day of celebration, against a bridge collapsing, against the birth of twins in a family, and so forth.

In marine insurance, Lloyds follows a unique procedure in the event an insured ship disappears, leaving no trace of sinking or other type of loss. After a designated length of time, the bell which was formerly on the ship Lutine is tolled in the association's meeting room. By this Act, Lloyds gives notice to the associated insurance companies that the ship in question is considered to be totally lost and that insurance coverages on the vessel are due to be paid.

Lloyds compiles a current list of all merchant vessels over 100 tons burden throughout the world which is published yearly in volume form called Lloyd's Register of Shipping. It is kept up to date with periodic corrections during the year.

For each ship, Lloyd's Register provides the vessel's official number, identifying signal code letters, the name of the vessel (and former name if it has been changed), the classification of the ship by Lloyds or a navigational registration bureau which rates the ship's seaworthiness and ability to perform special duties, the gross and net register tonnage of the vessel, the builders of the vessel—the year and place of construction, the name and address of the present owner of the vessel, the ship's length, breadth and depth, the place of registry, the ship's national flag, the type and power of her engines, her moulded depth, free board and draft, and the registration bureau, if other than Lloyds which has surveyed the ship.

All of this information is entered in Lloyd's Register only after a ship has actually been surveyed by a national registration bureau such as the American Bureau of Shipping, or by Lloyd's own surveyors who are located in all of the important ports of the world. In each survey, a ship is rated as to her seaworthiness, construction and suitability for the trade or the special purpose for which it was built. A top rating is *100 A 1*. This rating has become an expression synonymous for highest quality in areas outside shipping. A rating of 100 is given to iron and steel ships under the strict rules of survey issued by Lloyds in 1869. Less than a 100 rating— 90 or 80—shows the degree to which the vessel falls below the top rating of 100. The figures *A 1* indicate that the vessel is satisfactory in the opinion of the Committee for the special purpose for which it was built or the trade in which it operates.

Lloyd's Register and the carefully compiled rating given a ship is of great influence upon an insurance company planning to insure a vessel hull or the cargo it will carry. A poor rating is reflected in higher premiums charged because of the greater risk involved in insuring less than 100 A 1 ships. The same information is also of utmost value and usefulness for ship owners, operators, charterers and agents.

In some instances rather than depend solely on Lloyds, it is desirable to have an immediate survey of a vessel in order to determine its present condition, seaworthiness and suitability for the intended voyage when trying to affix a rate of premium to apply to an individual risk. To obtain such a survey, insurance companies have established associations, such as the San Francisco Board of Marine Underwriters, which employ surveyors to report on the conditions of ships and cargo so that insurance companies can be fully aware of an individual risk under consideration. This also serves to standardize the rates applicable to a risk and to familiarize companies with current market rates. Because of the unique nature of marine insurance underwriting, the consultation of companies over matter of rates is made excluded from the area of United States statutes on monopolistic practice.

Practically every marine insurance rate is a special computation, based on many extenuating circumstances such as the rating of the vessel, its present seaworthiness, the valuation of the vessel for insurance, the reputation of the vessel operator and the losses he has incurred in the past, the risks of the proposed voyage, the season of the year in which the voyage will be made, the anticipated lay-up time of the vessel, the risk inherent in cargo to be carried, the political and military situation in those countries along the ship's route, and the assurance that other insurance companies will be willing to underwrite in part the risk.

Losses are classified according to their seriousness to the ship. A vessel that sinks at sea is an actual total loss. A partially burned or stranded vessel might be impractical to recover or repair. This condition is called a constructive total loss. It is covered by a clause in the policy which states that a constructive total loss is proved when the cost of recovery and repair would exceed the insured value of the ship.

Particular average. Particular average is a partial loss less than a total or constructive total one. The loss is due to damage incurred by the perils of the sea—fire, collision, stranding, or sinking. To eliminate the cost of adjusting small claims, particular average clauses generally specify that losses will not be paid unless they exceed a minimum amount usually set at three per cent of the insured value of the hull. This is referred to as the franchise.

General average. General average claims arise when a voluntary sacrifice has been made for the benefit of ship and cargo. The claim under general average is therefore made in order to repay this sacrifice, not because of physical damage to an insured item of cargo or a ship.

The practice of adjusting these claims is so complex an operation, it may involve all of the insurance details outlined thus far, as well as ascertaining the amount of damage which may have happened in some distant sea, the transportation contracts between ship and cargo, whether laws of foreign countries are applicable, the differences of adjusting claims in various countries, the interests involved which may be scattered over the world, and details of insurance policies which may differ in coverage. To resolve all of these interests into an equitable settlement, a highly skilled marine insurance general average adjuster is required.

Occasions arise when a ship is in immediate danger and a sacrifice is either of the ship itself or of its cargo in order to save the vessel and enable it to continue its voyage. In such a situation, the one—cargo owner or carrier—who made the sacrifice is reimbursed by all of the parties having an interest in the voyage, the cargo, the vessel, and the freight money. Each contributes according to the value of his interest. In sacrifice cases *general average* is declared. This is a basic coverage in marine insurance and very necessary to ship and cargo, as a ship and cargo may arrive safely at destination yet still be subject to a proportionate contribution because of the sacrifice which made safe arrival possible. General average is added to the other basic coverages of a marine policy against the perils of the sea. The word "average" in technical marine usage is synonmous with "loss". General Average is a common loss, Particular Average—an individual loss.

To justify declaring a general average, the following circumstances must prevail:

1. The presence or rapidly approaching presence of a peril which threatens all interests in the voyage: ship, cargo and freight money. The danger must be in fact real or be considered so by the navigator of the vessel on the basis of his experience. The traditional perils of the sea are fire, collision, stranding, and sinking. Any of these contingencies is thus basis for declaring a general or particular average.

2. There must be a voluntary sacrifice, usually ordered by the master or someone in his behalf; an actual jettisoning of cargo during a storm or a beaching of the vessel to prevent sinking.

3. The act of sacrifice must be extraordinary rather than usual procedure in the operation of the ship. For instance, flooding of a hold to extinguish a fire which causes water to damage cargo is considered a sacrifice.

4. A sacrifice or expenditure must be reasonable. The order which results in sacrifice must be a logical move to meet a real potential peril, allowance is made for anxiety caused by danger.

5. The sacrifice must have been successful to the extent that

some property was saved or the continuation of the voyage was made possible. The payment of emergency expenditures for the discharging of cargo into lighters so as to lighten a ship and release it from the ground is a general average claim.

York-Antwerp Rules, 1950. The following international rules specify the conditions necessary for the declaration of general average:

York-Antwerp Rules, 1950

"There is a general average act when, and only when, any extraordinary sacrifice or expenditure is intentionally and reasonably made or incurred for the common safety for the purpose of preserving from peril the property involved in a common marine venture.

No jettison of cargo shall be made good as general average, unless such cargo is carried in accordance with the recognized custom of the trade.

Damage done to a ship and cargo or either of them, by or in consequence of a sacrifice made for the common safety, and by water which goes down a ship's hatches opened or other opening made for the purpose of making a jettison for the common safety, shall be made good as general average.

Damage done to a ship and cargo, or either of them, by water or otherwise including damage by beaching or scuttling a burning ship, in extinguishing a fire on board the ship, shall be made good as · general average; except that no compensation shall be made for damage to such portions of the ship and bulk cargo or to such separate packages of cargo, as have been on fire.

Loss of damage caused by cutting away the wreck or remains of spars, or of other things which have previously been carried away by sea-peril, shall not be made good as general average.

When a ship is intentionally run on shore, and all the circumstances are such that if that course were not adopted she would inevitably drive on shore or on rocks, no loss or damage caused to the ship, cargo, and freight, or any of them, by such intentional running on shore shall be made good as general average. In all other cases where the ship is intentionally run on shore for the common safety, the consequent loss or damage shall be allowed as general average.

Damage to or loss of sails and spars, or either of them, caused by forcing a ship off ground or by driving her higher up the ground, for the common safety, shall be made good as general average; but where the ship is afloat, no loss or damage caused to the ship, cargo, and freight, or any of them, by carrying a press of sail, shall be made good as general average.

Damage caused to machinery and boilers of a ship, which is ashore and in a position of peril, in endeavoring to refloat, shall be allowed in general average, when shown to have arisen from an actual intention to float the ship for the common safety at the risk of such damage; but where a ship is afloat no loss or damage caused by working the machinery and boilers, including loss or damage due to compounding of engines or such measures, shall under any circumstances be made good as general average.

When a ship is ashore and cargo and ship's fuel and stores or any of them are discharged as a general average act, the extra cost of lightening, lighter hire, and reshipping (if incurred) and the loss or damage sustained thereby shall be admitted as general average.

Ship's materials and stores, or any of them, necessarily burnt for fuel for common safety at a time of peril, shall be admitted as general average, when and only when, an ample supply of fuel had been provided; . . . . .

When a ship shall have entered a port or place of refuge, or shall have returned to her port or place of loading, in consequence of accident, sacrifice, or other extraordinary circumstances, which render that necessary for the common safety, the expenses of entering such port or place shall be admitted as general average; . . . . ."

Therefore, a voluntary and successful sacrifice or a part of a venture for the benefit of the whole is borne by all of the interests in the voyage. An owner who sustains loss by reason of sacrifice, in all justice, must be reimbursed. Maritime law requires that loss under general average be equitably apportioned between all of the interests involved according to the value of their interests.

Average adjustments. When a vessel which has survived a peril arrives in port of destination and a condition of general average is declared, the master, under law, is required to keep all interests together until the arrangements for the adjustment are made and security is given for the payment of charges which will be assessed each interest involved in the venture. A form of general average bond is prepared which contains the general average conditions, the sacrifices which were made and the expenses incurred. The signatories of the bond agree with the owners of the vessel to obligate themselves to pay the losses and expenses therein mentioned are shown to be either a charge on the cargo or the vessel when adjustment is completed. Neither delivery of cargo nor settlement of other accounts is made until a bond is executed. If goods have not been insured, a cargo owner is required to make a cash deposit sufficient to cover the estimated charges which may finally be assessed against his particular interest. If property has been insured under a marine policy, the adjuster usually accepts the assurance of the underwriters for such charges.

A general average adjustment is indicated briefly:

Value of vessel	$300,000
Value of cargo	400,000
Freight money	50,000
	$750,000

Value of cargo sacrificed under general average conditions—$7,500.

Vessel will contribute	30/75ths of $7,500 or	$3,000
Cargo will contribute	40/75ths of $7,500 or	4,000
Freight money	5/75ths of $7,500 or	500
		$7,500

Assuming that all of the cargo is owned by a single shipper, then his contribution is set at $4,000 for the general average loss and he will receive only a net reimbursement of $3,500 ($7,500 minus $4,000.) He is a partner in the general average loss and must therefore bear his share of the loss.

The adjustment proceeds with the ascertainment of the value of ship, of freight money, and of the value of each item of cargo which possibly number into the hundreds and may be the products of several countries. The amount of the sacrifice and expenses may have been incurred many miles from the port of destination where the adjustment may be handled. No two countries have the same laws, rules, regulations and customs relating to sacrifices and expenses covered and as to the method of adjustment. This lack of uniformity makes adjustment an extremely complicated procedure.

Efforts have been made to secure uniformity through international rules by meetings of the Association for the Reform and Codification of the Law of Nations which were held in 1864 at York, England, and again in 1877 at Antwerp, Belgium. These meetings resulted in a code known as the "York-Antwerp Rules" which were later revised in 1890, 1924, and again in 1950 and which are now cited in bills of lading as the "York-Antwerp Rules 1950". Marine policies provide that these rules be used as guides in the settlement of average claims. In the policy cited in this text, settlement is directed according to usages of the Port of San Francisco.

CHAPTER 17

Admiralty and Maritime Law

Origins of Admiralty and maritime jurisdiction. The Constitution of the United States grants judicial power over all cases of admiralty and maritime jurisdiction to the federal courts. (U.S. CONST. ART. 3. SEC. 2.) The words "admiralty" and "maritime" are not completely synonymous. Admiralty jurisdiction refers especially to that class of cases which originally came within the cognizance of the admiral for the administration and enforcement of the maritime laws of the particular country concerned. Its practice and application was limited to the waters and vessels of his own nation. Thus while in the early history of English law the administration of maritime law rested in courts of local jurisdiction, the latter were ultimately superceded by courts of Admiralty. These courts were held in the name of the Lord High Admiral, an appointee of the Crown, and this office gradually developed a judicial side just as the powers of equity gradually came into being via the office of the Chancellor. There are references to a court of Admiralty in England as early as 1357, and there is an existing record of a case heard by Sir Robert Herle, "Admiral of all the fleets" in the year 1361.

Maritime causes arise under maritime law which consists of principles of equity and mercantile usages which general convenience and a common sense of justice have established in all of the commercial countries of the world in matters relating to the sea. Thus English maritime law, which has of course moulded the American practice, reflects an Italian influence which was strongest in the late 15th and early 16th century as well as other Mediterranean mercantile customs which became a part of English law as a result of the revival and spread of Roman law into northern Europe in the 16th Century. In practice the maritime law takes into consideration the marine usages of all commercial countries so that a uniform justice will be administered to litigants even though they are of different nationalities and subject to the several codes of admiralty laws of their respective countries.

Proceedings in rem and in personam distinguished. Admiralty causes are divided into two classes: Proceedings *in rem* and proceedings *in personam*. Suits *in rem* are against the thing itself and the process and recovery is limited to the object in suit, as, S.S. *Washington*, Barge #39, or a tow of logs. Suits *in personam* direct the jurisdiction of the court against the *person* of the defendant and concern the rights and liabilities of the person. It is only in execution that such actions proceed against his property and then generally without restriction to the vessel or object in controversy. Suits are commenced by the libellant who files a libel in a U.S. District Court. A libel is similar to a complaint. The U.S. Marshall seizes a vessel by posting a notice of suit on the mast of the ship. Testimony is frequently taken before a U.S. Commissioner at various times when the vessel or her personnel or other interested parties are available. These depositions and interrogatories are then presented at time of trial to complete the offering of evidence. Attorneys who practice in Admiralty law are called *Proctors* when engaged in matters not before the Court and *Advocates* when appearing in Court, hence their full title, Proctor and Advocate in Admiralty.

Causes of action arising out of contracts, torts and crimes within the territorial boundaries of a state are usually within the jurisdiction of the courts of that state and are tried by state courts. However, some cause may fall within the jurisdiction of both state and federal courts and here there is a choice of jurisdictions. Causes may be removed upon petition, from state to federal courts where federal statute so provides or is in issue in the suit. Where the action is against the vessel itself, an action *in rem*, the jurisdiction of the federal court is exclusive of the state courts.

The designation *ship* or *vessel* is interchangeable in the law. A ship is an instrument of naval transportation and its form, rig or means of propulsion are merely matters of description. Legal terminology describes a ship with her tackle, apparel and furniture as follows: the hull and spars constitute the ship; the rigging is the tackle; the sails are the apparel; the anchors, chains are furniture; boats are boats; engines are engines.

The "high seas" are considered as the open ocean and "navigable waters" are those which are navigable and which fall within the territorial limits of a country or a state. "Navigable waters," which confer admiralty jurisdiction, are those which will float a vessel, even a canoe, in commerce. Tides do not limit the jurisdiction as it extends to rivers and lakes. The craft must be able to proceed in commerce but if it is merely floating and attached to the land it is classed as a shore structure.

When maritime jurisdiction exercised. Generally maritime jurisdiction is exercised in matters pertaining to ships either because of the subject matter on contract relating to a ship, or because the matter or event occurred at sea or on a vessel. The following are examples of maritime jurisdiction: All that concerns vessels and the acquiring of title to them; the rights and duties of the ship's company—captain and men; the rights and responsibilities of owners, charters and freighters; losses and sacrifices—averages—which happen to ship and cargo; marine insurance on ship and cargo; loans and advances on ship and cargo; contracts to repair a ship, and to rig, furnish and outfit her; material-man liens to enable the ship to navigate the sea; necessaries supplied to a vessel; sale of vessels and possessory actions to recover the ship; all cases of mariners' wages; mariner's interest in the voyage as in whaling, fishing; wharfage or dockage while lying at a pier; stevedoring for loading, stowage, and discharge of the vessel; contracts of affreightment, bills of lading; charter parties wherein a vessel or part is hired; contracts for carriage of passengers; pilotage for bringing a ship to port or taking her out to sea; contracts made by the master for the ship; maritime loans, and obligations incurred by the master for ship repairs; bottomry loans made on a particular voyage for the ship; *Respondentia* Bonds given to secure a loan on the cargo; contracts of insurance against the perils of the sea; cases of average contribution when a general sacrifice has been made; appropriation of cargo for the use of the ship; demurrage for detention of vessel; cases of salvage for voluntary assistance to the ship; enforcement of penalties by the United States or other nation; seizures made on navigable waters; ransome bills involving legality of capture as a prize; cases of torts on the high sea and navigable waters; personal injury on vessels; piracy, violation of property committed on the high seas; collisions of vessels; damage by vessels to shore structures.

When a ship is on the high seas, the law governing her is that of her own flag. But when she is in territorial waters of another nation the laws of the waters whereon she floats govern.

A suit *in rem*, arises when there is a maritime lien which gives the right to hold the ship itself responsible. Such liens may arise in maritime transactions involving seamen's wages, bottomry bonds, *respondentia* loans, repairs and supplies to vessels, affreightment contracts, tort and collision claims, towage, wharfage, stevedore service, salvage, pilotage, and general average.

Rights and immunities of carriers. Two federal statutes define the responsibilities of vessel owners for the cargoes their ships carry, these are the Harter Act, 1893, and the Carriage of Goods by Sea Act, 1936.

The following is an excerpt from the Carriage of Goods by Sea Act, (COGSA) and the entire Act is set out as Appendix II at the end of the book.

RIGHTS AND IMMUNITIES OF CARRIERS AND VESSELS

Apr. 16, 1936, sec. 4 (46 U. S. C. 1304). (1) Neither the carrier nor the ship shall be liable for loss or damage arising or resulting from unseaworthiness unless caused by want of due diligence on the part of the carrier to make the ship seaworthy.

(2) Neither the carrier nor the ship shall be responsible for loss or damage arising or resulting from—

(a) Act, neglect, or default of the master, mariner, pilot, or the servants of the carrier in the navigation or in the management of the ship;

(b) Fire, unless caused by the actual fault or privity of the carrier;

(c) Perils, dangers, and accidents of the sea or other navigable waters;

(d) Act of God;

(e) Act of war;

(f) Act of public enemies;

(g) Arrest or restraint of princes, rulers, or people, or seizure under legal process;

(h) Quarantine restrictions;

(i) Act or omission of the shipper or owner of the goods, his agent or representative;

(j) Strikes or lockouts or stoppage or restraint of labor from whatever cause whether partial or general: *Provided*, That nothing herein contained shall be construed to relieve a carrier from responsibility for the carrier's own acts;

(k) Riots and civil commotions;

(l) Saving or attempting to save life or property at sea;

(m) Wastage in bulk or weight or any other loss or damage arising from inherent defect, quality, or vice of the goods.

(n) Insufficiency of packing;

(o) Insufficiency or inadequacy of marks;

(p) Latent defects not discoverable by due diligence; and

(q) Any other cause arising without the actual fault and privity of the carrier and without the fault or neglect of the agents or servants of the carrier.

(3) The shipper shall not be responsible for loss or damage sustained by the carrier or the ship arising or resulting from any cause without the act, fault, or neglect of the shipper, his agents, or his servants.

(4) Any deviation in saving or attempting to save life or property at sea, or any reasonable deviation shall not be deemed to be an infringement or breach of this act or of the contract of carriage, and the carriers shall not be liable for any loss or damage resulting therefrom.

(5) Neither the carrier nor the ship shall in any event be or become liable for any loss or damage to or in connection with the transportation of goods in an amount exceeding $500 per package lawful money of the United States.

The Harter Act is national in its application whereas the Act of 1936 is intended to bring uniformity in international maritime usage. If he is to avoid liability, the Harter Act requires the vessel owner to have his vessel in seaworthy condition for the voyage; the Act of 1936 requires the owner to use due diligence to put his ship in a seaworthy condition.

The Harter Act was passed in 1893 to correct inequities arising from United States court decisions relative to vessel owners negligence. This earlier legislation has been almost completely replaced by the Carriage of Goods by Sea Act which was enacted in 1936. The Harter Act provided generally that it was unlawful for the carrier to insert a clause in any lading whereby it was relieved from loss or damage arising from negligence or fault in proper loading, stowage, custody, care, or proper delivery of any and all lawful merchandise or property committed to its charge.

Under the Act it is not lawful for any vessel transporting merchandise or property from or between ports of the United States of America and foreign ports, to insert in any lading any agreement whereby the obligations of the vessel owner to exercise due diligence properly to equip, man, provision, and outfit said vessel, and to make said vessel seaworthy and capable of performing the intended voyage, shall in any wise be lessened, weakened, or avoided.

Limitation of liability. It will be noted that under the two acts, if the vessel owner has used due diligence in making his ship seaworthy for the intended voyage, he will be relieved from liability for damage caused under the many contingencies of the Act of 1936. If such relief is not found to be available to him, then he has a final resort to limitation of his liability. When the vessel owner has been found liable, then, by petition he may ask that his liability be limited and he surrenders the vessel to the court to satisfy this liability. The amount of this limitation was fixed at the value of the vessel after the disaster. This, of course, would be practically nothing if the vessel were at the bottom of the high seas. The logic behind this limitation may be compared to that of stockholder in a defunct corporation where the stockholder's liability has been limited to his paid-up stock.

Limitation is available only to the real owner or the charterer as owner of the vessel, and he must surrender not only the ship but also any claims he may be entitled to receive passenger fares and freight money, subsidies, and every salvage asset of the ship, excepting insurance due to the owner.

When the limitation of liability is petitioned for in connection with personal injuries or death on seagoing vessels and his surrender does not bring the funds to an amount of $60 per ton of the vessel's gross register tonnage, then the owner must supply additional funds to bring the amount available to the $60 per ton gross register. This additional sum is required only in the case of claims for bodily injury or loss of life on "seagoing" vessels. Owners of small vessels and yachts may petition for limitation, but case decisions are not available to indicate whether they would be considered "seagoing" and thus liable for the additional contribution required in personal injury cases.

In determining the seaworthiness of a ship for an intended voyage, the courts examine into many technical details of marine architecture and engineering, into cargo handling and care, into the peculiarities of each trade in which the ship may engage, into the relative perils of each contemplated voyage, and into the competancy of the personnel who will man the ship. Consequently, a knowledge of the conditions that will make a ship unseaworthy is absolutely presumed to be a part of a ship owner's experience if he is to be relieved from liability by showing that he has used due diligence in providing against such contingencies.

When a vessel has been in a collision with another, the vital discussion will center around the movements of the vessels which led to the collision and wherein a fault might lie which contributed to the accident. If referred to a court, the decision will be that one vessel was at fault and the judgement in money for the damage caused will depend upon the finding made. If one vessel only was at fault, she will be required to settle the damage to her self and the other vessel. If both vessels were at fault, the amount of the damage will be added together and divided equally: if neither vessel was found at fault, then the damages will rest on each vessel in the amount each ship has been injured.

The following clause is usually added in bills of lading and charter parties to clarify the assessment of damages caused to cargo in the event of a collision wherein both vessels were at fault.

Both-to-Blame Collision Clause. If the ship comes into

collision with another ship as a result of the negligence of the other ship and any act, neglect or default of the Master, mariner, pilot or the servants of the Carrier in the navigation or in the management of the ship, the owners of the goods carried hereunder will indemnify the Carrier against all loss or liability to the other or non-carrying ship or her owners in so far as such loss or liability represents loss of, or damage to, or any claim whatsoever of the owners of said goods, paid or payable by the other or non-carrying ship or her owners to the owners of said goods and set off, recouped or recovered by the other or non-carrying ship or her owners as part of their claim against the carrying ship or carrier.

In the chapter herein on the Vessel at Sea, mention was made of two sets of rules, International and Inland, to prevent collisions of vessels. Illustrative of the difference to navigation prescribed for the same condition is the instance of two vessels approaching on courses that might involve a collision. Under the International rules, (Art. 19) the vessel A which sees vessel B's port side in daytime or B's red port light at night on A's own starboard side, has the duty of acting to avoid the collision. A is the "burdened" vessel and by rule she must slacken speed, stop or reverse. B is a "privileged" vessel and her duty under the rules (Art. 27) is to maintain her course and speed. Exception may be made, if, in order to avoid the accident, B at the instant that collision was imminent changes course or speed, The court will determine whether B by change of speed or course has abandoned her "privileged" status. Nor can B having the right of way, willfully smash into A.

Under Inland rules and in the same condition of meeting, the vessels may signal with their whistles their intention to change their courses. So, if vessel A blows one short blast on her whistle that is notice to B that A desires to change her course to starboard (or two blasts meaning a change of course to port.). B then signifies her understanding of A's intention to change course and B agrees to it by answering A's signal with the same number of blasts sent by A. Then both ships navigate according to their agreement. If B does not consent to the proposal of A, B blows a danger signal of not less than four short blasts on her whistle. *B* never "cross signals" by answering *A*'s one blast with two by *B*. The ship violating any of these provisions will probably be held responsible for the collision.

Salvage claims. These arise when a vessel has suffered some casualty at sea and is in need of assistance from some other vessel in order to prevent further damage or complete loss. The services rendered by the *salvor*, the assisting vessel, are rendered either on a contractual or a voluntary basis. If on a contractual basis, admiralty courts will examine the terms of the contract and the sums to be paid to be sure that the agreement was not made under duress occasioned by the difficulty from which the injured ship was suffering at the time.

Salvage is voluntary when not performed according to prior agreement. Such an instance would be if the vessel were abandoned and there was a real and imminent peril to the ship requiring assistance. The success of the salvage service is another necessary element to a salvage award. In the case of voluntary salvage, the courts are liberal in rewarding a salvor. Salvage cannot be claimed by those persons who owe a duty to the distressed ship, such as her master and crew. When the master of a vessel stays aboard to the last possible moment, it is for the purpose of placing the salvage charges on a contractual basis rather than abandoning vessel and having the courts award very liberal salvage claims on grounds that the services were performed voluntarily by the salvor. The salvor of a vessel does not acquire title to the salved vessel but only the right to assert a lien on the vessel for his services.

Status of seaman. The status of a seaman aboard a vessel was materially changed by the Merchant Marine Act of 1920, known as the Jones Act. In cases of injury or death prior to passage of the Act, a seaman was held by court decision to have been a fellow servant in relation to the other seaman whose act may have caused the injury. The injured seaman was considered to have accepted such risks as a part of his employment. He was therefore denied recovery for injury caused by negligence of the master or any member of the crew under this "fellow servant doctrine." Under the Jones Act the seaman's rights were given the same status as were provided for railway employees under the Federal Employers' Liability Act of 1908, which provided that the employer is liable to the injured employee (or in case of death, to the employee's survivor) for damages due in whole or part to the negligence of other employees or to the employer's negligence in the supply of equipment and appliances. The right of recovery is *in personam* against the carrier or ship owner, and not *in rem against the ship.*

The ship operator must make his ship seaworthy by the exercise of due diligence and furnish the proper tools for carrying out the duties of a seaman. Thus one seaman recovered for injuries sustained when he used a carving knife to serve hard ice cream and cut his hand. The jury found that he had not been furnished the proper instrument. *Ferguson* vs. *Moore-McCormack Lines*, 352 U.S. 524

The Jones Act did not supercede the seaman's right to proceed against the ship in a suit *in rem* for wages, maintenance and medical attention or to proceed *in personam* against the carrier or ship owner for unseaworthiness of the vessel or improper appliances.

The courts have rendered several decisions defining who are seamen under the provisions of the Jones Act. Under the statute a seaman is any person employed in any capacity on a vessel belonging to a citizen of the United States. *Sinko* vs. *LaCrosse Dredging Corp.* 352 U.S. 370 summarizes several cases determining the status of employees on ships relative their being a seaman under the Act. Is a deckhand working on a barge attached to the shore a seaman? Is a repairman on a liner, though never in transit, a seaman? Is the job of taking soundings a seaman's work? Is a harbor worker a seaman? Such issues as these are commonly met by the courts in cases hinging upon the applicability, or non-applicability —of this legislation.

International law of the sea. In addition to national legislation there is a large body of international law which is concerned with the regulation of maritime intercourse among the nations. The extent of this law, the extent of its enforcement, and the extent to which it is made a party of national law by treaty is, of course, ever changing.

At a conference of 86 nations meeting in Geneva during April 1958, five new treaties relating to the law of the sea were proposed. The proposals relate specifically to the following:

(1) The right of innocent passage of foreign ships through the undefined territorial waters of any nation and through straits used for international navigation.

(2) The need of a genuine link between ships and the nation whose flag they fly.

(3) Measures for fishery conservation on the high seas.

(4) Exclusive right of nations to explore the resources in their off-shore beds.

(5) The right of a landlocked nation to free access to the sea.

CHAPTER 18

Maritime Labor

Introduction. Labor relations in the maritime industry are subject to most of the major economic forces such as supply and demand which affect the labor market in shore industry. But in addition to these general factors labor on American merchant ships is peculiarly sensitive to government influences, direct competition from foreign labor and a traditional public contempt toward seafarers and waterfront workers.

Any study of this subject would therefore have to be made against the backdrop of these factors. The scope of this chapter is necessarily limited to the high lights of this controversial subject. A more detailed investigation of maritime labor would be rewarding to the student of ocean transportation. It is a fascinating subject just as the sea itself has been the subject of intense human interest from the dawn of history.

Nature of Seafaring and Waterfront Work. Merchant seaman have traditionally been considered irresponsible men with "a sweetheart (or wife) in every port." The public concept has been of men steering a course to the nearest bar when their ship touches a port or of longshoremen passing most of their non-working hours in gin mills. Writers have peddled this notion for years and employers, until recently, have exploited the concept to gain public support in their dealings with their maritime employees.

The truth is that seafarers and longshoremen are not much different from other laborers who work with manual skills such as plumbers, bricklayers, truck drivers or electricians. Anyone who has attended conventions of industry officials, salesmen or other management workers of virtually any type of occupation except the professions, will find this group not dissimilar in their basic interests from any other group.

One of the heritages from sailing ship days that still persists even in this day of nuclear propulsion for ships is that the common seaman should be considered as a ward of the government. He was so recognized in the last century and this concept has contributed to the general misconception of his occupation which the seafarer resents very much.

A good part of the militancy in maritime labor relations and the aggressive union activities aboard ships and ashore stem from an effort to prove that seafarers and dock workers are not second class citizens, that they are justly entitled to the privileges and respect acorded all American citizens.

Other factors have played an important role in the tumultuous course of maritime labor history in recent years. These include the youthfulness of the average seafarers and also the high turnover in the labor force as men desert the sea for work ashore. The casual character of the work itself and the confining nature of life aboard ship are other factors. All contribute toward the seafarers' restlessness, his determination to make economic gains at any cost and his loyalty to his union rather than to his employer.

Maritime work either at sea or ashore is by nature casual. A ship requires employees only when it is sailing or when it is being loaded or discharging cargo. Each voyage is a new commercial venture. Unless a ship is working, employment aboard it ceases. Ships frequently are laid up, creating temporary unemployment. There are few businesses which have more violent ups and downs than shipping.

Life at sea is like living in a world apart for crew members. Before the ship sails they must sign articles for the voyage, technically beginning their employment. When the voyage terminates, they sign off. Of course, the majority of a crew remains with the ship for subsequent voyages but this signing-on and signing-off process creates employment conditions found in no shore industry.

Seamen voluntarily remain ashore in preference to immediately shipping out again, looking to their union for future employment rather than to the owner of their last ship.

At sea every member of a ship's crew is by law subject to the absolute authority of the master. This abnormal condition also is a heritage of sailing ship days but there are sound reasons for maintaining such authority. There is no time during a storm or other threatening danger for a master to debate his orders with subordinates or to hold counsel with his officers. When an order is given it must be obeyed promptly. The very life of the ship and its crew may depend on the instantaneous execution of a command.

This does not mean that a master can abuse his privileges. He is still subject to civilian law which may be invoked when his ship reaches port.

Waterfront employment also is casual in nature because it depends on a ship being in port to take on or discharge cargo. When there are no ships in port there is no employment for most dock workers. This factor has tended to make pier workers more loyal to their union than their employers because they can count on their union to secure them other work when employment in one particular area slackens.

Government Influence in Maritime Labor Relations. The government has a big stake in its merchant marine. Many consider the commercial fleet a fourth arm of the nation's defense after the Army, Navy and Air Force. Without merchant vessels, skillfully manned, to carry supplies to the fighting fronts all over the world, the three other branches would be helpless.

A merchant fleet is also necessary during peacetime. The nation's foreign trade depends on vessels for carrying its products abroad. The United States has become a have not nation in recent years for many essential raw materials, notably ores and petroleum. Again ships must be available to maintain a constant flow of such materials to American ports. During World War I and, to some extent, World War II, freight rates rose to exorbitant levels before this nation entered either war because it had been dependent upon foreign vessels for its peacetime trade.

For this reason the government exercises closer supervision over maritime affairs than over most shore industry. The object of this interest is to assure an adequate force of skilled seamen, waterfront workers and ship-building labor in any emergency. The government properly considers such a labor force as vital to its defense and economic wellbeing as the merchant ships they man.

Ship Subsidies. The government long has recognized that costs are higher on American than on foreign ships. Yet the American ship owner must compete directly with foreign vessels on the high seas.

To encourage investment in and operation of a privately-owned American merchant fleet, the government has followed a policy of aiding owners agreeing to certain operating conditions. Before 1936 this aid was in the form of mail contracts and other indirect assistance. This type of aid was found to be unsatisfactory.

The Merchant Marine Act of 1936 provided for direct subsidies to American ships sailing in specified trade routes found to be essential to the commerce of the United States. To obtain subsidies shipowners must contract to maintain modern commercial vessels in such services and to employ American labor in repairing and operating them.

Subsidies are limited to dry cargo and passenger vessels operated in the essential routes. Thus, only 300 vessels are subsidized in the nation's oceangoing fleet of some 1,000 ships. The limitation has excluded tankers and bulk carriers, posing a serious problem for American owners of such vessels which also are operated in direct competition with foreign ships carrying lower paid crews. American owners have tended to meet this problem by registering their vessels under flags of friendly foreign nations, principally Panama and Liberia. This will be discussed later.

Government Jurisdiction. The government maintains direct supervision over maritime labor, exercising this function principally through the United States Coast Guard. This government agency acts as a licensing bureau and polices its permits. The master and all officers of any American merchant vessel must secure their licenses from the Coast Guard which administers examinations. Unlicensed seamen obtain credentials in a similar manner attesting to their experience ratings. A Coast Guard shipping commissioner signs on a crew for a vessel before it may sail to determine whether it is properly manned.

Perhaps more important is the Coast Guard's authority to suspend or revoke the license or papers of officers and seamen. This is done, however, only for flagrant violation of specific rules and regulations pertaining to the sea and after hearings. On the whole, the Coast Guard has acted in judicious fashion and has not unduly interfered in any collective bargaining relationships between ship management and labor.

Government interest in maritime labor is also expressed directly through training programs. It maintains the United States Merchant Marine Academy at Kings Point, Long Island, and contributes annually toward four state academies which also train deck and engine officers for merchant vessels.

The government has operated extensive maritime training facilities when war emergencies created a shortage of seafarers. Recently the government embarked on a special radar training program to acquaint officers of merchant ships with the proper method of using this effective, but frequently misused aid to navigation.

Labor Legislation. Maritime labor is subject to the same legislation as other labor unless specifically excluded. Considerable special legislation exists pertaining only to seafaring labor. It has been this Federal legislation which has created a climate in which seagoing and waterfront workers have made their greatest economic gains.

Passage of the National Industrial Recovery Act in 1933, followed by the National Labor Relations Act of 1935, made it possible for maritime unions of shore and seagoing labor to revive after being moribund for almost fourteen years. Provision of the labor acts enabled militant unions of such workers to force, for the first time, full recognition by employers of collective bargaining demands.

The first great legislative gain by seafarers was the Seamen's Act of 1916, passed despite tremendous employer opposition. This law prohibited practices which fostered the existence of crimp boarding houses and set a precedent by requiring, as a safety measure, that crews of American merchant vessels be able to comprehend the language in which orders were given.

This put an effective brake on the practice by shipowners of employing foreign crews, particularly Orientals, in lowest skilled ratings and tended to encourage a larger percentage of American citizenship among crew members. It was a preliminary step toward current legislation which requires that 90 per cent of the crew of any subsidized American ship be composed of United States citizens. The same law limits employment of non-citizens on American flag unsubsidized ships to 25 per cent of a ship's complement.

Such requirements have had far-reaching effects in the growth of militant maritime labor unions.

The Maritime Work Force.   Work performed in the maritime industry probably calls for more diversified skills than any other industry. At sea a ship is a self-contained community. There is no opportunity to send out for a carpenter, plumber, pipe-fitter or other technician if he is suddenly needed. He must be aboard.

Ashore the industry calls for less variety but here the range is still great, particularly in shipbuilding. Even in loading and unloading cargo there is need for specialized labor.

The work force on a merchant ship is divided into three basic departments: deck, engine and stewards. The deck department handles ship navigation and also supervises stowage of cargo. The engineer personnel operate the ship's power plant, electrical generators, air conditioning plants and other apparatus. The stewards look after the feeding of the crew and general housekeeping.

Some concept of the variety of skills going into the smooth functioning of a ship may be obtained from the table on page 169. The employment figures also indicate the casual nature of shipboard labor.

The number in any ship crew depends largely on the size of the vessel and upon its function. A typical freighter carries a crew of about forty men; a passenger liner like the United States employs almost 1,000, the majority in the stewards department. A tanker requires more men than a freighter because maintenance of the vessel's special pumping equipment requires special manpower.

Rating	All ports		Atlantic and Gulf Coasts ports		West Coast ports	
	Number of seamen	Average days worked	Number of seamen	Average days worked	Number of seamen	Average days worked
All seamen (except pursers and reliefmen)	85,541	212	63,976	215	19,885	201
All licensed seamen	16,308	233	10,889	231	3,739	238
Deck department	7,999	235	4,684	236	1,635	236
Masters	1,004	254	714	250	290	263
Chief mates	1,262	255	927	253	335	261
Second mates	1,339	244	1,044	245	395	242
Third mates	1,604	227	1,209	228	395	223
Fourth mates	1,060	198	765	199	—	193
Radio officers	1,680	234	—	—	—	—
Engine department	8,309	231	6,205	228	2,104	239
Chief engineers	1,378	259	1,106	254	272	279
First assistant engineers	1,354	243	1,026	240	328	251
Second assistant engineers	1,842	232	1,402	225	440	254
Third assistant engineers	1,834	231	1,386	230	448	233
Junior third assistant engineers	1,437	201	917	193	520	216
Licensed junior engineers	456	201	—	—	—	—
All unlicensed seamen	69,233	207	53,087	211	16,146	193
Deck department	24,613	210	18,587	214	6,026	196
Bosuns	1,727	228	1,440	233	287	198
Carpenters	640	219	—	—	—	—
Deck maintenance	3,111	219	2,140	216	971	226
Able-bodied seamen	15,525	220	9,607	224	2,918	209
Ordinary seamen	5,866	180	4,520	192	1,346	139
Engine department	19,746	206	14,880	209	4,866	197
Electrician	1,239	222	980	228	259	201
Second electrician	662	216	—	—	—	—
Oilers	5,789	221	4,480	224	1,309	208
Firemen, water tenders	4,901	208	3,760	210	1,141	204
Wipers	5,095	177	3,820	178	1,275	175
Stewards department	24,874	205	19,620	211	5,254	186
Chief stewards, all ships	1,649	258	1,300	276	349	191
Chefs, passenger	830	261	—	—	—	—
Cooks, passenger	505	249	—	—	—	—
Cooks, dry-cargo and tanker	1,038	216	700	228	338	190
Cooks and bakers, dry-cargo and tanker	1,162	222	960	222	202	220
Assistant cooks, passenger	560	241	—	—	—	—
Assistant cooks, dry-cargo and tanker	1,202	184	860	185	342	184
Stewards, passenger	1,455	211	—	—	—	—
Waiters, passenger	1,495	187	—	—	—	—
Messmen, all ships	11,877	195	9,460	199	2,417	191
Bellboys, passenger	440	187	—	—	—	—

Source: United States Department of Labor. "The Earnings and Employment of Seamen on U.S. Flag Ships." Bulletin No. 1238, Nov. 1958.

ANNUAL EMPLOYMENT July 1, 1956—June 30, 1957

(Number of Seamen and average days of employment by selected ratings in the United States Maritime Industry)

Commercial vessels are unloaded and loaded by longshoremen although one of the ship's officers is usually on hand to see that his vessel is stowed properly. The general conception of a longshoreman as an individual whose principal asset is a strong back is becoming obsolete. The widespread use of mechanized equipment within the narrow confines of a pier requires much more skill than the ability to lift.

Longshoremen work in gangs—groups of twelve to twenty men working together as teams. In many ports dock labor is hired by such work units and productivity is computed by the amount of cargo moved by a gang. A well integrated gang is prized by shore employers who will seek them out, if possible. The tendency to discriminate in favor of such star gangs was a basic cause, during the 1930's of a large number of labor disputes. The issue is avoided today by rotary hiring and seniority systems.

Maritime Unions. Maritime labor is virtually 100 per cent organized and the unions representing seagoing and shore labor are almost as numerous as their skills. While this is an obvious exaggeration, there are many unions in the industry and their number has contributed to the confusion and turbulence that have marked its labor relations.

Union rivalry has been a major complicating factor in maritime labor relations acting to make wage and fringe costs of American ship operations higher than they otherwise would have been. In testifying before a House Merchant Marine Committee investigating the complexity of maritime labor relations, Clarence G. Morse, chairman of the Federal Maritime Board, said:*

"Chief among these factors has been the bitter and longstanding rivalry among the unlicensed unions which had led them to membership raidings and to press for more and more economic gains, each trying to outdo the other. The lack of a common collective bargaining agreement termination date has also been responsible to a large extent for a chain reaction (or whipsaw) pattern of wage increases."

*"Hearings before the Committee on Merchant Marine and Fisheries, House of Representatives," 84th Congress, 1st Session, Page 73.

The major organizations are:

International Organization of Masters, Mates and Pilots, representing deck officers working in some 5,000 jobs on ships operated from the Atlantic, Pacific and Gulf Coasts.

National Marine Engineers Beneficial Association, representing engineer officers in about 5,500 jobs on ships operated from all three coasts.

Brotherhood of Marine Officers, representing deck and engineer officers of two major ship companies covering about 600 jobs on Atlantic Coast ships.

American Radio Association, representing approximately 650 radio officers on ships operated from the three coasts.

Radio officers Union of the Commercial Telegraphers Union, representing operators on about 400 jobs on ships from the three coasts.

American Merchant Marine Staff Officers Association, representing about 150 jobs on ships operated primarily along the Pacific Coast.

Staff Officers' Association of America, representing pursers in about 220 jobs on ships operated out of Atlantic and Gulf Coasts.

National Maritime Union, representing about 24,000 unlicensed deck, engine and stewards jobs on ships operated out of the Atlantic and Gulf Coasts.

Seafarers International Union, representing deck, engine and stewards unlicensed ratings out of the Atlantic and Gulf Coasts covering some 8,500 jobs.

Sailors Union of the Pacific, representing unlicensed personnel in three departments on ships operated out of the Pacific Coast covering about 10,000 jobs. The S.U.P. is affiliated with the S.I.U.

International Longshoremen's Association, representing some 80,000 dock workers on the Atlantic and Gulf Coasts.

International Longshoremen's and Warehousemen's Union representing some 25,000 dock workers on the Pacific Coast.

International Brotherhood of Longshoremen, uncertified rival of the I.L.A. with an uncertain membership.

In addition there are a number of independent unions for seagoing personnel, tugboat workers union and steamship office workers unions. The principal shipyard union is the Industrial Union of Marine and Shipbuilding Workers of America. This union has enjoyed marked stability in its collective bargaining relations. The general pattern for its negotiations has usually been set by the steel workers' bargaining negotiations rather than other maritime organizations. Shipyard labor and the smaller unions will not be treated further in this chapter.

Employer Groups. The lack of unity among maritime labor unions in recent years has been closely matched by employers. At one time waterfront management sought to play off one union against another. Unions picked up this technique rapidly and have become as skillful as management in applying it today.

The field of employer operations is the major reason for diverging resistence to labor demands. Subsidized companies have been accused, with some justification, of being softer in labor bargaining than unsubsidized ship lines which cannot pass off any increased labor costs to the government. Operators of tankers and ore ships find it expedient to conclude a swift agreement rather than run the risk of tying up an entire steel or petroleum industry of which they are only a small part.

West Coast ship operators have different labor problems than their colleagues on the East and Gulf Coasts. Efforts to persuade Pacific and Atlantic Coast operators to unite into one industry-wide bargaining unit have failed.

The principal employer groups dealing with seagoing labor are:

The American Merchant Marine Institute, representing a majority of the ship companies operating out of the Atlantic and Gulf Coasts. Actual negotiations are conducted by committees which may include some members who are not in the institute. None of the companies is bound by an agreement until it signs a separate contract with a union with which it has been negotiating. The AMMI deals with the N.M.U. for unlicensed crew members and with virtually all the unions representing licensed officers. Another loose group negotiates with the S.I.U. for Atlantic and Gulf Coast ships.

The Pacific Maritime Association represents American flag ship companies on the West Coast. Unlike the AMMI, the agree-

ments negotiated by PMA are binding on all companies authorizing PMA to bargain in their behalf. Contracts are executed by
PMA officials rather than by representatives of its member companies.

Separate employer groups in each Atlantic Coast port technically bargain with their dock workers for the area. However, the
general pattern for wages and other major issues is set by agreements reached between the I.L.A. and the New York Shipping
Association. This association, composed of 170 steamship and
stevedore companies bargains for foreign as well as American
employers. In its 1957 agreement with the NYSA, the International
Longshoremen's Association won coastwise bargaining on wages
hours, pension and welfare issues. This has started a trend within
the industry to concentrate all dock workers' bargaining for the
Atlantic and Gulf Coast in New York negotiations.

West Coast bargaining for longshoremen has been on an industry-wide basis since 1939. The employers group on the West
Coast, however, has gone through reorganization several times
in the last quarter century. Dock employers on the coast today are
represented by the Pacific Maritime Association.

Wages. Through militant union action the wages of American maritime workers have climbed further and more rapidly in
the last twenty years than those of any other nation's maritime
toilers. The take home pay has increased from 250 to 350 per cent
for seagoing labor while dock workers' pay has gone up 266 per
cent.

With increased wages workers have demanded and received
other forms of compensation unknown in the shipping industry
before World War II. Overtime has become an integral part of the
take-home pay of every American mariner, estimated at 40 per
cent of his over all wages. The work-week at sea has been reduced
to forty hours in five days. Since ships continue to sail seven days
a week, overtime must be paid for the work performed on the
two other days.

Maritime workers ashore and afloat now enjoy pensions, welfare plans and paid vacations, all paid from funds maintained by
employer contributions computed by the number of man hours
worked on each owner's ships.

In 1939 an able bodied seaman, the typical skilled unlicensed rating aboard American vessels, received $72.50 a month, his berth and board aboard ship and virtually no overtime. Today this rating calls for a base pay of $353.27 a month plus an overtime rate of $2.18 an hour. Overtime and penalty pay for doing work outside the scope of his regular duties has brought the able seaman's monthly wages nearer to $600.

A master of a freighter in 1939 received $350 a month, a chief engineer $310. Today the same ratings call for $1,280.78 and $1,175, respectively. Marine publications report that the master's wages on a typical British freighter would compare unfavorably with those of an ordinary seaman on the same size American merchant ship.

The table below, compiled from records of the American Merchant Marine Institute for East Coast seamen, illustrates the advances in basic wage costs for seafarers on American flag ships since 1941. The figures for mariners sailing from the West Coast are not much different.

MONTHLY BASE PAY FOR TYPICAL SHIP RATINGS IN 1941 AND 1958

Rating	1941	1958
Master	$350	$1,280.78
Chief Officer	205	710.35
Third Mate	160	578.23
Chief Engineer	310	1,175.10
1st Assistant Engineer	205	710.67
3d Assistant Engineer	160	579.15
Radio Officer	143.75	579.39
Chief Radio Officer	176	704.29
Boatswain	95	472.68
Able Seaman	82.50	353.27
Ordinary Seaman	65	274.37
Electrician	180	560.96
Oiler	92.50	353.27
Fireman	82.50	353.27
Chief Steward	130	460.96
Chief Cook	115	417.06
Messman	70	272.27

A study of "The Earnings and Employment of Seamen on

TABLE A-1. AVERAGE DAILY EARNINGS

(Average daily earnings of seamen manning seagoing ships in the
United States Maritime Industry by rating.

RATING	Number of seamen	Average daily earnings	All Ports Average daily premium Hours	Earnings
All seamen (except masters and cadets)	44,785	$20.19	2.8	$ 6.21
All licensed seamen	9,627	$29.80	2.8	$ 8.21
Deck department	4,820	29.04	3.2	9.22
Chief mates	882	35.94	3.3	10.59
Second mates	895	29.43	3.3	9.48
Third mates	903	27.64	3.3	9.19
Fourth mates	618	26.13	3.3	9.17
Radio officers	980	27.61	3.1	9.08
Chief pursuers, passenger	83	30.39	2.7	8.61
Pursers, dry-cargo and tanker	272	23.04	1.5	4.54
Assistant pursers, passenger	104	26.03	3.5	11.17
Engine department	4,807	30.56	2.5	7.19
Chief engineers	889	39.14	.5	1.87
First assistant engineers	881	35.09	3.1	9.64
Second assistant engineers	915	29.17	3.1	8.90
Third assistant engineers	992	26.87	2.9	8.16
Junior third assistant engineers	780	25.06	2.8	7.71
Licensed junior engineers	305	23.10	2.2	5.90
All unlicensed seamen	35,158	17.56	2.8	5.66
Deck department	13,709	16.70	2.8	5.28
Bosuns	908	22.44	3.1	6.97
Carpenters	429	21.48	2.9	6.85
Deck maintenance	1,656	18.96	2.6	5.88
Able-bodied seamen	5,503	19.50	3.3	7.30
Ordinary seamen	2,560	14.83	3.1	5.41
Engine department	10,095	17.34	2.4	5.00
Unlicensed junior engineers	308	16.94	1.2	2.51
Electricians	667	24.23	2.6	6.15
Second electricians	510	22.97	2.6	6.36
Engine maintenance	230	16.38	1.5	3.18
Oilers	2,720	17.38	2.9	5.93
Firemen, water tenders	2,749	17.56	3.0	6.13
Wipers	2,224	12.77	1.2	2.02
Stewards department	11,354	18.80	3.2	6.71
Chief stewards, passenger	50	32.04	4.0	8.64
Chief stewards, dry-cargo and tanker	833	22.94	3.2	6.99
Second stewards, passenger	65	26.19	4.7	10.18
Chefs, passenger	72	31.54	4.6	10.38
Cooks, passenger	358	24.39	3.8	8.39
Cooks, dry cargo and tanker	856	20.59	2.8	6.01
Cooks and bakers, dry-cargo & tanker	759	19.86	2.7	5.94
Assistant cooks, passenger	246	21.79	3.8	8.10
Assistant cooks, dry-cargo and tanker	857	18.49	2.7	5.85
Stewards, passenger	1,108	14.78	2.9	4.77
Waiters, passenger	1,103	15.51	3.3	5.50
Messmen, all ships	5,799	14.10	2.6	4.31
Bellboys, passenger	208	14.04	3.1	5.06

U. S. Flag Ships," recently completed by the United States Department of Labor (Bulletin 1238) reported that seamen, excluding masters and cadets, on United States flag vessels in May, 1957, had average daily earnings of $20.19. The average daily base pay amounted to $13.75 with "nearly all of the remainder accounted for by premium (overtime and penalty) pay practices in the industry."

Premium payments cover various forms of work done during regular working hours at sea as well as overtime. It may consist of war risk bonuses for sailing in dangerous waters, payment for extra services on passenger ships, penalty pay for sailing on vessels carrying dangerous or disagreeable cargo or for failure by the company to provide clean linen at specified intervals.

While the increase in longshoremen's wage rate has not been so precipitous, it has been substantial. With these increases has come more steady employment and the establishment of pension, welfare and vacation funds. In 1937, when the upward climb of longshore wage rates began, the hourly scale on the North Atlantic Coast was $1.05. A premium rate of $1.60 an hour was paid for week ends or work before 8 a.m. and after 5 p.m. on week days. On the West Coast the rates were 95 cents an hour for straight time during week days and $1.40 for overtime. The regular work day on the West Coast is only six hours, giving the longshoreman an extra two hours of overtime in a eight-hour working day.

In 1959 rates in the North Atlantic Ports had climbed to $2.80 an hour for straight time and $4.20 an hour for overtime. On the West Coast they are $2.63 an hour for straight time and $3.94½ for overtime.

Historical Background. The history of maritime labor has been marked by frequent, bitter and sometimes bloody clashes. As mentioned before, as many as 1,400 strikes, work stoppages and job actions occurred on the West Coast between 1934 and 1950 while East Coast pier and off-shore labor relations were high lighted by gang warfare and wildcat strikes as well as authorized work stoppages.

On both coasts ideological forces and union rivalries contributed to the tumult and confusion. Indeed, these factors have been as important as regular collective bargaining issues in prompting aggressive and militant union activities which have produced tremendous gains in wages, working conditions, fringe benefits and union security.

Underlying the strike has been the unions' and the workers' determination to control the hiring of dock and seagoing labor. Secondary, but also of fundamental importance, is the desire of the individual seaman or dock worker to prove he is a "first class citizen" by attaining the dignity of financial security.

From the poorly paid, overworked, underfed and frequently despised laborers of 1933, the maritime workers on sea and shore have emerged as affluent citizens, secure in their jobs through the protection of their unions.

Early Beginning. Although seamen's and longshoremen's unions have existed since the middle of the nineteenth century, they made little progress in collective bargaining before World War I. Initial organizational efforts were mostly successful on the West Coast where a shortage of manpower plus dependence on ships for coastwise trade created conditions where the demands of labor at least had to be heard.

The oldest seafaring union was organized by the marine engineers in 1875. The Sailors Union of the Pacific was created as the first seamen's union in 1885. The movement spread to the East Coast in the 1890's when the National Seamen's Union was organized. This union affiliated a year later with the American Federation of Labor and in 1895 changed its name to the International Seamen's Union.

The International Longshoremen's Association traces its beginnings to the 1890's when it began organizing on the Atlantic and later the Gulf and Pacific Coasts.

The first agreement between the Sailors Union of the Pacific and coastwise employers was signed in 1902. This was one year after longshore unions had suffered a bad setback in a strike in San Francisco. Five were killed and 336 injured in violence during the unsuccessful strike. In 1916 West Coast longshoremen walked out again and were decisively defeated.

But 1916 was a favorable year for seagoing labor. It was then that Congress passed the Seamen's Act, due largely to the persistent work of Andrew Furuseth, a pioneer seamen's labor leader. This act set certain standards for crews of American ships and halted some of the abuses of seamen's rights. The act also required that 75 per cent of the crew of any American ship be required to understand orders in the language given. This discouraged the use of Orientals and other foreigners as strikebreakers.

The outbreak of World War I also enabled organized maritime labor to make some gains. In August, 1917, a collective bargaining agreement was signed by Atlantic Coast shipowners, the United States Shipping Board and the International Seamen's Union. But this and subsequent agrements during the war were largely shotgun weddings betwen labor and management with the government holding the gun.

Collapse of Unionism. In 1920 the government lost interest in maintaining labor peace in the shipping industry. A year later employers severed relations with all unions and a strike to force recognition and to obtain improved wages was an utter failure. For the next thirteen years union membership decreased and ship owners and stevedore employers were in complete control of their industry.

During this period the worst abuses of labor revived. Overtime was eliminated, wages were reduced, speed-ups were enforced by discriminatory employment practices and blacklisting of labor for suspected union activity became common. Crimp joints (boarding houses where seafaring labor was recruited by encouraging men to go into debt to the boarding house owners) became important sources of new manpower.

The shipowners established Marine Service Bureaus for employment of seamen. The seafarers were required to carry discharge books on which their conduct in previous jobs was noted. The unions condemned these as "fink books" and the process as blacklisting.

The Jones-White Act of 1928, gave seaferers a little aid by providing that at least 50 per cent of the crews on ships receiving mail subsidies must be American citizens. But the oncoming depression eliminated the advantages this provision held forth. Competition for work, any kind of work, enabled shipowners to hire Americans as work-aways for the food and shelter they received on the ships. Able seamen were paid as little as $30 a month on some vessels. Food was poor, crew quarters and sanitary conditions rivaled the cramped conditions of the sailing ship era.

Contemporaries reported that conditions on the piers were "uncontrolled." A union statement in 1936 charged that the speed-up was practiced to reduce overtime and that longshoremen were often expected to run back for their next loads. Competition between gangs was encouraged with the result that men complained of an increase in accidents and deaths.

Revival of Unions. Such conditions set the stage for a resurgence of maritime unionism. The National Industrial Recovery Act provided the trigger. In calling for creation of "self-government industry codes" of prices, wages, hours and working conditions, the statute proclaimed the right of employees to bargain collectively without discrimination.

Union membership increased and by early 1934 the West Coast longshoremen, again under the banner of the International Longshoremen's Association, demanded an end to the shape-up, hiring through union controlled hiring halls and improved wages, hours and working conditions. Employers rejected the demands precipitating a strike despite government mediation efforts. A week after the dock workers quit they were joined by West Coast seamen's unions.

An employer attempt to break the strike resulted in the killing of two strikers and injuries to more than 100. Martial law was proclaimed by California's governor while teamster unions set the call for a general strike that would have crippled all business along the coast. Public revulsion against employer tactics caused management to offer arbitration which was accepted by the striking unions.

The arbitrators abolished the shape-up, substituting a union-employer controlled hiring hall. This broke the power of management to control hiring and reposed it in the union through selection of the dispatchers. The union instituted a rotary hiring system that still is being used on the West Coast in hiring dock labor.

The Sailors Union of the Pacific was not far behind in securing its union hiring hall and within a short time the employer Marine Service Bureaus were abolished.

Stimulated by the success of West Coast unions, rank-and-file groups in the moribund International Seamen's Union set up demands for similar gains. Led by Joseph Curran, some of the rank-

and-filers staged a sit-down strike on the Intercoastal liner *California*. While this strike failed as far as winning for the strikers their immediate demands, it pointed up dissatisfaction in the I.S.U. ranks with the union's conservative leadership.

The dissatisfaction came to a head when the leaders denounced Curran's group as mutineers and signed a contract with East Coast shipowners without consulting the union's membership. By 1937 Curran and his followers, through a series of sit-down strikes and other job action, had taken over the leadership of a majority of East Coast seamen, established the National Maritime Union and affiliated it with the Congress of Industrial Organizations.

As the I.S.U. passed out of existence, another remnant not sympathetic with Curran's aims organized the Seafarers International Union as an A.F.L. affiliate. This East Coast union has been as militant as the N.M.U. in securing economic gains for its members and rivalry between the two organizations has induced each to make demands which the other has felt called upon to equal or surpass.

The Hiring Hall. As one of its first demands the N.M.U. asked for and won the union hiring hall but the shipowners did not surrender readily. The first N.M.U. hiring hall was opened in 1938, two years after the Sailors Union of the Pacific had put theirs in operation. The Seafarers International Union on the East Coast had its own hiring hall soon after the N.M.U. Shipowners were still actively opposing union operation of hiring halls in 1941 and, in 1948, used the Taft-Hartley ban on the closed shop as another lever to win a part in managing the hiring of seamen. The attempt failed when all maritime unions struck on this principal issue.

The licensed officers were the last to gain control over the hiring of deck officers or engineers, their victory being deferred until after World War II. Today all American merchant ship crews, with the exception of Military Sea Transportation Service vessels, are hired through union hiring halls. The companies are guaranteed full selection of masters and chief engineers but must accept the unions' candidates for all other ratings unless they can produce a sound cause for rejecting candidates.

The net effect of this procedure is to make the seafarer loyal first to his union. The hiring halls are operated on a rotary basis. An unemployed seaman submits his card at the hall when he wishes to accept employment. As a job is posted, the man who have been the foundations of union successes in improving wages

The hiring halls and the union loyalty they have encouraged have been the foundations of union successes in improving wages and working conditions of their members. Leaders have carefully maintained impartial operation of these halls, a principle that has helped them continue in power.

Recently the unions and employers have worked out a seniority system under which seafarers are classified according to their length of service. A class A man, who has been going to sea for ten years would have preference for a berth over a class B man with only three years experience although the class B man may have been longer without a job.

Communist Influences. Communist ideology played a dominant role in maritime labor relations from 1935 until 1948. It was during this period that the West Coast experienced its greatest labor turbulence culmininating in an all-out fight in 1948 by employers against the longshoremen's union on an ideological issue. The employers lost their battle to oust suspected union leaders but won the war in that the settlement of the devastating strike produced a "new look" and stability in labor relations that has lasted since.

Two attempts were made betwen 1935 and 1948 to organize maritime labor on a nation-wide basis. Both attempts failed as leaders backed away from Communist influences.

The Communists gained their foothold among predominantly conservative Catholic and anti-Communist labor during the period of employer exploitation on the waterfronts prior to 1934. In this the trend was similar to that existing in other industrial fields. When the government set the stage for maritime unions to make their comeback, the leaders who took over from ultra-conservative union officers accepted help from virtually any source without asking many questions about political beliefs.

Employer resistance on the Pacific Coast to the resurgence of the International Longshoremen's Association brought to the front in 1934 a young rank-and-filer, Harry Renton Bridges. Another rank-and-filer, Harry Lundeberg, was rising fast in the Sailors Union of the Pacific. An alliance and later antagonism between these men did more to shape the course of events in West Coast maritime history than any other force.

Bridges and his lieutenants were conducting a life-and-death struggle for recognition in 1934 when Joseph P. Ryan, president of the I.L.A., arrived from the East Coast to take command of a bitter strike. The conservative Ryan formulated a compromise agreement with the employers which Bridges and his men rejected as a "sell-out." Ryan returned to the East Coast and Bridges went on to win.

In 1935 Bridges and Lundeberg formed the Maritime Federation of the Pacific, an organization that encompassed all West Coast maritime unions. The 1936 strike was conducted by the federation and turned out to be a success. However, when it ended a widening rift betwen Bridges and Lundeberg caused the latter to take the Sailors Union of the Pacific out of the federation. Lundeberg charged that Bridges and his supporters were motivated by Communist ideology and affiliated his union with the A.F.L. From then on the S.U.P. became a business union, interested solely in the benefits it could obtain for its members.

Bridges led almost all West Coast longshoremen out of the I.L.A. to form the International Longshoremen's and Warehousemen's Union in 1937 after Ryan refused assistance to the Pacific Coast strike effort. Bargaining relations were almost non-existent betwen Bridges union and employers from the union's inception. What agreements were obtained came about chiefly through government mediation and intercession. The union followed a policy of encouraging contract violations whenever a grievance arose.

It was during this period, until 1948, that almost 1,400 work stoppages of various lengths occurred on the Pacific Coast. Employers contended that union irresponsibility was prompted by the Communist ideology and pointed to waterfront labor's high productviity during World War II, after Russia was attacked, as partial proof of their contention.

In 1946 Bridges and a group of other C.I.O. maritime unions formed the Committee for Maritime Unity. Bridges and Curran were co-chairmen of the group. Within less than a year after its formation Curran had backed out of the C.M.U. and began instead a three-year struggle within his National Maritime Union to rid it of Communist influences. By 1949 Curran had succeeded and all East Coast maritime labor could be said to be comparatively free of open Communist protagonists.

The showdown battle on the West Coast began as a strike on Sept. 2, 1948, after the I.L.W.U. and the employers had almost reached an agreement through bargaining. As the work stoppage progressed, the employers issued public statements that they would refuse henceforth to bargain with any longshore leaders who would not sign affidavits provided under the Taft-Hartley law affirming that they were not Communists. Since many reputable labor leaders had already refused to sign such affidavits on grounds of principle, the issue produced an impasse from which the employers had to retreat. The C.I.O. stepped into the deadlock, aided by a businessmen's group, and their combined efforts brought a compromise agreement.

The pact found Bridges still in control of the I.L.W.U. while the employer bargainers were organized with more reasonable men in control. New grievance machinery was adopted in the new pact and scrupulous observance of this machinery by management and labor has led to more than a decade of unprecedented waterfront peace on the West Coast. Bridges union was later expelled by the C.I.O. as Communist dominated but no effort was made to replace it, a concession to Bridges' control.

Gangsters and Racketeers. As president of the I.L.A. Joseph P. Ryan dedicated his leadership to fighting the infiltration of Communism on the waterfront of the East Coast. In this he was eminently successful but he failed utterly to combat an almost equally destructful element—gangsters and racketeers.

Ryan's administration of the International Longshoremen's Association was similar in many respects to the rule of a king during the Middle Ages. The I.L.A. consisted of a group of independent locals which administered most of their affairs autonomously from the national office. Each local leader was boss of his own domain owing allegiance to the I.L.A. president just as a feudal baron owned allegiance to his king. And Ryan, like many feudal kings, was unable to get more than lip service from his followers.

This loose organization and the mutual resistance by Ryan and employers to any change in the shape-up system of hiring pier workers combined to provide a fertile field for the infiltration of gangsters. While Ryan was guarding the front door against the Communists, the racketeers were sneaking in the back way.

The control of hiring was the foundation of the labor racketeer's power. Without any system of seniority or rotary hiring, the employer could theoretically select his workers at the morning shape-up. Actually the hiring boss who selected the workers was a union member dominated by the racketeers who controlled the piers. Thus the man who sought work was expected to pay tribute in the form of kickbacks, patronize the local gangsters' loan sharks or bookmakers and assist the dock ruler in cargo pilferage schemes or even more serious crime.

Criminals graduated from the penitentiary to the docks. Gangsters waged bloody warfare for power. They made unilateral agreements with employers at a price, agreements which were enforced by "quickie" strikes called at the whim of the gang boss.

The employers, fearing rotary hiring as practiced on the West Coast, made no serious effort to resist increasing demands of racketeers. They worked with Ryan and, in return, the I.L.A. continued the shape-up system of hiring dock labor.

Rebellion against Ryan and the abuses began to take form in 1945 with an unsuccessful wildcat strike in New York. This was followed by another attempt to discredit Ryan in 1948. The most serious walkout occurred in 1950 when rebels closed the Port of New York for almost a month demanding the reopening of an agreement reached by Ryan which they charged was a "sell-out." The immediate objective was lost, the men returned to work under the obnoxious agreement but only after a fact-finding committee had been appointed to examine the entire waterfront situation.

The fact-finding committee's devastating report led to an investigation of the New York waterfront by the state's crime commission. Its report so shocked the public that the Legislatures of New York and New Jersey passed, with only one dissenting vote, a compact to establish a bi-state Waterfront Commission to wrest control of the piers from racketeers.

The Waterfront Commission of New York Harbor. The bi-state law gave this unique organization far-reaching powers intended to rid the piers of any persons considered to be objectionable to the public health and welfare. It had authority to register all longshoremen and to deny registration, after hearings, to men who were considered dangerous to law and order. It also had power to license hiring bosses, pier superintendents and stevedore companies which had to pass even more rigid standards than the dock workers. Unregistered longshoremen and unlicensed employers were not permited to work on the piers.

In the first year of its operations, beginning in December, 1953, the commission barred more than fifty hiring agents and about 600 longshoremen from waterfront employment because of their police records. On the other hand, it permitted several thousand men with criminal records to continue to work on the piers with the understanding that any misstep would bar them from future employment.

The I.L.A. conducted a persistent fight against the agency but lost every round in the courts and on the piers. By 1956 it had come to accept the agency and called off the work stoppages and demonstrations it had conducted to harass its operations. However, the union is continuing to fight the existence of such a bureau as a matter of principle. In this it has the support of many other labor organizations who fear the extension of such powers as a government effort to regiment labor.

Bargaining Elections. In an effort to clean labor's house, the American Federation of Labor expelled the erring I.L.A. in September, 1953, for corruption. It issued a temporary charter to the dissident group in New York to organize a new dock workers' union in that port and backed the group with a war chest of almost $1,000,000. I.L.A. locals in ports other than New York were invited to support the new union.

The ousted I.L.A. held an emergency convention in November, 1953, where Ryan resigned as president and William V. Bradley, president of the international union's tugboad affiliate, was installed as the new president. The majority of the I.L.A. locals voted to remain loyal to the old organization and to retain its identity as an independent, unaffiliated organization.

Thus the battle lines were drawn for three years of unprecedented turbulence on New York's waterfront. Strikes were called to combat inroads of the new union which took the name of International Brotherhood of Longshoremen. Demonstrations were also called against the Waterfront Commission. The I.L.A. received unexpected help early in its fight from John L. Lewis, president of the United Mine Workers of America. His union's loan of almost $500,000 went a long way toward the I.L.A.'s survival.

Four bargaining elections were conducted by the National Labor Relations Board to determine whether the I.L.A. or the International Brotherhood of Longshoremen should represent New York's dock workers. A victory for the brotherhood was conceded to mean a collapse of the I.L.A. as a national organization. However, the I.L.A. was victorious in each of the elections and the brotherhood eventually abandoned its effort in 1958.

The I.L.A.'s victories could be traced to three principal forces: 1. A hard core of regular work gangs attached to each pier remained loyal to the I.L.A. because they feared that a brotherhood victory would end their position of seniority in hiring dock labor; 2. A large group on the piers feared the influence of Paul Hall, head of the Seafarers International Union, who was the main support of the brotherhood's efforts; 3. A large amount of sentiment for the I.L.A. was generated because it was the underdog in concerted attacks by the A.F.L., the Waterfront Commission, the N.L.R.B. and by New York State's labor machinery.

The employers aided the I.L.A. to some degree in the long conflict The appointment of Alexander P. Chopin as head of their New York Shipping Association initiated a period of enlightened bargaining in which new grievance machinery was set up to resolve employee complaints as soon as they arose. This helped to eliminate the plague of "quickie strikes." Later the employers agreed to establishing a seniority system of employments and honest efforts were made by the union and the employers to make such a system work without resorting to rotary hiring.

During the entire conflict the I.L.A. continued to secure substantial wage and fringe benefits for its members under Bradley's leadership. This, too, tended to persuade the workers to maintain the old union as "the devil we know." Bradley also initiated some reform within the I.L.A.'s ranks to make it a more cohesive organization. Based on these reform efforts the union applied in 1959 for affiliation with the A.F.L.-C.I.O. Its application received the tacit support of Hall and other labor leaders who had been among its most bitter enemies three years previously.

Danger Warnings. The steadily mounting costs of American maritime labor have produced danger signals from two quarters. The seagoing unions have recognized both warnings and have reacted in vigorous fashion. Whether they can counteract the danger remains to be seen as this is written (1959).

The clearest warning came from the White House and from Congress. For three consecutive years the President has noted the growing expense of the nation's ship subsidy program with some alarm and has recommended that some limits be found. Congress has indicated that it is similarly alarmed. The budget submitted for 1959 was one of the largest for the post-war merchant fleet. It contained almost $150,000,000 for ship construction aid and $130,000,000 for operating subsidies. Virtually all the subsidy funds are traceable to the high costs of employing American citizens as seamen on the nation's ships.

COMPARISON OF WAGE COSTS ON
DOMESTIC AND FOREIGN SHIPS OF SIMILAR SIZE

Countries	Crew number	Costs (Monthly)
United States	48	$29,426
Denmark	43	7,990
France	47	10,274
Italy	41	7,713
Japan	56	6,273
Netherlands	55	7,567
Norway	43	7,145
United Kingdom		
White crew	54	6,444
Mixed crew	80	5,541

Source: House Committee on Merchant Marine and Fisheries, Hearings on Maritime Administration and Federal Maritime Board, 1955, Page 281.

Costs of operating American flag ships have reached a point where operators find it almost impossible to remain in business without subsidy or some other form of protection such as sailing their ships in domestic routes barred to foreign flag vessels. As explained previously, only ships operating in essential foreign trade routes carrying general cargo are eligible for subsidies. Thus operators of tankers, ore carriers or other bulk cargo ships can find no relief from high costs from this quarter.

The Effective Control Principle. Many operators of such ships have gone out of business or transferred their operations to another flag where there is more leeway in hiring crews. American owners of such ships have been concerned about this problem for more than a decade. Shortly after the end of World War II, the nation's military leaders, fearful that the country would lack adequate tanker and ore carrying tonnage as the trend toward higher American operating costs continued, evolved the effective control principle.

Under this principle American captial has been encouraged to build and operate ships to fly the flags of Panama, Liberia, Honduras and other nations closely allied with this country. American ships under these registries are declared to be under effective control of this country and available to its defense effort in the event of a future war. Meanwhile they are free of legal requirements imposed on American flag ships to hire high cost American crews.

The nation's maritime unions regard the operation of such vessels a serious threat to their security. In 1958, the Seafarers International Union and the National Maritime Union patched up a longstanding feud to begin a joint campaign against the practice of operating ships under the "flags of convenience" as the unions called them. The two unions not only secured assistance of other maritime organizations in this fight, they have also enlisted the active aid of the International Transport Workers Federation, composed of transport unions all over the world.

The American unions have adopted as their goal the organization of crews of American-owned Liberian and Panamanian flag ship to force the owners to pay equal wages and fringe benefits with American flag ships. The success of such a campaign seems to be in doubt because American owners have publicly affirmed their intention of either selling their tonnage outright or transferring it to traditional maritime nations rather than yield to the unions.

The Future. To say the future of maritime labor in this country is secure or insecure would require the services of an able soothsayer. Maritime union leadership has matured in the last twenty years and there is ample evidence that union members are aware of their responsibilities and of the dangers that face their employment.

Wage demands have become more reasonable in recent years. Several unions have passed up wage increases altogether in negotiating new agreements. Unions are seeking methods of spreading employment and still maintaining costs within reasonable bounds. But who can tell how long they will continue to do so as inflationary pressure mounts.

Management also has shown a tendency to co-operate with rather than fight their employees. Collective bargaining in 1958 was marked by only a small part of the animosity that prevailed in 1948. Employers have come to realize that a "happy ship" can be more profitable than one with a surly crew.

There are still many problems to be solved. Employers have virtually no way of getting rid of shirkers or goldbricks or malcontents. Production by longshoremen despite the "new look" on the West Coast and the reformed I.L.A. on the East Coast, has decreased. Dock workers are resisting adoption of automatic loading and unloading devices, provoking charges of featherbedding from employers. Overtime and penalty costs are still major burdens peculiar to American shipping. Regardless of their personal preference for registration under the American flag, the economic realities of costs and competition may give the American shipowner no other course than registration under "flags of necessity" whether these flags be Panamanian and Liberian or British and Norwegian.

CHAPTER 19

Ocean Shipping Via Canals

The three major canals of interest to ocean transportation are the Panama Canal, the St. Lawrence Seaway and the Suez Canal.

The Panama Canal. The Panama Canal extends across the Isthmus of Panama to connect the Atlantic and Pacific Oceans. It thus saves vessels the necessity of navigating around the southern tip of South America. In a voyage from North Pacific to North Atlantic ports on the American continent, for example, this represents a saving of 7,800 miles and many days of operation at sea.

The construction of such a canal was originally commenced by the French under Ferdinand de Lesseps, who had previously attained international fame as the successful builder of the Suez Canal. His company began work in 1880, but failed after an expenditure of some $300,000,000. In the years following the question of a canal route as between the one at Panama and one through Nicaragua was heatedly debated in the United States Congress. A majority favored the Nicaragua route. Survey estimates reported that route the more easily built into a canal, with fewer engineering uncertainties and a smaller estimated cost of construction. The choice of routes was ultimately made in favor of Panama, however, and in 1904 the United States took over the French concession and began construction.

At the present time the alternate route through Nicaragua is again a matter of Congressional concern. Development of a second canal is urged because of the heavy traffic through the existing canal and on grounds that the locks of the Panama Canal are not wide enough to accommodate the largest passenger ships and the newest navy aircraft carriers. The value of an alternate route as a matter of national defense, in case of attack upon the Panama Canal is also advanced. The Nicaragua canal originally proposed was to have been 184 miles long, including sea level sections of 46 miles on the Atlantic side and 12 miles on the Pacific side. There were to be 14 locks, 840 feet long by 84 feet wide to raise and lower the vessels from the midsection of the canal at a height of 145 feet above sea-level. A depth of 35 feet was proposed and it was estimated at that time that the canal could be built for $189,-000,000.

The Panama Canal was finished in 1914 at an expenditure of $375,000,000. It is 50 miles long including sea-level approaches of 15 miles. Ships are raised by six locks to a height at mid-section of 85 feet. The locks are 1,000 feet long and 110 feet in width. The controlling depth of the Canal is 42 feet. In passing through the canal, ships entering from the Atlantic side are further west than when they emerge on the Pacific end.

The locks are double, which permits ships to pass in both directions at the same time. Authority was given by Congress in 1939 to increase the size of the canal by adding a third lock parallel to the present locks. Construction was stopped in 1947 after an expenditure of $67,000,000. The estimate for building a sea level canal is $2,483,000,000.

In 1901, prior to the building of the canal, a treaty was negotiated between the United States and Great Britain, the Hay-Pauncefote treaty, provisions of which accorded to the United States the right to construct the canal together with full control of its management when completed. The United States agreed to use it on terms of equality. A decade later, in 1911, Congress passed the Panama Canal Act which exempted coast-wise American shipping from the payment of canal tolls. Great Britain protested this exemption as a contravention of the treaty giving equal terms to Great Britain and "all nations." The United States contended that foreign ships were excluded from U.S. coast-wise trade and therefore had no legitimate interest in what the U.S. did with their own vessels in that trade. England replied that the effect of the exemption would be to cast the burden of canal operation on foreign vessels and U.S. off-shore vessels. Congress finally repealed the exemption clause, at the urging of President Wilson, in 1914. Relatively recently the suggestion has again been made to help the American intercoastal trade by lowering the canal tolls to them while at the same time avoiding the question of discrimination against foreign vessels. As a means of accomplishing this, it is proposed that the United States government remit the tolls, which would be the unquestioned right of the government.

Canal tolls are based on the net register tonnage of the vessel and were originally set at $1.20 per ton of 100 cubic feet of the ship's cargo carrying capacity. It was estimated that the Canal's capacity was 80,000,000 tons per year and that lower rates would ultimately be granted. The present toll is $.90 per ton.

When American steamship lines several years ago petitioned the Canal Company for lower rates they were refused. The question of the rate of a toll for passage of the Canal was decided by the U.S. Supreme Court to be a matter discretionary with the Panama Canal Company, the agency designated by the United States to control and operate the canal under the Canal Zone Code. In this case, American shipping companies had brought a suit against the Company to prescribe new tolls for the use of the Canal in view of the fact that the Comptroller General of the United States had recommended a downward revision of the tolls. The Court held that under Secs. 411 and 412 of the Canal Zone Code, the Company has been authorized by Congress to change tolls to be levied and to prescribe the formula to be used in computing new tolls, and that judicial review of the Company's refusal to prescribe new tolls is barred. *Grace Line, Inc. et el. v Panama Canal Company* 356 U. S. 309 (Decided April 28, 1958).

The fiscal year ending June 30, 1958, was the best commercially in the 44 years of canal operation. A total of 9,189 commercial ocean-going vessels made the transit through the Canal. In December 1956, the one-billionth ton of cargo was carried through the Canal.

The St. Lawrence Seaway. U. S.—Canadian construction of the St. Lawrence Seaway will result in another waterway with a tremendous impact on ocean transportation. Work is underway to deepen the present 14 foot channel to an operating depth of 27 feet and to construct dams to raise the river and furnish hydro-electric power. Aside from the desirability of the additional power source, the Seaway will make it possible to bring iron ore from the new sources in Labrador and Venezuela to steel mills near the Great Lakes if and when ore from the Mesabi Range in Minnesota runs out and grain and general cargo originating in the area serviced by the Seaway can be shipped overseas without transfer. The Seaway builders claim that operation of the canal will be self-sustaining and will in time amortize the cost of construction. The original estimate of the United States' share of the cost was $87,000,000 which was raised to $135,000,000, by reason of increased building costs, but has again been re-estimated at $126,000,000.

The tolls committees for the St. Lawrence Seaway Development Corporation of the United States and the St. Lawrence Seaway Authority of Canada, have made public the proposed charges for traffic using the St. Lawrence Seaway*.

Proposed tolls for the Main Passages are broken down as follows:

For each passage through the entire seaway-Montreal to Lake Erie-a vessel will be assessed:

$0.06 a gross registered ton per vessel

$0.42 a ton for bulk cargo

$0.95 a ton for general cargo

For each passage—Montreal to or from Lake Ontario only, a vessel will be assessed:

$0.04 a gross registered ton per vessel

$0.40 a ton for bulk cargo

$0.90 a ton for general cargo

For partial transit through the seven locks between Montreal and Lake Ontario, a charge of 15% of the applicable toll for each of the locks used will be made

For each passage through the Welland Canal only, a vessel will be assessed:

$0.02 a gross registered ton per vessel

$0.02 a ton for bulk cargo

$0.05 a ton for general cargo

For partial transit, 50% of the toll irrespective of the number of locks used.

*Foreign Commerce Weekly, U. S. Department of Commerce, July 14, 1958.

The 2,000 pound ton will be the unit of weight used for assessment purposes. Passengers on commercial vessels will be charged for at the rate of $0.50 each for each lock transited.

These suggested tolls, according to the Tolls Committees, are believed to be sufficient to meet all financial requirements as the anticipated traffic develops. It is estimated that in the first year of operation traffic through the new seaway will rise to 25 million cargo tons. It is believed by the committees that by 1968 the tonnage will have risen to 50 million cargo tons.

Payments for passage of the seaway are to be made in two amounts. The proportion due Canada, 71% of the total charges, is to be made in Canadian funds. The other 29%, which is the proportion due the United States, is to be made in U. S. funds. according to the committees, the division of tolls is based upon current figures of estimated capital and operating costs and will be subject to variation as actual costs are determined.

Congress has placed the responsibility for the future operation of the United States' interests in the Seaway in a public corporation named, The St. Lawrence Seaway Development Corporation. Public Law 358–1958.

The Administrator of the Corporation has estimated that the completed Seaway will cost $450,000,000 and has made the following comparision with the seaway before being improved:

	Originally	Completed
Controlling depth of canal	14 feet	27 feet
Number of locks	21	7
Size of vessel accommodated		
length	253 feet	730 feet
breadth	44 feet	74 feet
Cargo capacity per ship	1,500 tons	25,000 tons

The Suez Canal. This vital Mid-Eastern link between the seas is 105 miles long and was built by Ferdinand de Lesseps. It was opened on November 17, 1869. In 1875 the British Prime Minister bought nearly half of the Universal Suez Canal Company shares from the Egyptian Khedive and the British shipping predominated the Canal and Britain by reason of her financial and economic interests was long recognized as the custodian of the Canal.

When opened in 1869, the Canal had a width of 177 feet at surface level and a depth of 26 feet. Today the Canal has a width of 510 feet and a depth of 46 feet, which permits the passage of vessels drawing up to 35 feet.

Typical of the distances saved by the Canal are, from Bombay to London, 4,460 miles; from Kuwait oil shipping facilities to New York, some 3,500 miles. The number of transits in 1956 was 14,666 vessels carrying 115 million tons of cargo. A convention was consumated in 1888 among maritime nations who agreed that the waterway was of economic, commercial and strategic international importance. It provided, for the benefit of all the world, that the international character of the Canal should be perpetuated for all time, irrespective of the expiration, in 1968, of the concession of the Universal Suez Canal Company.

In 1952, at the request of the Egyptian government, the British began the withdrawal of her troops guarding the Canal. Withdrawal was completed in 1956. Six weeks later the Egyptian government seized the Canal. British troops returned, and the Egypt-government by way of reprisal sank 15 ships in the Canal, effectively blocking it. In all there were 42 obstructions in the Canal. After prolonged negotiations in the United Nations, it was finally agreed to open the Canal and clear it of obstructions. The cost of clearing the Canal was estimated at $8,376,042 which was paid out of cash advanced by 11 countries. The United States contributed $5,000,000 towards that total.

The closing of the Canal caused charter rates to rise rapidly. The U.S. government formed a combination of American tankers to relieve the threatened oil shortage in Europe. Many shipyards received orders for the construction of new tankers of great size. The Canal was reopened. The orders for new tankers were delayed or cancelled. The charter rates came back down to the lowest figure in ten years. This quick cycle of events shows the importance of the Canal to world shipping and the sensitiveness of world shipping to international politics.

CHAPTER 20

World Fleets and Ports

Merchant Marine fleets of the world. Goods produced in one nation for consumption or manufacture in another may not require ocean transportation. If they do, it is the task of the world's merchant fleet to discharge this economic function. There are innumerable sources of information as to the composition and size of the merchant fleet.* The table on the page following lists the number of ocean-going vessels of 1,000 gross tons and over in the merchant fleets of the several nations listed.

U. S. foreign trade in U. S. ships. What are American objectives so far as our merchant marine is considered? The preamble of the Merchant Marine Act of 1936 states that the desirable size of the American merchant marine should be "sufficient to carry its domestic water-borne commerce and a substantial portion of the water-borne export and import commerce of the United States and to provide shipping service on all routes essential for maintaining the flow of such domestic and foreign water-borne commerce at all times."

In as much as the domestic commerce of the U. S. is restricted to American ships, the size of the fleet is purely a domestic matter. In foreign trade, the question of the size of the fleet engaged in

---

*The United States Department of Commerce has published a report on the merchant fleets of the world, entitled, *A Statistical Analysis of the World's Merchant Fleets Showing Age, Size, Speed and Draft By Frequency Groupings As of December 31, 1956.* This publication of the Maritime Administration was issued in December 1957. From this source and several others, The American Merchant Marine Institute published a Research Report on June 3, 1958, of the Merchant Fleets of the World.

WORLD MERCHANT FLEETS—VESSELS OF ALL TYPES
1939, 1958 and CURRENT CONSTRUCTION PROGRAMS

(Ocean-going vessels of 1,000 gross tons and over only)
(tonnage in 000s dwt)

I	II	III	IV	V
	In Existence		Building or	Potential
	September	January	On Order	Future Size
Country or Registry	1939	1958	Jan., 1958	(Col. III + IV)
U. S. (Private)	10,312	13,164	1,918	15,082
United Kingdom	21,857	23,724	10,006	33,730
Denmark	1,576	2,550	928	3,478
Finland	826	1,143	116	1,259
France	2,999	4,903	2,954	7,857
Germany	5,177	5,010	2,115	7,125
Greece	2,791	2,166	543	2,709
Italy	3,911	6,167	1,802	7,969
Japan	7,145	6,476	1,958	8,434
Liberia*	–	14,774	7,982	22,756
Netherlands	3,424	5,289	2,340	7,629
Norway	6,931	12,688	8,312	21,000
Panama	1,105	6,462	2,582	9,044
Spain	1,051	1,587	1,008	2,595
Sweden	2,033	4,309	1,881	6,190
U.S.S.R. #	2,204	3,584	404	3,988
Unknown	–	16	3,822	3,838
Major Countries				
Sub-total	73,342	114,012	50,671	164,683
Minor Countries	5,889	13,190	3,005	16,195
World Total	79,231	127,202	53,676	180,878

foreign commerce is to be judged by the effectiveness of foreign competition, as to what constitutes a "substantial portion" of the international commerce.

In the past typical percentages of the total of U. S. foreign commerce carried by American ships were:

1830	98.7	percent
1911-15	10.6	percent
1920	43.0	percent
1935	35.8	percent

*In 1939, Liberia had no ocean-going fleet under her registry.
#Includes Estonia, Latvia and Lithuania.

In more recent years these percentages are as follows:

U. S. OCEAN-BORNE FOREIGN DRY CARGO TRADE
Monthly Average
(Millions of Long Tons)

Year	Exports		Imports	
	Tons	Percent U. S. Flag	Tons	Percent U. S. Flag
1938	1.9	24	1.7	30
1946	4.0	71	1.4	65
1947	6.4	57	1.8	64
1948	3.8	46	2.1	55
1949	3.3	39	2.2	42
1950	2.3	36	2.5	38
1951	5.8	42	2.8	42
1952	4.9	31	2.8	42
1953	3.3	22	3.2	33
1954	3.6	23	3.2	31
1955	5.8	19	3.5	29
1956	7.7	17	4.0	27
1957	8.8	17	5.5	24
1958°	6.6	15	4.5	21

°On the basis of first 7 months only.
NOTE: Exclusive of cargo carried in military controlled vessels and trade
　　　with Canada.

From the above figures the effect of war is very evident in those years in which the United States built ships to carry their foreign commerce. During this time the fleets of other countries were engaged in the wartime service of their own nations.

The 50-50 law. The question of "substantial portion" has twice been raised in connection with administering the U. S. foreign aid program and in disposing of agricultural surpluses. Congress provided in the foreign aid program that 50% of the supplies being allocated to foreign lands must be carried in American bottoms. Foreign aid administrators, however, pointed out that by reason of difference in freight rates, $15 million dollars per month could be saved if the supplies were sent in foreign ships. Congress has insisted that its intent was that 50% of the foreign aid cargoes must be shipped in American ships.

At another time the Department of Agriculture, in its effort to dispose of the tremendous volume of agricultural commodities accumulated in the U. S. by reason of subsidies paid the farmers, devised a plan of selling the surpluses to foreign countries and taking their currency in payment. Foreign buyers objected strenuously to shipping via American ocean carriers, because of the higher costs and demanded the right to ship in their own vessels. The U. S., however, has classified such shipments as foreign aid and therefore subject to the 50-50 laws (Public Law 664, 83rd Congress). The Farm Bureau has attacked the 50-50 principle on grounds that if the American merchant marine needs aid it should be subsidized directly rather than through a penalty of foreign purchasers. Late in 1958 American tramp shipowners accused the Department of Agriculture of completely frustrating the 50-50 law. They have alleged that the Department, in chartering vessels to carry the surpluses, pays only the general charter market rate without allowance for the premium obtained by U. S. vessels under the operation of the 50-50 act.

The 50-50 Act provides an opportunity for U. S. flag vessels to secure preference on a few cargoes, but worldwide competition in the matter of rates is the more basic question that the American ship operator must solve in order to employ his vessel gainfully.

Operators need for information on foreign ports. In addition to the rate problem, the operator must give careful consideration to the range into which the vessel will be sent and the ports in which she will discharge. Ranges are the limits of the area in which are located ports wherein a vessel agrees to load cargo for discharge at another range of designated ports, e.g., the North Pacific Range (embracing Columbia River and Puget Sound ports) to the London-Liverpool range. The extent of a range is determined practically by the availability of cargo in the loading range and the demand for the cargo in the discharging range.

The conditions surrounding the port in which the vessel will be expected to discharge must be considered by the operator from the view points of safety for the vessel, availability of discharge facilities, delay to the ship in unloading, social unrest and international politics. If the destination of the ship is a major port, many of these questions are answered as a matter of record such as the list of services and facilities available in the port. In contrast to the many facilities available at a major port, many cities do not have protected harbors, and the vessel must discharge into lighters off shore while the weather permits.

Further inquiry must be made by the vessel operator concerning the facilities for the discharge and loading of his vessel. He must be informed as to whether the piers at which the ship will moor are strong enough to accommodate the ship, receive the cargo and warehouse the goods from the elements. The presence of cold-storage plants is necessary to receive refrigerated cargo, or oil tanks into which to pump cargo oil may be required. The availability of heavy lift cranes must be checked in case the vessel carries a piece of cargo too heavy for her own gear to handle.

The present condition of cargo handling at the port must be known so that the ship will not be unduly delayed by congestion of stevedoring services and berthing space. The prospect of waterfront strikes or political revolution should be anticipated. The presence of an epidemic of disease might cause the ship to be quarantined.

The customs of the port should be ascertained. The holidays and the number of hours the men will work in unloading vary. In some ports the stevedores will work only three consecutive days and then they will celebrate with their earnings while the ship waits. Failure to know custom house procedures and the port fees and fines can cause both delay and excessive cost.

Specific answers to such questions must be available to the vessel operator if he is to conduct his shipping business efficiently. He is presumably aware of current shipping conditions in his own port, but he must also be constantly advised by his overseas agents as to conditions in their respective ports. Other sources of such information include published reports of shipping conditions and other economic and political developments which might affect proposed voyages. In addition marine insurance companies issue reports on cargo handling and pilferage of cargo in various ports.

CHAPTER 21

Domestic Commerce of
The United States

Three areas of ocean carrier service in domestic commerce of the United States are regulated by the Government:

(1) The inter-coastal and coastwise ships

(2) The Great Lakes fleet

(3) Inland waters transportation

Intercoastal commerce. The operation of inter-coastal and coast-wise vessels involves all of the problems encountered in off-shore shipping with the exception of the world-wide competition in the matter of rates. By law foreign vessels cannot carry passengers and freight between United States ports. This eliminates competition from foreign sources and creates a domestic monopoly of commerce which is regulated by the interstate commerce laws of the United States.

In the inter-coastal service, freight rates are controlled directly by the Interstate Commerce Commission and indirectly by the tolls charged for the transit of the Panama Canal. The I.C.C. attempts to adjust rates on intercoastal traffic to make them competitive with trans-continental rail rates without discriminating in favor of either form of carrier. This intricate rate problem arose from the successful competition that vessels were able to give to the railroads in inter-coastal movement of goods. The railroads were bound by their transcontinental rates based generally on the distance hauled. To meet the lower vessel rates it became necessary for the railroads either to lower their through rates from coast to coast, and thus upset their entire rate structure, or to invoke the

I.C.C.'s permission to violate the long-and-short haul rule which requires that the roads cannot charge less for a long haul than a shorter one on the same road in the same direction. This would involve a rate discrimination against interior cities. This rate problem was critical before World War II, but during the war period shipping was requisitioned for war time service and the problem was less acute. Since then the former inter-coastal steamship lines claim that the present rate structure does not provide a satisfactory profit margin. Attempts have been made to solve the problem through savings in terminal charges and stevedoring costs of loading, stowing and discharging vessels by using seagoing, "roll on, roll off" ships, which handle the cargo loaded in motor truck trailers or trailer bodies. The "roll on, roll off" ship has yet to show the cost savings anticipated from its use. Except for use in the U. S. Navy, the cargo space occupied by the motor truck body and wheels has discouraged commercial application of the principle involved. Instead, carriers are tending more towards the use of the unmounted trailer body and loading it without use of the traction vehicle. See chapter on Cargo Handling.

Another item of cost to intercoastal vessels, is the Panama Canal tolls which are the direct administrative problem of the government. The tolls are levied on the underdeck, carrying capacity of the vessel in units of 100 cubic feet to a ton. The plea of the steamship operators for lower tolls is based on the accounting made by the government which includes with the cost of the canal operation many other items of broad, local administration in Panama and large sums for military protection of the Canal. It is contended that if these sums were debited to the general funds of the United States and to the military establishment, then the Canal would show a large operating profit which would permit the adjustment of the tolls.

To maintain the present rate structure and still come within the reservation of the Panama Canal treaty, the suggestion has been made that the United States remit the tolls to vessels owned and operated by domestic intercoastal common carriers. (See Chapter 19). Such grants in aid to the operation of intercoastal vessels are largely in the administrative discretion of the government and must come by Congressional action.

Coast-wise operation of larger vessels has been declining for many years due, perhaps, to the more flexible service offered by railroads and motor trucks on highways paralleling the Coast.

The Great Lakes fleet. The Great Lakes fleet likewise operates in a protected industry and has grown into a carrier service of tremendous size. The fleet is especially noted for its efficient carrying of grain and ore cargoes. Vessels have been especially designed and equipped to accommodate this service, and terminals have been prepared for the rapid loading and discharge of bulk cargoes. Competition, of course, comes from the railroads that serve the same areas, and one great handicap to operations is the freezing over of the lakes which prevents ship movements during five months of the year.

Further problems may arise from the exhausting of the ore supplies and possible competition by vessels using the St. Lawrence Seaway, when completed, to bring in ore from the lower St. Lawrence River or from foreign ports. For the present the Great Lakes operation seems to be stabilized.

The opening of the St. Lawrence Seaway is expected to revolutionize transportation on the Great Lakes. Harbors will be open to fairly large ocean-going vessels able to carry cargoes anywhere, and the fleet of ore carriers and grain vessels heretofore frozen in for months of the year may then go to sea in winter thus giving the ships a year-round continuous operation. Lake shore cities are busy building terminals in anticipation of the expected increase in traffic.

Inland waters commerce. Within the *inland waters* of the United States there are thousands of vessels engaged in intrastate and interstate commerce. These vessels form an efficient auxiliary to the seagoing ships in international commerce. To the larger ships, they bring cargo, supplies, fuels, water, repair machinery and heavy lift cranes. From the inbound ships, they take general cargo and special items. Their service is invaluable for the prompt and efficient delivery of cargo to points inaccessible to the ocean-going vessels.

The problems of inland carriers are largely local to the area in which the individual carrier is operating and are therefore peculiar to each carrier. It should be noted, however, that some of

Figure 17. The silhouettes illustrate the sizes and types of craft operating
on inland waterways.

the barge lines are entering seagoing service where protected
waters are available, as in the case of the Inside Passage to Alaska
from Puget Sound, through Canadian and Alaskan channels. Inland waters traffic is subject to national maritime laws and to
special regulation by the laws of each state in which the vessels

operate in intra-state commerce. Such shipping is also subject to the ordinances of the municipalities which control the harbors wherein the carriers transact their business.

The Mississippi River and its tributaries provide opportunity for a tremendous carrier service which maintains its business by offering much lower freight rates than the railroads which parallel the river. The barges in this service can load 1500 tons each and may be joined into a string of as many as 10 barges pushed by a twin-screw "towboat." Such a string of barges and its towboat measure as much as 950 feet in length and carry a cargo of 14,000 tons. This is the equivalent of the freight carried by 400 freight cars. It is possible to make a tow of 15 barges. The speed of the tow is about 6 miles per hour upstream and 12 miles per hour down stream.

The silhouettes reproduced in Figure 17 from a pamphlet by the U. S. Department of Commerce, illustrate the sizes and types of craft in common use operating on inland waterways.

CHAPTER 22

The United States Merchant Marine

American shipping must meet foreign competition in international trade both in the building of ships and in their operation. Because this service is performed on the high seas beyond the territorial jurisdiction of the United States, it cannot be given the protection afforded other industries by our tariff system. Under the tariff program the individual consumer pays for the protection of industry in higher prices paid for the commodity. Under the subsidy plan a similar burden is assumed by the general taxpayer.

In the mid-1930's a plea was directed to the Congress for government subsidy of the merchant marine on the following grounds: (1) In time of peace, subsidies granted by other nations or shipping combinations practicing discrimination or rebating methods, may well be used to the detriment of American shippers. The maintenance of fair competition alone calls for American-flag ships of sufficient tonnage to carry a reasonable portion of our foreign commerce; (2) In the event of a major war in which the United States is not involved, our commerce, in the absence of an adequate American merchant marine, might find itself seriously crippled because of its inability to secure bottoms for neutral peaceful foreign trade; (3) In the event of a war in which the United States itself might be engaged, American flag ships are obviously needed not only for naval auxiliaries but also for the maintenance of reasonable and necessary commercial intercourse with other nations

Merchant Marine Act of 1936. Congress passed the desired legislation in 1936 (Merchant Marine Act), and it has served since that time as a measure of the size and composition of our merchant marine.

The Merchant Marine Act (1936) includes this declaration of national policy: "It is necessary for the national defense and development of its foreign and domestic commerce that the United States shall have a Merchant Marine (a) sufficient to carry its domestic water-borne commerce and a substantial portion of the water-borne export and import foreign commerce of the United States and to provide shipping service on all routes essential for maintaining the flow of such domestic and foreign water-borne commerce at all times, (b) capable of serving as a naval and military auxiliary in time of war or national emergency, (c) owned and operated under the United States flag by citizens of the United States insofar as may be practicable, and (d) composed of the best-equipped, safest, and most suitable types of vessels, constructed in the United States and manned with a trained and efficient citizen personnel. It is hereby declared to be the policy of the United States to foster the development and encourage the maintenance of such a Merchant Marine."

Subsidies provided by the Act. The Act of 1936 provides for two types of subsidies to compensate the merchant marine for the lower building costs which prevail in foreign countries and the lower wage scale of foreign seamen. The first was the Constructional-differential subsidy, which was designed to compensate for the cheaper cost of building a vessel in foreign yards. This subsidy was not a direct payment to the American ship owner but went to equalize the cost of building in U.S. yards, so that the shipbuilding industry could be preserved and given work.

The other subsidy was the Operational-differential subsidy paid to put the American ship operator on a parity with the foreign shipowner who employs seaman at a far lower wage scale than that prevailing in the United States. This subsidy is passed on to the crew and for other operating expenses in order to place the U.S. ship in a position to compete. For example the U.S. ordinary seaman gets from $239 to $335 per month in base pay while an Italian ordinary seaman gets about $29 per month. Items considered in determining the Operating-differential subsidy include: wages and subsistence of officers and crew; cost of insurance; maintenance of vessel; repairs not compensated for by insurance; and other items of operating cost.

When the operator makes a profit on the operation of the vessel, he is required to repay the Government one half of the net profit in excess of 10% per annum on the capital necessarily used in the operation of the subsidized vessel with profits and losses to be averaged over a ten year period. In the ten year period 1938 to 1950, under this recapture clause the government has been repaid more than one-half of the subsidies expended.

Items to be considered in arriving at the Constructional-differential subsidy include: amount of the subsidy; appropriate design of the vessel; ability of the applicant to carry out his commitment; national defense features to be included in the vessel, and whether or not the vessel was operated on an essential route. The amount of the subsidy is not to exceed 33⅓% of the cost of the vessel, with certain exceptions. Earnings in excess of 10% are to be repaid to the Government under the recapture clause on the contract cost of the vessel.

The Federal Maritime Board lists the following qualifications for shipbuilding to be eligible for government subsidy: Cargo vessels, 9000 tons and over, must have a minimum speed of 18 knots. Four basic designs will be considered: *Island*—350 feet long, draft 21 feet, 5,000 tons deadweight; *Freedom*—417 feet long, 26½ foot draft, 8,500 tons deadweight; *Clipper*—460 feet long, draft 28 feet, 10,800 tons deadweight; *Seafarer*—494 feet long, draft 29 feet 9 inches, 13,500 tons deadweight.

The Federal Maritime Board and Maritime Administration were created in 1950 to succeed the Maritime Commission. They were placed in the Department of Commerce but exercise a considerable autonomy within the Department. Its functions are to review and approve steamship conference agreements to prevent discrimiatory practices and to regulate shipping rates between the continental United States and its possessions and territories.

Essential Trade Routes. The Maritime Administration has been commissioned to make a study of these trade routes for the purpose of building and maintaining a merchant marine to serve them in the best interests of the foreign trade of the United States and an efficient merchant marine.

Section 211 of the Merchant Marine Act, 1936, directs the Maritime Commission to determine the essential ocean routes for the promotion, development, expansion, and maintenance of the foreign commerce of the United States. The payment of operating-differential subsidies is limited to vessels plying the routes and services determined by the Maritime Administration to be essential. The criteria used in determining esential trade routes are, in brief:

1. Economic
   Comparison of area trade to total trade
   Significance of trade to economy of U.S.
   Domestic industrial relocation and development
   Trade inhibitors

2. Geopolitical
   Commercial and political ties, lines of communication
   Political-economic relationships

3. National Defense
   Importance of trade routes to defense
   Stockpile considerations
   Increased export influence in adjacent areas

4. Steamship Economics
   Delimiting trade area
   Description of trade area
   Service requirements of area
   Vessel characteristics
   Competitive vessels and service

Trade routes regarded as essential to the United States, by the Maritime Commission (May 1957) are the following:

1. U.S. Atlantic Ports (Maine to Key West)—East Coast South America
2. U.S. Atlantic Ports—West Coast South America
3. U.S. Atlantic Ports— East Coast Mexico

4. U.S. Atlantic Ports—Caribbean Ports

5. U.S. North Atlantic Ports (Maine to Cape Hatteras)—United Kingdom and Erie

6. U.S. North Atlantic Ports—Scandinavian, Baltic Ports

7. U.S. North Atlantic Ports—German North Sea Ports

8. U.S. North Atlantic Ports—Belgium and Netherlands

9. U.S. North Atlantic Ports—Atlantic France and Northern Spain

10. U.S. North Atlantic Ports—Mediterranean, Black Sea, Portugal, Spain, Morocco

11. U.S. South Atlantic Ports (Cape Hatteras to Key West)—United Kingdom and Eire, Continental Europe, Scandinavian and Baltic ports North of Portugal

12. U.S. Atlantic Ports— Far East

13. U.S. South Atlantic & Gulf Ports (Cape Hatteras to Texas)—Mediterranean, Black Sea, Atlantic Spain, Portugal, Morocco

14. U.S. Atlantic & Gulf Ports—West Africa,

15A. U.S. Atlantic Ports—South and East Africa, Madagascar

15B. U.S. Gulf Ports—(Key West to Mexican border)— South and East Africa

16. U.S. Atlantic & Gulf Ports—Australia

17. U.S. Atlantic, and Pacific Ports— Indonesia, Malaya Southwest Asia

18. U.S. Atlantic & Gulf Ports—India, Burma, Persian Gulf, Red Sea

19. U.S. Gulf Ports—Caribbean ports

20. U.S. Gulf Ports—East Coast South America

21. U.S. Gulf Ports—United Kingdom, Eire, Continental Europe, North of Portugal

22. U.S. Gulf Parts—Far East

23. U.S. Pacific Ports—Caribbean ports

24. U.S. Pacific Ports—East Coast South America

25. U.S. Pacific Ports—West Coast Mexico, Central America and South America

26. U.S. Pacific Ports—United Kingdom and Eire, Havre Hamburg Range

27. U.S. Pacific Ports—Australia, Asia, Indonesia, Malaya, Pakistan
28. U.S. Pacific Ports—India, Burma, Persian Gulf, Red Sea
29. California Ports—Far East
30. Washington and Oregon Ports—Far East
31. U.S. Gulf Ports—West Coast South America
32. U.S. Great Lakes—Western Europe
33. U.S. Great Lakes—Caribbean Ports

Size of U. S. Merchant Marine fleet. Changes in the composition of the American merchant marine fleet are reflected in the table* that follows.

	Jan. 1, 1954	Jan. 1, 1955	Jan. 1, 1956	Jan. 1, 1957	Jan. 1, 1958	Jan. 1, 1959
Grand total of Vessels	3,348	3.277	3,241	3,175	3,125	3,127
Active vessels	1,348	1,271	1,072	1,099	983	960
Vessels in reserve	1,964	2,006	2,169	2,076	2,142	2,167
Seamen employed (Est.)	66,350	60,100	56,329	58,148	55,537	51,761
Private construction, vessels	29	9	16	78	109	82
Government construction	16	12	16	12	6	3

#1,012 privately owned
2,113 publicly owned

The American Merchant Marine Institute, Inc., is constantly engaged in the study of and reporting upon the U.S. merchant marine and has issued research reports showing the condition of the fleet at the end of 1958. The following excerpts are from a report on the U. S. Flag Privately Owned Tanker Fleet (February 3, 1959, 59-1) and U. S. Flag and Privately Owned Dry Cargo and Passenger Carrying Fleet (February 10, 1959 59-2).

U. S. FLAG PRIVATELY OWNED TANKER FLEET

	Number	DWT 000's
June, 1939	377	4,217
January, 1949	490	7,206
January, 1950	461	6,873
January, 1951	448	6,673
January, 1952	457	6,806
January, 1953	443	6,774
January, 1954	443	6,956
January, 1955	405	6,635
January, 1956	362	6,017
January, 1957	341	5,848
January, 1958	328	5,782
January, 1959	334	6,138

*From data compiled by the Federal Maritime Board.

U. S. FLAG AND PRIVATELY OWNED DRY CARGO AND PASSENGER CARRYING FLEET

(Ocean-going vessels of 1,000 gross tons & over only)

	Number	DWT 000's
June, 193?	852	5,981
January, 1949	690	6,832
January, 1950	736	7,385
Januray, 1951	729	7,357
January, 1952	842	8,666
January, 1953	823	8,556
January, 1954	806	8,388
January, 1955	730	7,618
January, 1956	713	7,517
January, 1957	718	7,626
January, 1958	684	7,352
January, 1959	673	7,254

Innovations—Present and Future. The industry is currently witnessing many improvements in vessel design and manner of operation as well as new developments and changes in cargo handling. Some of the innovations have been tried and some are in the process of development.

The "Roll-on, Roll-off" ship has already been alluded to. A variation of this is the "lift-on, lift-off" type of cargo handling wherein the body of the trailer, fully loaded, is taken aboard either with the ship's gear or with a shoreside crane. Other proposals have been made for the loading of railroad cars and trailers on wheels through large ports in the stern of the vessel.

Oil tanker owners have also expressed interest in this wheeled cargo. Plans are projected to construct a bridge over the main deck of the tanker, where its loading valves are placed, and use this space for truck and trailer traffic of about 58 vehicles per trip.

Besides oil carrying, tankers are being designed to carry liquids other than oil. A tanker with stainless steel compartments has commenced carrying fresh orange juice from Florida to New York and will be able to transport capacity loads of 1,500,000 gallons under refrigeration. It is claimed that the cost of this voyage is only $15,000 compared to a sum of $256,000 if the same quantity were hauled by motor truck.

Beer is being carried by a tanker in Holland from the brewery to the aging plant, a distance of 50 miles, at a saving of over 50% compared with rail tank expense.

Wet paper pulp is being carried by tankers from British Columbia to California saving the expenses of pressing and drying the pulp, transporting it as dry cargo and re-wetting again in the process of paper making.

Propane gas is being transported in tankers from Houston to Newark carrying 1.2 million gallons per trip in half the time required for the trip by tank cars and with a capacity equal to that of 1,200 railroad tank cars.

The closing of the Suez Canal resulted in the planning of large tankers designed to carry oil more cheaply around the southern tip of Africa than through the canal with its tolls. The size of these tankers planned and building is 100,000 tons dwt. Smaller ships of 50,000 tons dwt., with speeds up to 19 knots, may be able to affect economical delivery of crude oil from the Persian Gulf to Philadelphia at three cents per gallon.

In vessel hull design, a proposal to put hydrofoils on merchant ships has been accepted by the Maritime Administration and a contract awarded for study of the plan. The hydrofoil is similar to the use of wings on an airplane or a water ski. Its use is expected to increase the speed of a ship by some 50%, with the same power.

Other new developments or proposals include the use of anti-rolling fins, for passenger ships. These are said to be capable of reducing the roll of a large vessel to one-and-one-half degrees in a 40-knot gale which normally would have produced a fifteen-degree roll.

Ships are being built with a completely smooth inner skin which will greatly facilitate cleaning of the vessel's hold after carrying certain cargoes. The space between the skins of the ship can be used for fuel or ballast.

The atomic-powered ship is a success from an operational viewpoint. Plans for reducing cost to make such vessels commercially competitive are under consideration. The success of nuclear power was dramatically shown by the cruise of the submarine *Nautilus* from the Bering Sea to England under the North Polar ice cap.

CHAPTER 23

Reports From The Lookouts

A statement of progress. A recent report* of the Federal Maritime Board and The Maritime Administration has summarized their activities for the period reported and provided some indication of future developments. The report (1) assessed the relationships between the government and the privately owned and operated American maritime industry; (2) forecast improvement for American overseas trade and commerce; (3) outlined present and future shipbuilding plans: (4) reported on the progress of the nuclear ship *Savannah;* (5) discussed research and development in the maritime field.

The cooperation and effective action between the Federal Maritime Board, the Maritime Administration, and the shipping industry in carrying out the aims of the Merchant Marine Act of 1936 contributed to American economic improvement and national security. Most significant was the understanding, guidance, support, and criticism from the Merchant Marine and Fisheries Committee, and the Interstate and Foreign Commerce Committee of Congress.

The American shipbuilding industry is engaged in peacetime ship construction with 34 cargo ships and 58 tankers, totaling nearly 3 million deadweight tons, building in American yards at this time. In 1958 American shipyards built and converted a record tonnage of nearly 1,000,000 deadweight tons including four new passenger-cargo ships, two of 15,000 gross tons capable of carrying 300 passengers each, and two of 18,000 gross tons capable of carrying 300 passengers each.

*Year end statement, December 25, 1958.

The government and privately owned American shipping have joined in a program to avoid block obsolescence of the American flag fleet. There were 53 new tankers on order in the U.S. yards for delivery during the years 1959 and 1960 of which 37 were for addition to the U.S. fleet. Except for the Great Lakes operation, bulk carriers were not being ordered for U.S. flag operation.

Three other ship deliveries of note occurred in 1958 in which the Maritime Administration acted as construction agent. The first was the conversion of the passenger-cargo ship *Atlantic* intended to pioneer a new American "one-class" passenger service between the United States and Europe. The second vessel built was the *U.S.N.S. Comet,* a roll-on roll-off ship, which has been reported as successful by the Military Sea Transportation Service in the transport of military wheeled devices. The third vessel was the *U.S.N.S. Point Barrow* which is a landing-ship dock type capable of servicing bases where dock facilities are at a minimum.

In 1958 the keel was laid of the world's first nuclear merchant ship, the *N.S. Savannah.* The ship will be launched in 1959 and trials and operation are scheduled for the latter part of that year and in 1960.

The report pointed out that research and development in 1958 by the Maritime Administration was directed along practical lines such as developing better and more easily maintained crews' quarters and plastic lifeboats which are expected to require no maintenance. Other studies included hydrofoil experiments designed to give a vessel much greater speed (80 knots) by converting its bottom into planes to use the principle of the hydroplane. Underwater cargo craft are being studied to make use of some of the advantages of submerged vessel hulls. Other projects being tested on the Administration's experimental ships are the free piston and the gas turbine for power purposes and the reversible propeller for vessel maneuvering. Also being tested are level luffing movable cranes for cargo handling.

There is a growing interest in container ships which are expected to lower cargo handling costs and quicken the turnaround of the vessel's voyage. The containers lessen damage and pilferage claims and accomplish better integration between land and sea transport. The construction of the containers is being studied and the "lift-on lift-off" type of vessels which would use the containers.

The major project for 1959 is the replacement of older ships with special consideration to be given to replacement of tramp vessels and bulk carriers. For military defense requirements attention will be given to specialized vessels such as roll-on roll-off and reefer ships.

Educational activities, in addition to training in the nuclear field, encompass the training of Merchant Marine Cadets at the U.S. Merchant Marine Academy at Kings Point, Long Island, New York and the courses being conducted in radar uses and interpretation and instruction in atomic, biologic and chemical warfare defenses at New York, San Francisco and New Orleans.

The Federal Maritime Board, in the performance of its regulatory functions, continued its investigation of practices of foreign freight forwarders and other persons subject to the shipping acts.

SIZE of U.S. MERCHANT MARINE, 1958 and 1959.

On January 1, 1958

	Government	Private	Total
Ships in active service	41	942	983
Inactive vessels	2072	70	2142
Total fleet	2113	1012	3125
Vessels building	6	109	115
Subsidized vessels			307

On January 1, 1959

	Government	Private	Total
Ships in active service	25	935	960
Inactive vessels	2095	72	2167
Total fleet	2120	1007	3127
Vessels building	3	82	85
Subsidized vessels			312

Manpower—December 1958

Training 1,900   Seamen 51,700   Shipbuilders 56,200   Longshoremen 72,500
Taken from the Federal Maritime Board and Maritime Administration's resume of Merchant Marine data sheets released January 1959, for the period January 1, 1958 to January 1, 1959.

Cargo Containers. A recent report* by the Federal Maritime Board and Maritime Administration traces and compares the evolution of cargo containers aboard ship in the United States and

*"Survey and Analysis of Cargo Containers for Cargo Ships," U.S. Department of Commerce, PB 151230, January 1959.

in Western Europe. It includes a summary of current activity looking toward standardization of sizes, weights, and materials of containers. The "Survey and Analysis" covers sizes of European containers as well as the ability of foreign transportation media— railroads, canal barges and truck— to handle American containers as well as our ability to handle European containers. Part of the study is devoted to transfer of containers and their coordination with rail and truck transport services for maximum effectiveness in containerizing cargoes for long-distance, door-to-door delivery on through bills of lading from origin to destination. This brief, introductory report is intended to serve an interim purpose, pending completion of a comprehensive survey to be brought out by several committees currently dealing with this subject under the direction and guidance of the American Standards Association.

Recent Research. Progress in research on a commercial submarine also has been reported. Such research will serve as a basis for the preliminary design of a fast, subsurface freighter employing water-jet propulsion of advanced concept. In effect, the vessel will "fly" through the water. This research is directed toward the improvement of sea vehicles more suitably to employ the potentialities of nuclear energy. The hull of such a ship, when underway, would not be visible above the sea, having only a thin strut or fin piercing the surface like a knife.

On the surface, supported by the fin, would be a gondola to accommodate living quarters, navigating bridge and running lights. The cigar-shaped hull would have positive buoyancy and float to the surface when not in motion. The gondola, riding the waves, would permit conventional navigation and an air-breathing prime mover, as well as a normal environment for human beings. Underway, a triaxial control system would furnish steering control, longitudinal and transverse stabilization and the necessary downward force to keep the novel ship at its proper cruising depth. It would at all times operate with excess positive buoyance and the hull would be kept submerged by hydrodynamic forces. The ultimate power force for driving the propulsion jet pumps is expected to be nuclear.

Research into shipboard organization and activities on an oceangoing freighter is also currently underway for the Maritime

Administration. The four-part project will be concerned with (1) watch standing (2) maintenance and underway repair, (3) subsistence and lodging, and (4) general operations.

The problem is to identify opportunities for economy in operation of a freight vessel at sea and the practice of these economies. The procedure will be to place monetary values on manpower, equipment and material required to perform these tasks and to explore the possibilities of new and better methods of accomplishing them. The importance of the study lies in the fact that the average oceangoing freight vessel spends about one half of its life at sea and the efficiency of the vessel during this time is determined by organization, practices, traditions, and regulations which upon study and analysis may reveal areas where cost reduction and operational efficiency may be obtained.

PROBLEMS AND CHALLENGES FOR THE FUTURE

Building new vessels. The cost of shipbuilding in American shipyards is far higher than in foreign yards. A study by the Committee of American Steamship Lines states: "Japan can build a 12,500 ton diesel freighter for about $2,950,000. The German price would be about $3,263,000. In a U.S. yard the cost would run $10,000,000 and up". Congress has recognized the necessity of maintaining an adequate merchant marine and renewing the vessels becoming obsolete by providing the constructional differential subsidy plan. Under this plan together with vessels being privately built a $3 billion shipbuilding program has been commenced and is accomplishing the desired result of preserving the shipbuilding skills in the American yards. The amount of construction is a record for peacetime activity.

New type vessels. Two recent accomplishments in the building of new type vessels have caught the interest of the American vessel operators. The first was the laying of the keel of the first nuclear-powered passenger-cargo ship. She will be named the "*Savannah*" in honor of the American steamship *Savannah* which in 1819 was the first vessel using steam power to cross the Atlantic Ocean. The further development of nuclear powered ships is a matter of engineering, planning and experimentation.

The first large seagoing roll-on roll-off ship constructed in this country went into service in January, 1958. Although the ship was built for the Military Sea Transportation Service, it will serve as a model for other vessels to be built for private operation. Its operation was considered successful from a military standpoint and other vessels of this type are under construction. From the viewpoint of operation as a private cargo carrier, the opinions of steamshipmen differ and some declare that the operation of this type of vessel is not financially practical because of the waste of cargo space taken up by the wheels of the vehicles being transported.

International Maritime Consultative Organization. IMCO is a new agency set up under the United Nations organization for the purpose of study and correction of maritime problems on an inter-governmental basis. The organization was officially established by the United Nations upon acceptance by Japan on March 17, 1958 thus completing the requirement of acceptance by 21 nations. The headquarters will be in London and its Assembly will meet every two years.

The purposes of this specialized organization are to promote cooperation among governments in solving technical problems of international shipping; to encourage general adoption of the highest practical standards for the safety and efficiency of navigation; to seek the removal of discriminatory action and unnecessary reservations by governments affecting international shipping; and to provide for the consideration of matters concerning unfair practices by shipping concerns.

The formation of IMCO has been under consideration for nine years and the advisability of the United States joining the organization has been urged upon by the U.S. Department of State but the Department has not acted.

Ships under flags of convenience. The seriousness and the complexity of this problem may be judged from the statements and the actions of the several agencies interested in its solution.

The registering of American owned ships under foreign flags is caused by the opportunity of ship operation more cheaply under foreign wage scales, and lower taxation by those nations. Illustrating the financial reason for these registrations, some of these ships changed back to U.S. registry to take advantage of the opportunity to secure cargoes under provisions of the 50-50 law requiring that percentage of government cargoes be carried in U.S. flag vessels.

The diversity of nationalities between the ownership of vessels and their flag of operation can cause international complications. Maritime nations meeting in Geneva recognized this condition and proposed a treaty requiring an identity of ownership and operation under the same flag.

Late in 1958 maritime unions staged a four-day protest against low wage conditions on these vessels under flags of convenience and many ships in various ports of the world were immobilized for that period. The unions announced that further action will be taken against the vessels by the maritime unions.

To protect themselves the vessel owners formed an association of their interests under the title flags of necessity to meet foreign competition of foreign vessels maintaining the same scale of pay of which the maritime unions complained.

The matter of avoidance of U. S. taxes by vessals under flags of convenience was referred to the House Committee on Ways and Means which issued an informal statement that the problem should be dealt with by some other method than taxation as the taxation of foreign corporations presented serious problems in situations where some of the stockholders are nationals of foreign countries.

The Office of Defense and Civilian Mobilization considers that these vessels, owned by U. S. citizens but flying flags of convenience of countries such as Panama and Liberia, are a part of this country's mobilization potential and they have a role in greater defense planning. However, such ships are customarily replaced by foreign shipyards and would therefore be unsuitable for military purposes, for example, their lack of equipment to handle military vehicles on a roll-on roll-off basis.

Stabilized ocean freight rates. The question of whether the steamship conferences will be able to maintain the uniform, published freight rates is critical in view of the United States Supreme Court decision that the Conferences' dual rate system is illegal. Without this weapon, the stability of rates will depend in each instance upon the strength of the particular Conference and the acceptance of the situation by the shippers. Congress passed a resolution to hold the dual rate system in effect, except in the cause under litigation, until 1960 to provide time for a study of the situation to arrive at some solution.

The opponents of the dual rate system immediately filed suit in a U. S. Court to have Congress' action declared improper in maintaining a system which the Supreme Court had already found to be illegal.

Vessel operational costs. The higher cost of operation of vessels under the American flag over those sailing under foreign flags is generally attributed to the major cost of maritime wages.

The Federal Maritime Board and the Maritime Administration published in January of 1959 (NR 59-10) a study on "The Earnings and Employment of Seamen on U.S. Flag Ships, July 1, 1956–June 30, 1957". The combined calculation of average daily earnings with average annual employment was set out for selected ratings: second mates, $8,110; messmen, $3,285; cooks, $5,345; ablebodied seamen, $4,607. The great difference in U. S. and foreign wage scales has been thus expressed by one spokesman for the maritime industry: "On American ships we pay $19,000 in wages per month. On a German ship, the wages are $4,100 per month".

It is the duty of the Federal Maritime Board to determine the fairness and reasonableness of wages upon which the operational differential subsidy is paid. Congress has been very cautious in the appropriations for both the operational differential and constructional differential subsidies even though much of the subsidies has been recaptured in the event of the profitable operation of the subsidized ship. The sums allocated by Congress are very small in comparision with the appropriations for agriculture subsidies and foreign aid.

The year-end statement of the Federal Maritime Board and the Maritime Administration showed that there were 23 less ships in active service on January 1, 1959 as compared with January 1, 1958 and the number of seaman employed was about 2,000 less. The maritime unions are aware of this decline and set as one of their goals the building up of job opportunities in the industry and the capture of runaway ships under flags of convenience.

Americans' use of American ships. To bring understanding and support by the American public for their merchant marine is the purpose of such organizations as the American Merchant Marine Institute, Inc. and the Committee of American Steamship Lines. Their officers and the heads of steamship lines appear before various meetings to express the aims and the needs of the U.S. merchant marine. The following are conclusions made by those leaders of the maritime industry:

> "Why is it then that an American does not always choose an American vessel, rates and service being equal? It is hard to believe and still we know the situation exists.
>
> "American-flag shipping has never sought a monopoly of the sea lanes, nor will it. We recognize that ships of other nations give good service. American-flag lines have opened up trade areas over the entire world; have instituted trade promotion departments; have placed thousands of shippers in communication with buyers abroad; have placed thousands of American importers in connection with shippers from other countries. But once the trade is developed, vessels of other nations come in until now they are carrying nearly 80 per cent."

U. S. flag vessels carry only 20% of U. S. foreign trade. In seeking the answer to the question of foreign vessels carrying U. S. overseas trade in a ratio of 4 to 1, it should be noted that a considerable portion of this commerce would move in shipments of a size large enough to attract tramp vessels or other charterers. Tramp vessels under the American flag registry are having a difficult time meeting the competitive rates set by foreign flag vessels which have the advantage of operation on a very much lower wage scale. It is very practical for the American shipper to take advantage of the lowest available freight rate to meet competition in his particular commodity either from foreign sources or from his American counterpart.

To analyze accurately the reason that Americans use foreign vessels in large ratio, statistics would have to be accumulated showing the percentage of U. S. cargo moving in foreign tramps, the percentage moving in the U. S. tramps but subsidized under the 50-50 law, and the percentage carried in American owned ships sailing under convenience flags of other nations and make allowances for financial advantages to the shippers in each of these conditions.

The transportation of that large portion of American commerce with foreign nations which is carried in conference line ships is an area that furnishes equal conditions of competition. The ships have the same rating, their schedules are similar and their ocean freight rates are identical. The quality of the service rendered to the shippers is the deciding factor in the procurement of the cargoes. The items of such service were discussed in a previous chapter herein on the Procurement of Cargoes.

Popular education. The Committee of American Steamship Lines has developed community programs wherein whole U. S. communities are roused to enthusiasm by the presentation of maritime facts. "The programs substitute information for ignorance—facts for fallacies—enthusiasm for antipathy." The Committee will have accomplished its mission if it can revive among the American people that powerful allure of GOING TO SEA.

CHARACTERISTICS—LIBERTY SHIP—EC2-S-C1

Single Screw Steamer with Flush Deck, Raked Stem, Cruiser Stern

Length over all	441'6"
Length between perpendiculars	416'0"
Length at Load Waterline	428'0"

REGISTER: Length   422.8'   Beam 57.0'   Depth   34.85'

Extreme Beam	57'0"
Molded Beam	56'10¾"
Molded Depth to Main Deck at Side	37'4"

Lightweight	3877 Tons
Fixed Ballast	408 Tons
Deadweight	10368 Tons (Ballast to be deducted)
Displacement, SW	14245 Draft 27'8⅞"
Gross Tonnage	7176 Tons
Net Tonnage	4375 Tons
Panama Canal Gross Tonnage	7246.61 Tons
Panama Canal Net Tonnage	5042.86 Tons
Suez Canal Gross Tonnage	6696.32 Tons
Suez Canal Net Tonnage	5279.38 Tons

Light Draft	8'9½" (unballasted)
Loaded Draft	27'8⅞" (Summer Load Line)
Molded Draft	27'8"

Sustained Sea Speed 11 knots (70 RPM 1520 SHP)

Fuel Consumption 135 — 160 Bbls/day

Cruising Radius 20,850 miles

Freeboard to Center of Disc	9'8¾"
Fresh Water Allowance for all Freeboards	7¼"
Tropical line above Center of Disc	7"
Winter line below Center of Disc	7"
Maximum loadline above Center of Disc	1' 2¼"
(Tropical Fresh)	

Draft   28'11⅛"   Displacement 14550 Tons

General Cargo Capacity Bale Cu. 499,573 Cu.Ft. Grain Cu.Ft. 562,508 Cu.Ft.

Fuel Oil in Double Bottoms	6743 Bbls	1017 Tons
Fuel Oil in Deep Tanks (#3)	4643 Bbls	666 Tons
Fuel Oil in Settlers	670 Bbls	102 Tons
Total Fuel Capacity	12036 Bbls	1785 Tons
Potable Water		56 Tons
Reserve Feed Water (#4DB)		132 Tons

Fore Peak	141 Tons (FW)	After Peak	151 Tons (FW)
#1 Deeptanks	220 Tons (FW)	After Peak	228 Tons (SW)
#2 Deeptanks	410 Tons (FW)	After Peak	420 Tons (SW)

| Two Bower Anchors | 8410 lbs. each |
| One Stream Anchor | 3195 lbs. |

240 Fathoms of 2 1/16" Stud link chain, 120 fathoms for each anchor in 15 fathom shots.

Anchor Windlass is Steam driven, handling both anchor chains on independently locking wildcats, fitted with individual brake bands and is capable of hoisting both anchors from a depth at 30 fathoms with a minimum chain speed of 30 feet per minute.

CARGO DATA

Cargo Holds

There are five cargo holds with two complete decks in each. Three are forward of machinery space, two are aft. All hatches have strong beams and wood hatch covers. Weather hatches have tarpaulins for water tightness.

Cargo Handling Gear

There are three masts, one between #1 and #2 hatches, one between #2 and #3 hatches and one between #4 and #5 hatches. Each hatch has 5 ton booms port and starboard. In addition a 15 ton boom is fitted at #4 hatch and a 50 ton boom at #2 hatch. There are no king posts.

HATCH	LOCATION	NO. OF BOOMS	CAPACITY	LENGTH
#1	Aft	2	5	55
#2	Forward	2	5	55
#2	Forward	2	5	55
#3	Forward	1	30	51
#4	Aft	2	5	55
#4	Aft	1	15	51
#5	Forward	2	5	47

Winches

There are 10 cargo winches as follows:

    8—WA Riddell Company, DBL, RED, 2 cylinders
      Size 7" x 12", 10,000# at 125ft./min., 5000# at 250 ft./min.
    2—American Hoist and Derrick Company

Main Engine

    1—Direct acting condensing triple expansion, 3 cylinder type, developing 2500 HP at 76 RPM. Steam pressure 220# G. Maximum steam temperature 440° F, vacuum 26" Hg — Connected to main engine: reversing engine, turning engine, wet air pump, 2 bilge pumps, evaporator pump.

RPM	76
Indicated HP	2191.6
Mean indicated pressure, HP cyl	92.9
Mean indicated pressure, 1 P cyl	. 38.4
Mean indicated pressure, LP cyl	10.6
Steam pressure at Throttle, #/sq in G	215.1
Steam pressure at HP receiver #/sq in G	205.8
Steam pressure at 1 P receiver #/sq in G	64.0
Steam pressure at LP receiver #/sq in G	10.05
Steam at Throttle, °F (Max.)	440.0
Vacuum, inches Mercury	26.0
Exhaust temperature °F	112.0

Boilers

Two water tube, cross drum, sectional header, 3 pass, straight tube type with connection type superheaters. Burning Bunker 6 Fuel Oil — Each boiler capable of sustained operation at 30% excess evaporation.

Heating surface, Sq. Ft.	4852
Superheater Surface, Sq. Ft.	260 (Approx.)
Furnace Volume, Cu. Ft.	770
Normal evaporation, #/sq. ft./HS	4.5
Design pressure, lbs./sq. in.	250
Drum pressure lbs./sq. in.	230
Superheater outlet pres., lbs./sq./in.	220
Superheater outlet temp. °F	450
Auxiliary Steam Pressure #/sq. in. G	220.6
Desuperated Steam temperature °F	337.1
Uptake temperature, Port °F	330.7
Uptake temperature, Stbd. °F	345.0
Air pressure at burner front, port H_2O	.34
Air pressure at burner front, Stbd. H_2O	.26

Main Condenser

The main condenser is of the two-pass type with about 3000 sq. ft. of cooling surface and is designed to maintain 26″ vacuum with cooling water at 80°F, circulating water outlet temperature 101°F. There are 1360 aluminum straight tubes, 10′4″ long, ¾″ OD.

Auxiliary Condenser

The auxiliary condenser has about 700 sq. ft. of cooling surface and is of the two-pass type. It is designed to maintain 20″ vacuum with cooling water at 80° F and has 510 aluminum brass straight tubes, 6′—11⅞″ long, ¾″ OD. Number 18 BWG, ferruled on both ends.

Propeller

Single, four bladed bronze—Pitch varies from 12.6′ at the hub to 16.5′ from 5R to tip. Diameter is 18′6″.

HOLDS	HOLD CAPACITIES GRAIN CU. FT.	BALE CU. FT.	HATCH OPENING LENGTH & WIDTH
Hold #1	41,257	36,083	35'9" x 20'
'Tween Deck #1	42,924	39,322	35'9" x 20'
Hold #2	98,860	92,008	35' x 20'
'Tween Deck #2	46,744	42,630	35' x 20'
Hold #3	68,459	59,793	20' x 20'
'Tween Deck #3	27,970	23,904	20' x 20'
Hold #4	58,840	52,574	30' x 20'
'Tween Deck #4	35,277	29,689	30' x 20'
Hold #5	58,620	51,571	35' x 20'
'Tween Deck #5	34,570	30,864	35' x 20'
TOTAL	513,522	458,438	

DEEP TANKS	GRAIN CU. FT.	BALE CU. FT.
#1 Port Forward	3639	2729
#1 Stbd. Forward	3639	3004
#2 Port Aft	7473	5294
#2 Stbd. Aft	7473	5578
TOTAL	22,224	16,605

TANK CAPACITIES

FUEL OIL	BBLS.	FUEL OIL TONS	SALT WATER TONS
No. 1 Double Bottom	878	132	144
No. 2 Double Bottom, port	1042	157	170
No. 2 Double Bottom, stbd.	1042	157	170
No. 3 Double Bottom, port	768	116	126
No. 3 Double Bottom, stbd.	762	115	125
No. 5 Double Bottom, port	766	116	125
No. 5 Double Bottom, stbd.	766	116	125
No. 6 Double Bottom	719	108	118
No. 3 Deep Tank, port	2363	356	387
No. 3 Deep Tank, stbd.	2280	344	373
F.O. Settling Tank, port	335	51	
F.O. Settling Tank, stbd.	335	51	
TOTAL	12,056	1819	1863

BALLAST TANKS	SW TONS 100% FULL AT 35
Fore Peak Tank	145
After Peak Tank	155
TOTAL	300

FRESH WATER TANKS

	Tons — 100% full at 36
#4 Double Bottoms, port	66
#4 Double Bottom, stbd.	66
Fresh Water Tank, fwd #4 'Tween Deck, port	28
Fresh Water Tank, fwd #4 'Tween Deck, stbd.	28
TOTAL	188

SHIPS STORES

	Cu. Ft.
Boatswains Stores (second deck)	3034
Boatswains Stores (on flat between 2nd and upper deck)	3492
Cabin Stores (2nd deck)	4329
Linen Locker	585
Bonded Stores	186
Ship's Refrigerated Stores	1918 (See below)
TOTAL	13,544

FEFRIGERATED SPACES

	Cu. Ft.
Meat	801
Fish	173
Vegetables	768
Dairy	176
TOTAL	1918

APPENDIX II

(PUBLIC—NO. 521—74TH CONGRESS S. 1152)

AN ACT RELATING TO THE CARRIAGE OF GOODS BY SEA.

Be it enacted by the Senate and House of Representatives of the United States of America in Congress assembled, That every bill of lading or similar document of title which is evidence of a contract for the carriage of goods by sea to or from ports of the United States, in foreign trade, shall have effect subject to the provisions of this Act.

TITLE I

SECTION 1. When used in this Act—

(a) The term "carrier" includes the owner or the charterer who enters into a contract of carriage with a shipper.

(b) The term "contract of carriage" applies only to contracts of carriage covered by a bill of lading or any similar document of title, insofar as such document relates to the carriage of goods by sea, including any bill of lading or any similar document as aforesaid issued under or pursuant to a charter party from the moment at which such bill of lading or similar document of title regulates the relations between a carrier and a holder of the same.

(c) The term "goods" includes goods, wares, merchandise, and articles of every kind whatsoever, except live animals and cargo which by the contract of carriage is stated as being carried on deck and is so carried.

(d) The term "ship" means any vessel used for the carriage of goods by sea.

(e) The terms "carriage of goods" covers the period from the time when the goods are loaded on to the time they are discharged from the ship.

RISKS

SEC. 2. Subject to the provisions of section 6, under every contract of carriage of goods, by sea, the carrier in relation to the loading, handling, stowage, carriage, custody, care, and discharge of such goods, shall be subject to the responsibilities and liabilities and entitled to the rights and immunities hereinafter set forth.

RESPONSIBILITIES AND LIABILITIES

SEC. 3. (1) The carrier shall be bound, before and at the beginning of the voyage, to exercise due diligence to—

(a) Make the ship seaworthy;

(b) Properly man, equip, and supply the ship;

(c) Make the holds, refrigerating and cooling chambers, and all other parts of the ship in which goods are carried, fit and safe for their reception, carriage, and preservation.

(2) The carrier shall properly and carefully load, handle, stow, carry, keep, care for, and discharge the goods carried.

(3) After receiving the goods into his charge the carrier, or the master or agent of the carrier, shall, on demand of the shipper, issue to the shipper a bill of lading showing among other things—

(a) The leading marks necessary for identification of the goods as the same are furnished in writing by the shipper before the loading of such goods starts, provided such marks are stamped or otherwise shown clearly upon the goods if uncovered, or on the cases or coverings in which such goods are contained, in such a manner as should ordinarily remain legible until the end of the voyage.

(b) Either the number of packages or pieces,, or the quantity or weight, as the case may be, as furnished in writing by the shipper.

(c) The apparent order and condition of the goods: *Provided,* That no carrier, master, or agent of the carrier, shall be bound to state or show in the bill of lading any marks, number, quantity, or weight which he has reasonable ground for suspecting not accurately to represent the goods actually received, or which he has had no reasonable means of checking.

(4) Such a bill of lading shall be prima facie evidence of the receipt by the carrier of the goods as therein described in accordance with paragraphs (3) (a), (b), and (c), of this section: *Provided,* That nothing in this Act shall be construed as repealing or limiting the application of any part of the Act, as amended, entitled "An Act relating to bills of lading in interstate and foreign commerce", approved August 29, 1916 (U.S.C., title 49, secs. 81–124), commonly known as the "Pomerene Bills of Lading Act."

(5) The shipper shall be deemed to have guaranteed to the carrier the accuracy at the time of shipment of the marks, number, quantity, and weight, as furnished by him; and the shipper shall indemnify the carrier against all loss, damages, and expenses arising or resulting from inaccuracies in such particulars. The right of the carrier to such indemnity shall in no way limit his responsibility and liability under the contract of carriage to any person other than the shipper.

(6) Unless notice of loss or damage and the general nature of such loss or damage be given in writing to the carrier or his agent at the port of discharge before or at the time of the removal of the goods into the custody of the person entitled to delivery thereof under the contract of carriage, such removal shall be prima facie evidence of the delivery by the carrier of the goods as described in the bill of lading. If the loss or damage is not apparent, the notice must be given within three days of the delivery.

Said notice of loss or damage may be endorsed upon the receipt for the goods given by the person taking delivery thereof.

The notice in writing need not be given if the state of the goods has at the time of their receipt been the subject of joint survey or inspection.

In any event the carrier and the ship shall be discharged from all liability in respect of loss or damage unless suit is brought within one year after delivery of the goods or the date when the goods should have been delivered: *Provided,* That if a notice of loss or damage, either apparent or concealed, is not given as provided for in this section, that fact shall not affect or prejudice the right of the shipper to bring suit within one year after the delivery of the goods or the date when the goods should have been delivered.

In the case of any actual or apprehended loss or damage the carrier and the receiver shall give all reasonable facilities to each other for inspecting and tallying the goods.

(7) After the goods are loaded the bill of lading to be issued by the carrier, master, or agent of the carrier to the shipper shall, if the shipper so demands, be a "shipped" bill of lading: *Provided,* That if the shipper shall have previously taken up any document of title to such goods, he shall surrender the same as against the issue

of the "shipped" bill of lading, but at the option of the carrier such document of title may be noted at the port of shipment by the carrier, master, or agent with the name or names of the ship or ships upon which the goods have been shipped and the date or dates of shipment, and when so noted the same shall for the purpose of this section be deemed to constitute a "shipped" bill of lading.

(8) Any clause, covenant, or agreement in a contract of carriage relieving the carrier or the ship from liability for loss or damage to or in connection with the goods, arising from negligence, fault, or failure in the duties and obligations provided in this section, or lessening such liability otherwise than as provided in this Act, shall be null and void and of no effect. A benefit of insurance in favor of the carrier, or similar clause, shall be deemed to be a clause relieving the carrier from liability.

RIGHTS AND IMMUNITIES

SEC. 4. (1) Neither the carrier nor the ship shall be liable for loss or damage arising or resulting from unseaworthiness unless caused by want of due diligence on the part of the carrier to make the ship seaworthy, and to secure that the ship is properly manned, equipped, and supplied, and to make the holds, refrigerating and cool chambers, and all other parts of the ship in which goods are carried fit and safe for their reception, carriage, and preservation in accordance with the provisions of paragraph (1) of section 3. Whenever loss or damage has resulted from unseaworthiness, the burden of proving the exercise of due diligence shall be on the carrier or other persons-claiming exemption under this section.

(2) Neither the carrier nor the ship shall be responsible for loss or damage arising or resulting from—

(a) Act, neglect, or default of the master, mariner, pilot, or the servants of the carrier in the navigation or in the management of the ship;

(b) Fire, unless caused by the actual fault or privity of the carrier;

(c) Perils, dangers, and accidents of the sea or other navigable waters;

(d) Act of God;

(e) Act of war;

(f) Act of public enemies;

(g) Arrest or restraint of princes, rulers, or people, or seizure under legal process;

(h) Quarantine restrictions;

(i) Act or omission of the shipper or owner of the goods, his agent or representative;

(j) Strikes or lockouts or stoppage or restraint of labor from whatever cause, whether partial or general: *Provided,* that nothing herein contained shall be construed to relieve a carrier from responsibility for the carrier's own acts;

(k) Riots and civil commotions;

(l) Saving or attempting to save life or property at sea;

(m) Wastage in bulk or weight or any other loss or damage arising from inherent defect, quality, or vice of the goods;

(n) Insufficiency of packing;

(o) Insufficiency or inadequacy of marks;

(p) Latent defects not discoverable by due diligence; and

(q) Any other cause arising without the actual fault and privity of the carrier and without the fault or neglect of the agents or servants of the carrier, but the burden of proof shall be on the person claiming the benefit of this exception to show that neither the actual fault or privity of the carrier nor the fault or neglect of the agents or servants of the carrier contributed to the loss or damage.

(3) The shipper shall not be responsible for loss or damage sustained by the carrier or the ship arising or resulting from any cause without the act, fault, or neglect of the shipper, his agents, or his servants.

(4) Any deviation in saving or attempting to save life or property at sea, or any reasonable deviation shall not be deemed to be an infringement or breach of this Act or of the contract of carriage, and the carrier shall not be liable for any loss or damage resulting therefrom: *Provided, however,* That if the deviation is for the purpose of loading or unloading cargo or passengers it shall, prima facie, be regarded as unreasonable.

(5) Neither the carrier nor the ship shall in any event be or become liable for any loss or damage to or in connection with the transportation of goods in an amount exceeding $500 per package

lawful money of the United States, or in case of goods not shipped in packages, per customary freight unit, or the equivalent of that sum in other currency, unless the nature and value of such goods have been declared by the shipper before shipment and inserted in the bill of lading. This declaration, if embodied in the bill of lading, shall be prima facie evidence, but shall not be conclusive on the carrier.

By agreement between the carrier, master, or agent of the carrier, and the shipper another maximum amount than that mentioned in this paragraph may be fixed: *Provided,* That such maximum shall not be less than the figure above named. In no event shall the carrier be liable for more than the amount of damage actually sustained.

Neither the carrier nor the ship shall be responsible in any event for loss or damage to or in connection with the transportation of the goods if the nature or value thereof has been knowingly and fraudulently misstated by the shipper in the bill of lading.

(6) Goods of an inflammable, explosive, or dangerous nature to the shipment whereof the carrier, master or agent of the carrier, has not consented with knowledge of their nature and character, may at any time before discharge be landed at any place or destroyed or rendered innocuous by the carrier without compensation, and the shipper of such goods shall be liable for all damages and expenses directly or indirectly arising out of or resulting from such shipment. If any such goods shipped with such knowledge and consent shall become a danger to the ship or cargo, they may in like manner be landed at any place, or destroyed or rendered innocuous by the carrier without liability on the part of the carrier except to general average, if any.

SURRENDER OF RIGHTS AND IMMUNITIES AND INCREASE OF RESPONSIBILITIES AND LIABILITIES

SEC. 5. A carrier shall be at liberty to surrender in whole or in part all or any of his rights and immunities or to increase any of his responsibilities and liabilities under this Act, provided such surrender or increase shall be embodied in the bill of lading issued to the shipper.

The provisions of this Act shall not be applicable to charter parties; but if bills of lading are issued in the case of a ship under a charter party, they shall comply with the terms of this Act. Nothing in this Act shall be held to prevent the insertion in a bill of lading of any lawful provision regarding general average.

SPECIAL CONDITIONS

Sec. 6. Notwithstanding the provisions of the preceding sections, a carrier, master or agent of the carrier, and a shipper shall, in regard to any particular goods be at liberty to enter into any agreement in any terms as to the responsibility and liability of the carrier for such goods, and as to the rights and immunities of the carrier in respect of such goods, or his obligation as to seaworthiness(so far as the stipulation regarding seaworthiness is not contrary to public policy), or the care or diligence of his servants or agents in regard to the loading, handling, stowage, carriage, custody, care, and discharge of the goods carried by sea: *Provided*, That in this case no bill of lading has been or shall be issued and that the terms agreed shall be embodied in a receipt which shall be a nonnegotiable document and shall be marked as such.

Any agreement so entered into shall have full legal effect: *Provided*, That this section shall not apply to ordinary commercial shipments made in the ordinary course of trade but only to other shipments where the character or condition of the property to be carried or the circumstances, terms, and conditions under which the carriage is to be performed are such as reasonably to justify a special agreement.

Sec. 7. Nothing contained in this Act shall prevent a carrier or a shipper from entering into any agreement, stipulation, condition, reservation, or exemption as to the responsibility and liability of the carrier or the ship for the loss or damage to or in connection with the custody and care and handling of goods prior to the loading on and subsequent to the discharge from the ship on which the goods are carried by sea.

Sec. 8. The provisions of this Act shall not affect the rights and obligations of the carrier under the provisions of the Shipping Act, 1916, or under the provisions of sections 4281 to 4289, inclusive, of the Revised Statutes of the United States, or of any amendments thereto; or under the revisions of any other enactment for the time being in force relating to the limitation of the liability of the owners of seagoing vessels.

TITLE II

SECTION 9. Nothing contained in this Act shall be construed as permitting a common carrier by water to discriminate between competing shippers similarly placed in time and circumstances, either (a) with respect to their right to demand and receive bills of lading subject to the provisions of this Act; or (b) when issuing such bills of lading, either in the surrender of any of the carrier's rights and immunities or in the increase of any of the carrier's responsibilities and liabilities pursuant to section 5, title I, of this Act, or (c) in any other way prohibited by the Shipping Act, 1916, as amended.

SEC. 10. Section 25 of the Interstate Commerce Act is hereby amended by adding the following proviso at the end of paragraph 4 thereof: *"Provided, however,* That insofar as any bill of lading authorized hereunder relates to the carriage of goods by sea, such bill of lading shall be subject to the provisions of the Carriage of Goods by Sea Act."

SEC. 11. Where under the customs of any trade the weight of any bulk cargo inserted in the bill of lading is a weight ascertained or accepted by a third party other than the carrier or the shipper, and the fact that the weight is so ascertained or accepted is stated in the bill of lading, then, notwithstanding anything in this Act, the bill of lading shall not be deemed to be prima facie evidence against the carrier of the receipt of goods of the weight so inserted in the bill of lading, and the accuracy thereof at the time of shipment shall not be deemed to have been guaranteed by the shipper.

SEC. 12. Nothing in this Act shall be construed as superseding any part of the Act entitled "An Act relating to navigation of vessels, bills of lading, and to certain obligations, duties, and rights in connection with the carriage of property", approved February 13, 1893, or of any other law which would be applicable in the absence of this Act, insofar as they relate to the duties, responsibilities, and liabilities of the ship or carrier prior to the time when the goods are loaded on or after the time they are discharged from the ship.

Sec. 13. This Act shall apply to all contracts for carriage of goods by sea to or from ports of the United States in foreign trade. As used in this Act the term "United States" includes its districts, territories, and possessions: *Provided, however,* That the Philippine Legislature may by law exclude its application to transportation to or from ports of the Philippine Islands. The term "foreign trade" means the transportation of goods between the ports of the United States and ports of foreign countries. Nothing in this Act shall be held to apply to contracts for carriage of goods by sea between any port of the United States or its possessions, and any other port of the United States or its possessions: *Provided however,* That any bill of lading or similar document of title which is evidence of a contract for the carriage of goods by sea between such ports, containing an express statement that it shall be subject to the provisions of this Act, shall be subjected hereto as fully as if subject hereto by the express provisions of this Act: *Provided further,* That every bill of lading or similar document of title which is evidence of a contract for the carriage of goods by sea from ports of the United States, in foreign trade, shall contain a statement that it shall have effect subject to the provisions of this Act.

Sec. 14. Upon the certification of the Secretary of Commerce that the foreign commerce of the United States in it competition with that of foreign nations is prejudiced by the provisions, of any of them, of title I of this Act, or by the laws of any foreign country or countries relating to the carriage of goods by sea, the President of the United States may, from time to time, by proclamation, suspend any or all provisions of title I of this Act for such periods of time or indefinitely as may be designated in the proclamation. The President may at any time rescind such suspension of title I hereof, and any provisions thereof which may have been suspended shall thereby be reinstated and again apply to contracts thereafter made for the carriage of goods by sea. Any proclamation of suspension or rescission of any such suspension shall take effect on a date named therein, which date shall be not less than ten days from the issue of the proclamation.

Any contract for the carriage of goods by sea, subject to the provisions of this Act, effective during any period when title I hereof, or any part thereof, is suspended, shall be subject to all provisions of law now or hereafter applicable to that part of title I which may have thus been suspended.

SEC. 15. This Act shall take effect ninety days after the date of its approval; but nothing in this Act shall apply during a period not to exceed one year following its approval to any contract for the carriage of goods by sea, made before the date on which this Act is approved, nor to any bill of lading or similar document of title issued, whether before or after such date of approval in pursuance of any such contract as aforesaid.

SEC. 16. This Act may be cited as the "Carriage of Goods by Sea Act."

Approved, April 16, 1936.

APPENDIX III

AMERICAN HULLS (PACIFIC)

1. Touching the Adventures and Perils which we, the said Assurers, are contented to bear and take upon us, they are of the Seas, Men-of-War, Fire, Enemies, Pirates, Rovers, Thieves, Jettisons, Letters of Mart and Counter-Mart, Surprisals, Takings at Sea, Arrests, restraints and detainments of all Kings, Princes and Peoples, of what nation, condition or quality soever, Barratry of the Master and Mariners and of all other like Perils, Losses and Misfortunes that have or shall come to the Hurt, Detriment or Damage of the said Vessel, &c., or any part thereof. And in case of any Loss or Misfortune, it shall be lawful for the Assured, their Factors, Servants and Assigns, to sue labor and travel for, in, and about the Defense, Safeguard and Recovery of the said Vessel, &c., or any part thereof, without prejudice to this Insurance, to the Charges whereof, the Assurers will contribute according to the Rate and Quantity of the sum herein insured. And it is expressly declared and agreed that no act of the Assurers or Assured in recovering, saving or preserving the property insured shall be considered as a waiver or acceptance of abandonment.

2. And it is further agreed that if the Ship hereby Insured shall come into collision with any other Ship or Vessel, and the Assured or Charterers shall in consequence thereof or the Surety for either or both of them in consequence of their undertaking become liable to pay and shall pay by way of damages to any other person or persons any sum or sums in respect of such collision, this Company will pay the Assured or Charterers such proportion of such sum or sums so paid as its subscription hereto bears to the value of the Ship hereby insured, provided always that its liability in respect of any one such collision shall not exceed its proportionate part of the value of the Ship hereby Insured; and in cases in which the liability of the Ship has been contested, or proceedings have been taken to limit liability, with the consent in writing of a majority of the underwriters on the hull and machinery (in amount), this Company will also pay a like proportion of the costs which the Assured or Charterers shall thereby incur, or be compelled to pay; but when both Vessels are to blame, then unless the liability of the Owners or Charterers of one or both of such Vessels becomes limited by law, claims under this clause shall be settled on the principle of cross-liabilities as if the Owners or Charterers of each Vessel had been compelled to pay to the Owners or Charterers of the other of such Vessels such one-half or other proportion of the latters damages as may have been properly allowed in ascertaining the balance or sum payable by or to the Assured or Charterers in consequence of such collision.

3. Provided always that this Clause shall in no case extend to any sum which the Assured or Charterers may become liable to pay or shall pay for removal of obstructions under statutory powers, for injury to harbours, wharves, piers, stages, and similar structures, consequent on such collision; or in respect to the cargo or engagements of the insured vessel, or for loss of life or personal injury.

4. Should the Vessel hereby insured come into collision with or receive salvage services from another Vessel belonging wholly or in part to the same Owners or Charterers, or under the same management, the Assured or

Charterers shall have the same rights under this policy as they would have were the other Vessel entirely the property of owners not interested in the Vessel hereby insured; but in such case the liability for the collision or the amount payable for the services rendered, shall be referred to a sole arbitrator to be agreed upon between the Underwriters and the Assured or Charterers.

5.   Provided that in the event of any claim being made by Charterers under the above clauses, they shall not be entitled to recover in respect of any liability to which the Owners of the Ship, if interested in this Policy at the time of the collision in question, would not be subject, nor to a greater extent than the Shipowners would be entitled in such event to recover.

6.   In port and at sea, in docks and graving docks, and on ways, grid-irons and pontoons, at all times, in all places, and on all occasions, services and trades whatsoever and wheresoever, under steam or sail, with leave to sail with or without pilots, to tow and assist vessels or craft in all situations, and to be towed and to go on trial trips.

7.   Should the vessel at the expiration of this Policy be at sea, or in distress, or at a port of refuge or of call, she shall, provided previous notice be given to the Underwriters, be held covered at a pro rata monthly premium, to her port of destination.

8.   Held covered in case of any breach of warranty as to cargo, trade, locality or date of sailing, provided notice be given, and any additional premium required be agreed immediately after receipt of advices.

9.   Should the vessel be sold or transferred to new management, then, unless the Underwriters agree in writing to such sale or transfer, this Policy shall thereupon become cancelled from date of sale or transfer, unless the Vessel has cargo on board and has already sailed from her loading port or is at sea in ballast, in either of which cases such cancellation shall be suspended until arrival at final port of discharge if with cargo, or at port of destination if in ballast. A pro rata daily return of net premium shall be made. The foregoing provisions with respect to cancellation in the event of sale or change of management shall apply even in the case of insurance "for account of whom it may concern."

10.   This insurance also specially to cover (subject to the free of average warranty) loss of or damage to hull or machinery directly caused by the following:—

> Accidents in loading discharging or handling cargo, or in bunkering or taking in fuel.
>
> Explosions on shipboard or elsewhere.
>
> Bursting of boilers, breakage of shafts or any latent defect in the machinery or hull (excluding however, the cost and expense of repairing or renewing the defective part).
>
> Negligence of Master, Mariners, Engineers or Pilots.

provided such loss or damage has not resulted from want of due diligence by the Owners of the Vessel, or any of them, or by the Managers.

> Masters, Mates, Engineers, Pilot or Crew not to be considered as part owners within the meaning of this clause should they hold shares in the Vessel.

11.   General Average, Salvage and Special Charges payable as provided in the contract of affreightment, or failing such provisions, or there be no contract of affreightment, payable in accordance with the Laws and Usages of the

Port of San Francisco. Provided always that when an adustment according to the laws and usages of the port of destination is properly demanded by the owners of the cargo, General Average shall be paid in accordance with same.

When the contributory value of the Vessel is greater than the valuation herein the liability of these Underwriters for General Average contribution (except in respect to amount made good to the Vessel) or Salvage shall not exceed that proportion of the total contribution due from the Vessel that the amount insured hereunder bears to the contributory value; and if because of damage for which these Underwriters are liable as Particular Average the value of the Vessel has been reduced for the Purpose of contribution, the amount of the Particular Average claim under this Policy shall be deducted from the amount insured hereunder and these Underwriters shall be liable only for the proportion which such net amount bears to the contributory value.

12.   In the event of expenditure for Salvage, Salvage Charges or under the Sue and Labor Clause, this Policy shall only be liable for its share of such proportion of the amount chargeable to the property hereby insured as the insured value, less loss and for damage, if any, for which the Underwriters are liable bears to the value of the salved property. Provided that where there are no proceeds or there are expenses in excess of the proceeds, the expenses, or the excess of the expenses, as the case may be, shall be approportioned upon the basis of the sound value of the property at the time of the accident and this Policy without any deduction for loss and/or damage shall bear its pro rata share of such expenses or excess of expenses accordingly.

13.   Average payable on each valuation separately or on the whole, without deduction of thirds, new for old, whether the average be particular or general.

14.   Donkey boilers, winches, cranes, windlasses, steering gear, and electric light apparatus shall be deemed to be part of the hull, and not part of the machinery. Refrigerating machinery and insulation not covered unless expressly included in this Policy.

15.   Warranted free from particular average under 3 per cent, but nevertheless, when the Vessel shall have been stranded, sunk, on fire, or in collision with any other Ship or Vessel, Underwriters shall pay the damage occasioned thereby, and the expense of sighting the bottom after stranding shall be paid if reasonably incurred, even if no damage be found.

16.   From the cost of cleaning and painting the bottom of a Vessel, (exclusive of dry-dock charges) recoverable in average, there shall be deducted one-twelfth for every month since the Vessel was last painted, but no allowance shall be made for cleaning and painting on account of exposure to air unless the Vessel has been more than twenty-four hours on the dock.

17.   Grounding in the Panama Canal, Suez Canal, or in the Manchester Ship Canal or its Connections, or in the River Mersey above Rock Ferry Slip, or in the River Plate (above a line drawn from the North Basin, Buenos Aires, to the mouth of the San Pedro River) or its tributaries, or in the Danube or Demerara Rivers or on the Yenikale Bar, shall not be deemed to be a stranding.

18.   The warranty and conditions as to average under 3 per cent, to be applicable to each voyage as if separately insured and a voyage shall be deemed to commence at one of the following periods to be selected by the Assured when making up the claim, viz.: at any time at which the Vessel (1) begins to load cargo or (2) sails in ballast to a loading port. Such voyage shall be

deemed to continue during the ensuing period until either she has made one outward and one homeward passage (including an intermediate ballast passage if made) or has carried and discharged two cargoes whichever may first happen, and further, in either case, until she begins to load a subsequent cargo or sails in ballast for a loading port. When the Vessel sails in ballast to effect damage repair such sailing shall not be deemed to be a sailing for a loading port although she loads at the repairing port. In calculating the 3 per cent. above referred to, particular average occuring outside the period covered by this Policy may be added to particular average occuring within such period provided it occur upon the same voyage (as above defined), but only that portion of the claim arising within such period shall be recoverable hereon. The commencement of a voyage shall not be so fixed as to overlap another voyage on which a claim is made on this or the preceding Policy.

19.   In no case shall Underwriters be liable for unrepaired damage in addition to a subsequent total loss sustained during the term covered by this Policy.

20.   In ascertaining whether the Vessel is a constructive total loss the insured value shall be taken as the repaired value, and nothing in respect of the damaged or break-up value of the Vessel or wreck shall be taken into account.

21   In the event of total or constructive total loss, no claim to be made by the Underwriters for freight, whether notice of abandonment has been given or not.

22.   In the event of accident whereby loss or damage may result in a claim under this Policy, notice shall be given in writing to the Underwriters, where practicable, prior to survey, so that they may appoint their own surveyor if they so desire. The Underwriters shall be entitled to decide the port to which a damaged Vessel shall proceed for docking or repairing (the actual additional expense of the voyage arising from compliance with Underwriters' requirements being refunded to the Assured) and Underwriters shall also have a right of veto in connection with the place of repair or repairing firm proposed and whenever the extent of the damage is ascertainable the majority (in amount) of the Underwriters may take or may require to be taken tenders for the repair of such damage.

In cases where a tender is accepted with the approval of Underwriters, an allowance shall be made at the rate of 30 per cent. per annum on the insured value for each day or part thereof from the time of the completion of the survey until the acceptance of the tender provided that it be accepted without delay after receipt of Underwriters' approval.

No allowance shall be made for any time during which the Vessel is loading or discharging cargo or bunkering or taking in fuel.

Due credit shall be given against the allowance as above for any amount recovered:—

(a)   in respect of fuel and stores and wages and maintenance of the Master, Officers and Crew or any member thereof allowed in General or Particular Average;

(b)   from third parties in respect of damages for detention and/or loss of profit and/or running expenses;

for the period covered by the tender allowance or any part thereof.

In the event of failure to comply with the conditions of this clause 15 per cent. shall be deducted from the amount of the ascertained claim.

23.   Warranted that the amount insured for account of the Assured and/or

their managers on Disbursements, Commissions and/or similar interests, "policy proof of interest" or "full interest admitted" or on excess or increased value of Hull or Machinery, however described, shall not, except as indicated below, exceed 10 per cent. of the insured valuation of the Vessel, but the Assured may in addition thereto effect "policy proof of interest" or "full interest admitted" insurance on any of the following interests:

(a) Premiums (reducing or not reducing monthly) to any amount actually at risk, and

(b) Freight and/or Chartered Freight and/or Anticipated Freight and/or Earnings and/or Hire or Profits on Time Charter and/or Charter for series of voyages for any amount not exceeding in the aggregate 15 per cent. of the insured valuation of the Vessel; and if the actual amount at risk on any or all of such interests shall exceed such 15 per cent. of the insured valuation of the Vessel, the Assured and/or their managers may, without prejudice to the warranty, insure whilst at risk the excess of such interests reducing as earned, and

(c) Risks excluded by the "F. C. & S. Clause", and

(d) Loss or damage in consequence of strikes, lockouts, political or labor disturbances, civil commotions, riots, martial law, military or usurped power or malicious act.

Provided always that a breach of this warranty shall not afford the Underwriters any defense to a claim by mortgagees or other third parties who may have accepted this Policy without notice of such breach of warranty nor shall it restrict the right of the Assured and/or their managers to insure in addition General Average and/or Salvage Disbursements whilst at risk.

24. At the expiration of this Policy to return_____per cent net for every thirty consecutive days the Vessel may be laid up in port out of commission and not under average (provided that no return be made for any thirty-day period in which an accident happens for which claim is made on Underwriters or during which repairs for Underwriters' account are effected); and to return _____per cent, net for every thirty days of unexpired time if it be mutually agreed to cancel this Policy, but no returns whatsoever to be paid in case of loss of the Vessel.

In the event of the Vessel being laid up in port for a period of thirty consecutive days a part only of which attaches to this Policy it is hereby agreed that the laying up period in which either the commencing or ending date of this Policy falls shall be deemed to run from the first day on which the Vessel is laid up and that on this basis Underwriters shall pay such proportion of the return due in respect of a full period of thirty days as the number of days attaching hereto bear to thirty.

Notwithstanding the foregoing this Policy is:

(a) Warranted free from any claim for loss, damage, or expense caused by or resulting from capture, seizure, arrest, restraint or detainment, or the consequences thereof or of any attempt thereat, or any taking of the Vessel, by requisition or otherwise, whether in time of peace or war and whether lawful or otherwise; also from all consequences of hostilities or warlike operations (whether there be a declaration of war or not), but the foregoing shall not exclude collision, explosion or contact with any fixed or floating object (other than a mine or torpedo), stranding, heavy weather or fire unless caused directly (and independently of the nature of the voyage or service which the vessel concerned or, in the case of a collision, any other vessel involved therein, is performing) by a hostile act by or against a belligerent power, and for the purpose of this warranty "power" includes any authority maintaining naval, military or air forces in association with a power; also warranted free, whether in time of peace or war, from all loss, damage or expense caused by any weapon of war employing atomic fission or radioactive force.

Further warranted free from the consequences of civil war, revolution, rebellion, insurrection, or civil strife arising therefrom, or piracy.

If war risks are hereafter insured by endorsement on the Policy, such endorsement shall supersede the above warranty only to the extent that their terms are inconsistent and only while such war risk endorsement remains in force.

(b) Warranted free from liability in general average for deck cargo jettisoned.

(c) Warranted to be subject to English law and usage as to liability for and settlement of any and all claims.

Index

NOTES

NOTES

NOTES

NOTES

NOTES

NOTES

NOTES

NOTES

NOTES

NOTES